Taste of Home

Bring a Dish!

MORE THAN 350 CROWD-PLEASING POTLUCK, CHURCH SUPPER, AND STAY-AT-HOME MEALS!

© 2017 by RDA Enthusiast Brands, LLC,
1610 N. 2nd St., Suite 102, Milwaukee, WI 53212. All Rights Reserved.

Taste of Home is a registered trademark of RDA Enthusiast Brands, LLC

Printed in the United States of America

Photographs by Taste of Home Photography Studio, Milwaukee, WI

Floral background by vodoleyka/Getty Images; linen background by Lava4images/Getty Images;
photo of tag by taska2000/Getty Images

Book design by Carol Angstadt

ISBN 978-1-62336-827-2   direct hardcover

2 4 6 8 10 9 7 5 3 1   direct hardcover.

Contents

Introduction

Whether you're heading to a church potluck, special brunch, holiday meal, or just a simple family dinner, coming up with new and interesting recipes can be a challenge. But with *Taste of Home Bring a Dish!,* you're sure to find a crowd pleaser for every occasion. This book is packed with more than 350 delicious appetizers, entrées, casseroles, side dishes, salads, desserts, and more—all from home cooks just like you.

Each dish will be the star of the buffet table with these recipes that are almost too good to cut into. You'll be the talk of the party when your dish is the first to disappear, especially with offerings like Patricia Collins's hearty Tomato–French Bread Lasagna (page 210). If you want a dessert that stands out from the rest, Erma Fox's Chocolate Chiffon Cake (page 358) is the cake to make!

Discover more than 100 "last-minute, throw together" recipes, conveniently labeled in each chapter. Everyone will love the flavors and colors in Terry McCarty's quick and easy Balsamic Chicken Pasta Salad (page 74), which takes less than 30 minutes to make. Or, try a crowd-favorite appetizer like Nicole Marcotte's Warm Bacon Cheese Spread (page 166), which is served right in the bread bowl, making cleanup a breeze.

When you do have time to plan, you'll find 100 of our most-loved "slow cooker" and "make & bake" recipes to choose from. Your guests will be impressed to learn that a decadent dessert like Krista Lanphier's iconic Pink Grapefruit Cheesecake (page 374) came from a slow cooker!

Not just for large potlucks, *Taste of Home Bring a Dish!* offers recipes perfect for small get-togethers with friends or for dinner any night of the week. Schelby Thompson's Parmesan Chicken (page 249) is easy enough to be a family weekday meal yet impressive enough to serve to guests. Make this chicken for dinner and never have leftovers!

Craving something different for dinner tonight? Here you'll find simple recipes you can toss in the oven and relax while they cook. Try Sherri Melotik's simple Pan-Roasted Chicken and Vegetables (page 243). This one-dish meal tastes like it needs hours of hands-on time but takes just minutes to prep.

Along with hundreds of potluck-favorite, family-approved, home-cooked recipes, you'll find tips and tricks from real home cooks to make each dish perfect. Learn the easiest way to transport your hot dishes with the clever method on page 54. Want to keep track of everyone's best-loved dish? Discover this handy way to track your family's favorites on page 347.

With *Taste of Home Bring a Dish!,* each foolproof recipe is sure to be a hit.

Breakfast for a Bunch

Calico Scrambled Eggs

PREP/TOTAL TIME: 20 MINUTES ● **YIELD:** 4 SERVINGS

When you're short on time and scrambling to get a meal on the table, this recipe is "eggs-actly" what you need. There's a short ingredient list, and cooking is kept to a minimum. Plus, with green pepper and tomato, it's colorful.

—Taste of Home Test Kitchen

8 large eggs	1 tablespoon butter
$\frac{1}{4}$ cup 2% milk	$\frac{1}{2}$ cup chopped green pepper
$\frac{1}{8}$ to $\frac{1}{4}$ teaspoon dill weed	$\frac{1}{4}$ cup chopped onion
$\frac{1}{8}$ to $\frac{1}{4}$ teaspoon salt	$\frac{1}{2}$ cup chopped fresh tomato
$\frac{1}{8}$ to $\frac{1}{4}$ teaspoon pepper	

1. In a bowl, whisk the first five ingredients until blended. In a 12-inch nonstick skillet, heat butter over medium-high heat. Add green pepper and onion; cook and stir until tender. Remove from pan.

2. In same pan, pour in egg mixture; cook and stir over medium heat until eggs begin to thicken. Add tomato and pepper mixture; cook until heated through and no liquid egg remains, stirring gently.

NUTRITIONAL FACTS
1 CUP: 188 calories, 13 g fat (5 g saturated fat), 381 mg cholesterol, 248 mg sodium, 4 g carbohydrate (3 g sugars, 1 g fiber), 14 g protein

Quick Tip If you just don't have time to cook for the church supper, ask if you can contribute paper plates, napkins, or plastic eating utensils. Or, volunteer to set up the dinner tables or promise to help clean up after the event.

Brunch Scramble

PREP/TOTAL TIME: 30 MINUTES • **YIELD:** 6 SERVINGS

When I have overnight guests, I serve this speedy skillet dish for breakfast. Onion, green pepper and mushrooms add a bounty of flavor they love.

—Valerie Putsey, Winamac, Indiana

1 medium red onion, chopped	¾ cup half-and-half cream
1 medium green pepper, chopped	1½ teaspoons salt
1 jar (4½ ounces) sliced mushrooms, drained	¼ teaspoon pepper
3 tablespoons butter	1½ cups shredded cheddar cheese
12 large eggs	1 tablespoon minced chives

1. In a large skillet, saute the onion, green pepper and mushrooms in butter until crisp-tender.

2. Meanwhile, in a large bowl, whisk the eggs, cream, salt and pepper. Add egg mixture to vegetables in skillet; cook and stir over medium heat until eggs are almost set. Sprinkle with cheese and chives. Cover and cook until eggs are completely set.

NUTRITIONAL FACTS
1 EACH: 357 calories, 27 g fat (15 g saturated fat), 485 mg cholesterol, 1050 mg sodium, 7 g carbohydrate (4 g sugars, 1 g fiber), 20 g protein

Spiral Omelet Supreme

PREP: 20 MINUTES ● **BAKE:** 20 MINUTES ● **YIELD:** 8 SERVINGS

You can substitute 2 cups of any combination of your favorite omelet fillings for the vegetables in this recipe. A serrated knife works well for slicing it.

—*Debbie Morris, Hamilton, Ohio*

4	ounces cream cheese, softened	1	cup sliced fresh mushrooms
¾	cup 2% milk	1	small onion, chopped
¼	cup plus 2 tablespoons grated Parmesan cheese, divided	2	teaspoons canola oil
2	tablespoons all-purpose flour	1½	cups shredded part-skim mozzarella cheese
12	large eggs	1	plum tomato, seeded and chopped
1	large green pepper, chopped	1¼	teaspoons Italian seasoning, divided

1. Preheat oven to 375°. Line the bottom and sides of a greased 15x10x1-inch baking pan with parchment paper; grease the paper and set aside.

2. In a small bowl, beat cream cheese and milk until smooth. Beat in ¼ cup Parmesan cheese and flour until blended. In a large bowl, beat eggs; add cream cheese mixture and mix well. Pour into prepared pan. Bake 20–25 minutes or until set.

3. Meanwhile, in a large skillet, saute the pepper, mushrooms and onion in oil until crisp-tender. Keep warm.

4. Turn omelet onto a work surface; peel off parchment paper. Sprinkle with the vegetable mixture, mozzarella cheese, tomato and 1 teaspoon Italian seasoning. Roll up jelly-roll style, starting with a short side. Place on a serving platter. Sprinkle with remaining Parmesan cheese and Italian seasoning.

NUTRITIONAL FACTS
1 SLICE: 268 calories, 19 g fat (9 g saturated fat), 351 mg cholesterol, 314 mg sodium, 6 g carbohydrate (3 g sugars, 1 g fiber), 19 g protein

Slow Cooker Frittata Provencal

PREP: 30 MINUTES ● **COOK:** 3 HOURS ● **YIELD:** 6 SERVINGS

This recipe ensures that a delectable dinner is ready when I walk in the door from work. The meatless slow cooker meal also makes an elegant brunch for lazy weekend mornings.

—*Connie Eaton, Pittsburgh, Pennsylvania*

$\frac{1}{2}$ cup water

1 tablespoon olive oil

1 medium Yukon Gold potato, peeled and sliced

1 small onion, thinly sliced

$\frac{1}{2}$ teaspoon smoked paprika

12 large eggs

1 teaspoon minced fresh thyme or $\frac{1}{4}$ teaspoon dried thyme

1 teaspoon hot pepper sauce

$\frac{1}{2}$ teaspoon salt

$\frac{1}{4}$ teaspoon pepper

1 log (4 ounces) fresh goat cheese, coarsely crumbled, divided

$\frac{1}{2}$ cup chopped soft sun-dried tomatoes (not packed in oil)

1. Layer two 24-inch pieces of aluminum foil; starting with a long side, fold up foil to create a 1-inch-wide strip. Shape strip into a coil to make a rack for bottom of a 6-qt. oval slow cooker. Add water to slow cooker; set foil rack in water.

2. In a large skillet, heat oil over medium-high heat. Add potato and onion; cook and stir 5-7 minutes or until potato is lightly browned. Stir in paprika. Transfer to a greased 1$\frac{1}{2}$-qt. baking dish (dish must fit in slow cooker).

3. In a large bowl, whisk eggs, thyme, pepper sauce, salt and pepper; stir in 2 ounces cheese. Pour over potato mixture. Top with tomatoes and remaining goat cheese. Place dish on foil rack.

4. Cook, covered, on low 3 hours or until eggs are set and a knife inserted near the center comes out clean.

NOTE: This recipe was tested with sun-dried tomatoes that are ready-to-use without soaking. When using other sun-dried tomatoes that are not oil-packed, cover with boiling water and let stand until soft. Drain before using.

NUTRITIONAL FACTS
1 WEDGE: 245 calories, 14 g fat (5 g saturated fat), 385 mg cholesterol, 338 mg sodium, 12 g carbohydrate (4 g sugars, 2 g fiber), 15 g protein

Black Bean & White Cheddar Frittata

PREP: 20 MINUTES • **COOK:** 15 MINUTES • **YIELD:** 6 SERVINGS

This is one of my favorite comfort foods for breakfast or even a quick dinner. I like to make it with lime salsa. But if you're looking for something with more kick, use hot salsa or add some chipotle pepper.

—*Aysha Schurman, Ammon, Idaho*

- 6 large eggs
- 3 large egg whites
- ¼ cup salsa
- 1 tablespoon minced fresh parsley
- ¼ teaspoon salt
- ¼ teaspoon pepper
- 1 tablespoon olive oil
- ⅓ cup finely chopped green pepper
- ⅓ cup finely chopped sweet red pepper
- 3 green onions, finely chopped
- 2 garlic cloves, minced
- 1 cup canned black beans, rinsed and drained
- ½ cup shredded white cheddar cheese
     Optional toppings: minced fresh cilantro, sliced ripe olives and additional salsa

1. Preheat broiler. In a large bowl, whisk the first six ingredients until blended.

2. In a 10-inch ovenproof skillet, heat oil over medium-high heat. Add peppers and green onions; cook and stir 3–4 minutes or until peppers are tender. Add garlic; cook 1 minute longer. Stir in beans. Reduce heat to medium; stir in egg mixture. Cook, uncovered, 4–6 minutes or until nearly set. Sprinkle with cheese.

3. Broil 3–4 inches from heat 3–4 minutes or until light golden brown and eggs are completely set. Let stand 5 minutes. Cut into wedges. If desired, serve with toppings.

NUTRITIONAL FACTS
1 WEDGE (CALCULATED WITHOUT TOPPINGS): 183 calories, 10 g fat (4 g saturated fat), 196 mg cholesterol, 378 mg sodium, 9 g carbohydrate (2 g sugars, 2 g fiber), 13 g protein

Tomato Herb Frittata

PREP: 20 MINUTES ● **BAKE:** 15 MINUTES ● **YIELD:** 6 SERVINGS

Fresh herbs and garlic really add to the flavor of this hearty, savory and filling egg dish. Every slice is brimming with cheesy eggs and bright tomatoes.

—Candy Summerhill, Alexander, Arkansas

9 large eggs
1¼ cups shredded part-skim mozzarella cheese, divided
½ cup 2% milk
1 tablespoon minced fresh basil or 1 teaspoon dried basil
1 tablespoon minced fresh oregano or 1 teaspoon dried oregano

1 teaspoon minced fresh thyme or ¼ teaspoon dried thyme
½ teaspoon salt
¼ teaspoon pepper
1½ cups grape tomatoes
2 tablespoons olive oil
2 garlic cloves, minced
Thinly sliced fresh basil, optional

1. Preheat oven to 400°. In a small bowl, whisk the eggs, ¾ cup cheese, milk, herbs, salt and pepper; set aside.

2. In a 10-inch ovenproof skillet, saute tomatoes in oil until tender. Add garlic; cook 1 minute longer. Pour egg mixture into pan; sprinkle with remaining cheese.

3. Bake for 12–15 minutes or until eggs are completely set. Let stand for 5 minutes. Cut into wedges. Garnish with sliced basil if desired.

NUTRITIONAL FACTS
1 SLICE: 227 calories, 16 g fat (6 g saturated fat), 332 mg cholesterol, 425 mg sodium, 4 g carbohydrate (3 g sugars, 0 fiber), 16 g protein

Oven Denver Omelet

PREP/TOTAL TIME: 30 MINUTES ● **YIELD:** 6 SERVINGS

I like omelets but don't always have time to stand by the stove. That's why I favor this oven-baked variety that I can quickly pop into the oven at a moment's notice. My family frequently requests this for Sunday brunch. They always empty the dish.

—Ellen Bower, Taneytown, Maryland

8 large eggs	1 cup finely chopped fully cooked ham
½ cup half-and-half cream	¼ cup finely chopped green pepper
1 cup shredded cheddar cheese	¼ cup finely chopped onion

1. Preheat oven to 400°. In a large bowl, whisk eggs and cream. Stir in the cheese, ham, green pepper and onion. Pour into a greased 9-inch square baking dish.

2. Bake for 25 minutes or until golden brown.

NUTRITIONAL FACTS
1 EACH: 235 calories, 16 g fat (8 g saturated fat), 326 mg cholesterol, 506 mg sodium, 4 g carbohydrate (2 g sugars, 0 fiber), 17 g protein

Greek Zucchini & Feta Bake

PREP: 40 MINUTES ● **BAKE:** 30 MINUTES + STANDING ● **YIELD:** 12 SERVINGS

Looking to highlight your meal with something light, indulgent and golden on top? Turn to this Greek-style egg bake.

—Gabriela Stefanescu, Webster, Texas

2 tablespoons olive oil, divided

5 medium zucchini, cut into $\frac{1}{2}$-inch cubes (about 6 cups)

2 large onions, chopped (about 4 cups)

1 teaspoon dried oregano, divided

$\frac{1}{2}$ teaspoon salt

$\frac{1}{4}$ teaspoon pepper

6 large eggs

2 teaspoons baking powder

1 cup (8 ounces) reduced-fat plain yogurt

1 cup all-purpose flour

16 ounces feta cheese, cubed

$\frac{1}{4}$ cup minced fresh parsley

1 teaspoon paprika

1. Preheat oven to 350°. In a Dutch oven, heat 1 tablespoon oil over medium-high heat. Add half of the zucchini, half of the onions and $\frac{1}{2}$ teaspoon oregano; cook and stir 8–10 minutes or until zucchini is crisp-tender. Remove from pan. Repeat with remaining oil and vegetables. Return previously cooked vegetables to pan. Stir in salt and pepper. Cool slightly.

2. In a large bowl, whisk eggs and baking powder until blended; whisk in yogurt and flour just until blended. Stir in cheese, parsley and zucchini mixture. Transfer to a greased 13x9-inch baking dish. Sprinkle with paprika.

3. Bake, uncovered, 30–35 minutes or until golden brown and set. Let stand 10 minutes before cutting.

NOTE: If desired, thinly slice 1 medium zucchini and toss with 2 teaspoons olive oil; arrange over casserole before sprinkling with paprika. Bake as directed.

NUTRITIONAL FACTS
1 PIECE: 231 calories, 13 g fat (7 g saturated fat), 128 mg cholesterol, 583 mg sodium, 16 g carbohydrate (6 g sugars, 2 g fiber), 12 g protein

Quick Tip

According to the American Egg Board, eggs can be used up to five weeks after the date printed on the carton. The date on the carton is actually the last day the eggs can be sold.

Bacon and Eggs Casserole

PREP: 20 MINUTES • **BAKE:** 40 MINUTES • **YIELD:** 10 SERVINGS

Because it requires so little time to prepare and is such a great hit with family and friends alike, this is a favorite of mine to make for brunches. Served with a fruit salad, hot muffins and croissants, it's excellent for an after-church brunch.

—*Deanna Durward-Orr, Windsor, Ontario*

4	bacon strips	1	cup (8 ounces) sour cream
18	large eggs	¼	cup sliced green onions
1	cup whole milk	1 to 1½	teaspoons salt
1	cup shredded cheddar cheese	½	teaspoon pepper

1. Preheat oven to 325°. In a large skillet, cook bacon over medium heat until crisp. Remove to paper towels to drain.

2. In a large bowl, beat eggs. Add milk, cheese, sour cream, onions, salt and pepper.

3. Pour into a greased 13x9-inch baking dish. Crumble bacon and sprinkle on top. Bake, uncovered, for 40–45 minutes or until a knife inserted in center comes out clean. Let stand for 5 minutes.

NUTRITIONAL FACTS
1 EACH: 289 calories, 22 g fat (10 g saturated fat), 420 mg cholesterol, 508 mg sodium, 4 g carbohydrate (3 g sugars, 0 fiber), 16 g protein

Amish Breakfast Casserole

PREP: 15 MINUTES ● **BAKE:** 35 MINUTES + STANDING ● **YIELD:** 12 SERVINGS

We enjoyed a hearty breakfast bake during a visit to an Amish inn. When I asked for the recipe, one of the ladies told me the ingredients right off the top of her head. I modified it to create this version my family loves. Try breakfast sausage in place of bacon.

—Beth Notaro, Kokomo, Indiana

1 pound sliced bacon, diced
1 medium sweet onion, chopped
6 large eggs, lightly beaten
4 cups frozen shredded hash brown potatoes, thawed

2 cups shredded cheddar cheese
1½ cups (12 ounces) 4% cottage cheese
1¼ cups shredded Swiss cheese

1. Preheat oven to 350°. In a large skillet, cook bacon and onion over medium heat until bacon is crisp; drain. In a large bowl, combine remaining ingredients; stir in bacon mixture. Transfer to a greased 13x9-inch baking dish.

2. Bake, uncovered, 35–40 minutes or until a knife inserted near the center comes out clean. Let stand 10 minutes before cutting.

NUTRITIONAL FACTS
1 PIECE: 273 calories, 18 g fat (10 g saturated fat), 153 mg cholesterol, 477 mg sodium, 8 g carbohydrate (3 g sugars, 1 g fiber), 18 g protein

Quick Tip — **When serving on a buffet, try to keep hot egg dishes hot, and cold egg dishes cold. Casseroles and other dishes containing eggs should be cooked to 160°. Use a food thermometer to be sure.**

Slow Cooker Ham & Eggs

PREP: 15 MINUTES ● **COOK:** 3 HOURS ● **YIELD:** 6 SERVINGS

This dish is great anytime of the year, but I love serving it on holiday mornings. It's basically a hands-free recipe that helps me create a fun meal for family.

—*Andrea Schaak, Jordan, Minnesota*

6 large eggs
1 cup biscuit/baking mix
²⁄₃ cup 2% milk
¹⁄₃ cup sour cream
2 tablespoons minced fresh parsley
2 garlic cloves, minced

¹⁄₂ teaspoon salt
¹⁄₂ teaspoon pepper
1 cup cubed fully cooked ham
1 cup shredded Swiss cheese
1 small onion, finely chopped
¹⁄₃ cup shredded Parmesan cheese

1. In a large bowl, whisk the first eight ingredients until blended; stir in remaining ingredients. Pour into a greased 3- or 4-qt. slow cooker.

2. Cook, covered, on low 3–4 hours or until eggs are set. Cut into wedges.

NUTRITIONAL FACTS
1 SERVING: 315 calories, 18 g fat (9 g saturated fat), 256 mg cholesterol, 942 mg sodium, 17 g carbohydrate (4 g sugars, 1 g fiber), 21 g protein

Hash Brown Pancetta Casserole

PREP: 25 MINUTES ● **BAKE:** 30 MINUTES + STANDING ● **YIELD:** 8 SERVINGS

Eggs, hash browns, cheese, spinach, pancetta and fabulous flavor—this casserole has everything! You could also substitute provolone or Swiss cheese for the fontina.

—Gilda Lester, Millsboro, Delaware

- 1 large onion, finely chopped
- 1 tablespoon olive oil
- 2 garlic cloves, minced
- 1 package (10 ounces) frozen chopped spinach, thawed and squeezed dry
- ¼ teaspoon salt
- ¼ teaspoon pepper
- 2 ounces sliced pancetta or bacon, finely chopped
- 3 cups frozen shredded hash brown potatoes, thawed
- 8 large eggs
- 2 cups 2% milk
- 1 cup shredded fontina cheese, divided
- 1 cup shredded cheddar cheese, divided
- ¼ cup minced fresh parsley
- 1 tablespoon Worcestershire sauce
- 1 teaspoon ground mustard
- ¼ teaspoon ground nutmeg
  Freshly ground pepper and additional fresh parsley, optional

1. Preheat oven to 350°. In a large skillet, saute onion in oil until tender. Add garlic; cook 1 minute longer. Stir in the spinach, salt and pepper. Remove from the heat.

2. In another skillet, cook pancetta over medium heat until crisp. Remove to paper towels with a slotted spoon; drain.

3. In a greased 13x9-inch baking dish, layer the hash browns, spinach mixture and pancetta. In a large bowl, whisk the eggs, milk, ½ cup fontina cheese, ½ cup cheddar cheese, parsley, Worcestershire sauce, mustard and nutmeg; pour over casserole. Sprinkle with remaining cheeses.

4. Bake, uncovered, for 30–35 minutes or until a knife inserted near the center comes out clean. Let stand for 10 minutes before cutting. If desired, sprinkle with freshly ground pepper and garnish with additional parsley.

NUTRITIONAL FACTS
1 PIECE: 291 calories, 19 g fat (9 g saturated fat), 253 mg cholesterol, 557 mg sodium, 13 g carbohydrate (5 g sugars, 2 g fiber), 18 g protein

Italian Sausage Egg Bake

PREP: 20 MINUTES + CHILLING • **BAKE:** 50 MINUTES • **YIELD:** 12 SERVINGS

This hearty entree warms up any breakfast or brunch menu with its herb-seasoned flavor.

—*Darlene Markham, Rochester, New York*

8 slices white bread, cubed

1 pound Italian sausage links, casings removed and sliced

2 cups shredded sharp cheddar cheese

2 cups shredded part-skim mozzarella cheese

9 large eggs, lightly beaten

3 cups 2% milk

1 teaspoon dried basil

1 teaspoon dried oregano

1 teaspoon fennel seed, crushed

1. Place bread cubes in a greased 13x9-inch baking dish; set aside. In a large skillet, cook sausage over medium heat until no longer pink; drain. Spoon sausage over bread; sprinkle with cheeses.

2. In a large bowl, whisk the eggs, milk and seasonings; pour over casserole. Cover and refrigerate overnight.

3. Remove from the refrigerator 30 minutes before baking. Bake, uncovered, at 350° for 50–55 minutes or until a knife inserted near the center comes out clean. Let stand for 5 minutes before cutting.

NUTRITIONAL FACTS
1 PIECE: 316 calories, 20 g fat (10 g saturated fat), 214 mg cholesterol, 546 mg sodium, 13 g carbohydrate (5 g sugars, 1 g fiber), 21 g protein

Hash Brown Egg Brunch

PREP: 20 MINUTES ● **COOK:** 4 HOURS ● **YIELD:** 10 SERVINGS

Slow cookers aren't just for making dinner. I make this often if we're having company overnight. I can prep it the night before, and when we all get up in the morning, breakfast is waiting.

—*Barb Keith, Eau Claire, Wisconsin*

1 package (30 ounces) frozen shredded hash brown potatoes, thawed	1½ cups shredded cheddar cheese
1 pound bacon strips, cooked and crumbled	12 large eggs
1 medium onion, chopped	1 cup 2% milk
1 medium green pepper, chopped	½ teaspoon salt
	½ teaspoon pepper

1. In a greased 5-qt. slow cooker, layer a third of each of the following: potatoes, bacon, onion, green pepper and cheese. Repeat layers twice. In a large bowl, whisk eggs, milk, salt and pepper; pour over layers.

2. Cook, covered, on high 30 minutes. Reduce heat to low; cook, covered, 3½ to 4 hours or until a thermometer reads 160°.

NUTRITIONAL FACTS
1 CUP: 315 calories, 17 g fat (8 g saturated fat), 289 mg cholesterol, 589 mg sodium, 20 g carbohydrate (3 g sugars, 2 g fiber), 20 g protein

Elegant Smoked Salmon Strata

PREP: 30 MINUTES + CHILLING • **BAKE:** 55 MINUTES + STANDING • **YIELD:** 12 SERVINGS

This fancy overnight egg bake is ideal for guests. In the morning, you can simply let it come to room temperature and whip up side dishes as it bakes. Then get ready for compliments!

—*Lisa Speer, Palm Beach, Florida*

4   cups cubed ciabatta bread
2   tablespoons butter, melted
2   tablespoons olive oil
2   cups shredded Gruyere or Swiss cheese
2   cups shredded white cheddar cheese
10 green onions, sliced
$\frac{1}{2}$ pound smoked salmon or lox, coarsely chopped

8   large eggs
4   cups 2% milk
4   teaspoons Dijon mustard
$\frac{1}{4}$ teaspoon salt
$\frac{1}{4}$ teaspoon pepper
    Creme fraiche or sour cream and minced chives

1. In a large bowl, toss bread cubes with butter and oil; transfer to a greased 13x9-inch baking dish. Sprinkle with cheeses, onions and salmon. In another bowl, whisk the eggs, milk, mustard, salt and pepper; pour over top. Cover and refrigerate overnight.

2. Remove from the refrigerator 30 minutes before baking. Cover and bake at 350° for 30 minutes. Uncover; bake 25–30 minutes longer or until a knife inserted near the center comes out clean. Let stand for 10 minutes before serving. Serve with creme fraiche and chives.

NUTRITIONAL FACTS
1 PIECE: 359 calories, 21 g fat (11 g saturated fat), 194 mg cholesterol, 845 mg sodium, 21 g carbohydrate (6 g sugars, 1 g fiber), 22 g protein

Brie and Sausage Brunch Bake

PREP: 30 MINUTES + CHILLING ● **BAKE:** 50 MINUTES + STANDING ● **YIELD:** 12 SERVINGS

I've made this brunch bake for holidays, as well as for a weekend at a friend's cabin, and I always get requests for the recipe. It is make-ahead convenient, reheats well and even tastes great the next day.

—*Becky Hicks, Forest Lake, Minnesota*

1 pound bulk Italian sausage	8 large eggs
1 small onion, chopped	2 cups heavy whipping cream
8 cups cubed day-old sourdough bread	1 tablespoon Dijon mustard
1/2 cup chopped roasted sweet red peppers	1 teaspoon pepper
1/2 pound Brie cheese, rind removed, cubed	1/2 teaspoon salt
2/3 cup grated Parmesan cheese	3/4 cup shredded part-skim mozzarella cheese
2 tablespoons minced fresh basil or 2 teaspoons dried basil	3 green onions, sliced

1. In a large skillet, cook sausage and onion over medium heat until meat is no longer pink; drain.

2. Place bread cubes in a greased 13x9-inch baking dish. Layer with sausage mixture, red peppers, Brie and Parmesan cheeses and basil. In a large bowl, whisk eggs, cream, mustard, pepper and salt; pour over top. Cover and refrigerate overnight.

3. Remove from the refrigerator 30 minutes before baking. Preheat oven to 350°. Bake, uncovered, 45–50 minutes or until a knife inserted near the center comes out clean.

4. Sprinkle with mozzarella cheese. Bake 4–6 minutes or until cheese is melted. Let stand 10 minutes before cutting. Sprinkle with green onions.

NUTRITIONAL FACTS
1 PIECE: 424 calories, 31 g fat (17 g saturated fat), 237 mg cholesterol, 779 mg sodium, 17 g carbohydrate (2 g sugars, 1 g fiber), 19 g protein

Take-It Tip **When you bring a dish to pass at a potluck, add a label or create a small card to place in front of the item. This tells guests what they're enjoying and notes whom they should see for the recipe!**

Crustless Spinach Quiche

PREP: 25 MINUTES ● **BAKE:** 40 MINUTES ● **YIELD:** 8 SERVINGS

I served this dish at a church luncheon, and I had to laugh when one gentleman told me his distaste for vegetables. He, along with many others, were surprised how much they loved this veggie-filled quiche!

—*Melinda Calverley, Janesville, Wisconsin*

1 cup chopped onion
1 cup sliced fresh mushrooms
1 tablespoon vegetable oil
1 package (10 ounces) frozen chopped spinach, thawed and well drained

⅔ cup finely chopped fully cooked ham
5 large eggs
3 cups shredded Muenster or Monterey Jack cheese
⅛ teaspoon pepper

Preheat oven to 350°. In a large skillet, saute onion and mushrooms in oil until tender. Add spinach and ham; cook and stir until the excess moisture is evaporated. Cool slightly. In a large bowl, beat eggs; add cheese and mix well. Stir in spinach mixture and pepper; blend well. Spread evenly into a greased 9-inch pie plate or quiche dish. Bake for 40–45 minutes or until a knife inserted in the center comes out clean.

NUTRITIONAL FACTS
1 PIECE: 255 calories, 19 g fat (10 g saturated fat), 180 mg cholesterol, 482 mg sodium, 5 g carbohydrate (2 g sugars, 2 g fiber), 17 g protein

Golden Corn Quiche

PREP: 20 MINUTES ● **BAKE:** 35 MINUTES + STANDING ● **YIELD:** 8 SERVINGS

I serve cut-up fresh fruit with this comforting quiche, which my vegetarian son really enjoys. You could also pair it with a slice or two of ham. Try it for brunch or dinner.
—*Donna Gonda, North Canton, Ohio*

1 unbaked pastry shell (9 inches)	1 tablespoon all-purpose flour
1⅓ cups half-and-half cream	1 tablespoon sugar
3 large eggs	1 teaspoon salt
3 tablespoons butter, melted	2 cups frozen corn, thawed
½ small onion, cut into wedges	

1. Preheat oven to 375°. Let pastry shell stand at room temperature for 10 minutes. Line unpricked pastry shell with a double thickness of heavy-duty foil. Bake for 5 minutes. Remove foil; bake 5 minutes longer.

2. In a blender, combine the cream, eggs, butter, onion, flour, sugar and salt; cover and process until blended. Stir in corn; pour into crust.

3. Bake for 35–40 minutes or until a knife inserted near the center comes out clean. Let stand for 10 minutes before cutting.

NUTRITIONAL FACTS
1 PIECE: 285 calories, 17 g fat (9 g saturated fat), 116 mg cholesterol, 473 mg sodium, 26 g carbohydrate (5 g sugars, 1 g fiber), 6 g protein

Cheesy Egg Puffs

PREP: 15 MINUTES • **BAKE:** 35 MINUTES • **YIELD:** 2½ DOZEN

My father loves to entertain, and these buttery egg delights are one of his favorite items to serve at brunch. The leftovers are perfect to reheat in the microwave on busy mornings, so Dad always stashes a few aside for me to take home once the party is over.

—Amy Soto, Winfield, Kansas

½ pound fresh mushrooms, sliced	1 teaspoon baking powder
4 green onions, chopped	½ teaspoon salt
1 tablespoon plus ½ cup butter, cubed, divided	10 large eggs, lightly beaten
½ cup all-purpose flour	4 cups shredded Monterey Jack cheese
	2 cups (16 ounces) 4% cottage cheese

1. Preheat oven to 350°. In a skillet, saute the mushrooms and onions in 1 tablespoon butter until tender. In a large bowl, combine the flour, baking powder and salt.

2. In another bowl, combine eggs and cheeses. Melt remaining butter; add to egg mixture. Stir into dry ingredients along with mushroom mixture.

3. Fill greased muffin cups three-fourths full. Bake for 35–40 minutes or until a knife inserted near the center comes out clean. Carefully run the knife around edge of muffin cups before removing.

NUTRITIONAL FACTS
2 EACH: 275 calories, 21 g fat (12 g saturated fat), 194 mg cholesterol, 486 mg sodium, 6 g carbohydrate (2 g sugars, 0 fiber), 16 g protein

Quick Tip The next time you have to grate a large block of cheese for a church supper specialty, spritz the grater with nonstick cooking spray before you begin. Not only will this help the cheese grate with ease, but you'll find that cleanup is an absolute snap.

Twice-Baked Breakfast Potatoes

PREP: 30 MINUTES • **BAKE:** 15 MINUTES • **YIELD:** 8 SERVINGS

Leftover baked potatoes were the inspiration for this impromptu meal. The bacon and sausage combo makes it a hearty breakfast dish, but it makes a filling lunch or dinner as well.

—William Brock, Amelia, Ohio

4 large baking potatoes	³⁄₄ cup shredded cheddar cheese, divided
1 tablespoon butter	¹⁄₂ cup minced chives, divided
4 large eggs, beaten	1 tablespoon minced fresh parsley
10 ounces bulk sausage	¹⁄₂ teaspoon salt
¹⁄₄ cup sour cream	¹⁄₂ teaspoon pepper
8 bacon strips, cooked and crumbled	Additional sour cream, optional

1. Preheat oven to 375°. Scrub potatoes; pierce several times with a fork. Place on a microwave-safe plate. Microwave, uncovered, on high for 15–17 minutes or until tender, turning once.

2. Meanwhile, in a large skillet, melt butter over medium-high heat. Add the eggs; cook and stir until set. Remove and set aside. In the same skillet, cook sausage over medium heat until no longer pink; drain and set aside.

3. When potatoes are cool enough to handle, cut each in half lengthwise. Scoop out pulp, leaving thin shells. In a large bowl, mash the pulp with sour cream. Stir in the bacon, ¹⁄₂ cup cheese, ¹⁄₄ cup chives, parsley, salt, pepper, eggs and sausage. Spoon into potato shells.

4. Place on a baking sheet. Bake, uncovered, for 12–15 minutes or until heated through. Sprinkle with remaining cheese and chives. Serve with additional sour cream if desired.

NUTRITIONAL FACTS
1 EACH: 354 calories, 18 g fat (8 g saturated fat), 146 mg cholesterol, 562 mg sodium, 35 g carbohydrate (4 g sugars, 3 g fiber), 14 g protein

Eggsquisite Breakfast Casserole

PREP: 20 MINUTES ● **BAKE:** 55 MINUTES + STANDING ● **YIELD:** 12–16 SERVINGS

I developed this recipe over 20 years ago. The rich warm sauce tastes especially great on cold winter mornings. I hope your family enjoys it as much as mine!

—*Bee Fischer, Jefferson, Wisconsin*

- 1 pound sliced bacon, diced
- 2 packages (4½ ounces each) sliced dried beef, cut into thin strips
- 1 can (4 ounces) sliced mushrooms
- ½ cup all-purpose flour
- ⅛ teaspoon pepper
- 4 cups whole milk
- 16 large eggs
- 1 cup evaporated milk
- ¼ teaspoon salt
- ¼ cup butter, cubed
- Chopped fresh parsley, optional

1. Preheat oven to 350°. In a large skillet, cook bacon until crisp. Remove bacon to paper towels to drain; discard all but ¼ cup drippings. In the same skillet, add the beef, mushrooms, flour and pepper to the drippings; cook until thoroughly combined. Gradually add milk; cook and stir until thickened. Stir in bacon; set aside.

2. In a large bowl, whisk eggs, evaporated milk and salt. In another large skillet, heat butter until hot. Add egg mixture; cook and stir over medium heat until eggs are completely set.

3. Place half of the eggs in a greased 13x9-inch baking dish; pour half the sauce over the eggs. Repeat layers. Cover and bake for 55–65 minutes or until a knife inserted near the center comes out clean. Let stand 5 minutes before serving.

NUTRITIONAL FACTS
1 PIECE: 240 calories, 16 g fat (7 g saturated fat), 245 mg cholesterol, 634 mg sodium, 9 g carbohydrate (5 g sugars, 0 fiber), 15 g protein

Ham & Cheese Breakfast Strudels

PREP: 25 MINUTES ● **BAKE:** 10 MINUTES ● **YIELD:** 6 SERVINGS

These get the morning off to a great start! Sometimes I assemble the strudels ahead and freeze them individually before baking.

—Jo Groth, Plainfield, Iowa

3 tablespoons butter, divided
2 tablespoons all-purpose flour
1 cup 2% milk
⅓ cup shredded Swiss cheese
2 tablespoons grated Parmesan cheese
¼ teaspoon salt
5 large eggs, lightly beaten
¼ pound ground fully cooked ham
(about ¾ cup)

6 sheets phyllo dough (14x9-inch size)
½ cup butter, melted
¼ cup dry bread crumbs

TOPPING:

2 tablespoons grated Parmesan cheese
2 tablespoons minced fresh parsley

1. In a small saucepan, melt 2 tablespoons butter. Stir in flour until smooth; gradually add milk. Bring to a boil; cook and stir 2 minutes or until thickened. Stir in cheeses and salt.

2. In a large nonstick skillet, melt remaining butter over medium heat. Add eggs to pan; cook and stir until almost set. Stir in ham and cheese sauce; heat through. Remove from heat.

3. Preheat oven to 375°. Place one sheet of phyllo dough on a work surface. (Keep remaining phyllo covered with plastic wrap and a damp towel to prevent it from drying out.) Brush with melted butter. Sprinkle with 2 teaspoons bread crumbs. Fold in half lengthwise; brush again with butter. Spoon ½ cup filling onto phyllo about 2 inches from a short side. Fold side and edges over filling and roll up. Brush with butter. Repeat with remaining phyllo, butter, bread crumbs and filling.

4. Place on a greased baking sheet; sprinkle each with 1 teaspoon cheese and 1 teaspoon parsley. Bake 10–15 minutes or until golden brown. Serve immediately.

NUTRITIONAL FACTS
1 EACH: 439 calories, 33 g fat (18 g saturated fat), 255 mg cholesterol, 754 mg sodium, 20 g carbohydrate (4 g sugars, 1 g fiber), 16 g protein

Freeze It **After topping strudels with cheese and parsley, freeze unbaked on a waxed paper–lined baking sheet until firm. Transfer to a freezer container; return to freezer. To use, bake strudels as directed, increasing time to 30–35 minutes or until heated through and golden brown.**

New Mexico Green Chili Breakfast Burritos

PREP/TOTAL TIME: 25 MINUTES • **YIELD:** 6 SERVINGS

Here in the Southwest, we wrap everything up in a tortilla. Breakfast burritos in every possible combination are very popular in New Mexico.

—*Angela Spengler, Clovis, New Mexico*

6 large eggs
3 large egg whites
1 jalapeno pepper, seeded and minced
  Dash cayenne pepper
4 breakfast turkey sausage links, casings removed

¾ cup shredded reduced-fat Mexican cheese blend
1 can (4 ounces) chopped green chilies, drained
6 whole wheat tortillas (8 inches), warmed
6 tablespoons salsa

1. In a small bowl, whisk the eggs, egg whites, jalapeno and cayenne; set aside.

2. Crumble sausage into a large skillet; cook over medium heat until no longer pink. Drain. Push sausage to the sides of pan. Pour egg mixture into center of pan. Cook and stir until set. Sprinkle with cheese and chilies. Remove from the heat; cover and let stand until cheese is melted.

3. Place ⅓ cup mixture off center on each tortilla. Fold sides and end over filling and roll up. Top with salsa.

NOTE: Wear disposable gloves when cutting hot peppers; the oils can burn skin. Avoid touching your face.

NUTRITIONAL FACTS
1 BURRITO WITH 1 TABLESPOON SALSA: 290 calories, 12 g fat (3 g saturated fat), 232 mg cholesterol, 586 mg sodium, 25 g carbohydrate (2 g sugars, 2 g fiber), 19 g protein

Sausage Breakfast Burritos

PREP/TOTAL TIME: 20 MINUTES • **YIELD:** 8 SERVINGS

These are a fun and filling way to serve scrambled eggs, and the zippy flavor will wake up your taste buds.

—*Brenda Spann, Granger, Indiana*

1 pound bulk pork sausage	1 tablespoon butter
1 small onion, chopped	6 large eggs, beaten
½ green pepper, chopped	8 flour tortillas (8 inches), warmed
1 can (4 ounces) mushroom stems and pieces, drained	1 cup shredded cheddar cheese
	Salsa, optional

1. In a large skillet, brown sausage. Drain, reserving 2 tablespoons drippings. Saute the onion, green pepper and mushrooms in drippings until tender.

2. In another skillet, melt butter over medium-high heat. Add eggs; cook and stir until set.

3. Divide sausage mixture among tortillas; top with eggs and cheese. Fold bottom of tortilla over filling and roll up. Serve with salsa if desired.

NUTRITIONAL FACTS
1 BURRITO: 751 calories, 43 g fat (17 g saturated fat), 390 mg cholesterol, 1333 mg sodium, 57 g carbohydrate (4 g sugars, 1 g fiber), 33 g protein

Good-Morning Granola

PREP: 15 MINUTES ● **BAKE:** 20 MINUTES + COOLING ● **YIELD:** 7½ CUPS

This is ridiculously easy to make and has lots of healthy ingredients. It's a great way to start your day or to keep you going. With pretty packaging, it makes a nice gift or bake sale item.

—Mary Bilyeu, Ann Arbor, Michigan

4 cups old-fashioned oats	½ cup honey
½ cup toasted wheat germ	2 teaspoons canola oil
½ cup sliced almonds	1 teaspoon vanilla extract
2 teaspoons ground cinnamon	1 cup dried cherries
⅛ teaspoon salt	1 cup dried cranberries
½ cup orange juice	Reduced-fat plain yogurt, optional

1. Preheat oven to 350°. In a large bowl, combine the first five ingredients; set aside. In a small saucepan, combine orange juice, honey and oil. Bring to a boil, stirring constantly. Remove from heat; stir in vanilla. Pour over oat mixture and mix well.

2. Transfer to a 15x10x1-inch baking pan coated with cooking spray. Bake 20–25 minutes or until golden brown, stirring every 10 minutes. Cool completely on a wire rack.

3. Stir in dried fruits. Store in an airtight container. Serve with yogurt if desired.

NUTRITIONAL FACTS
½ CUP: 206 calories, 4 g fat (0 saturated fat), 0 cholesterol, 21 mg sodium, 40 g carbohydrate (21 g sugars, 4 g fiber), 5 g protein

Baked Blueberry & Peach Oatmeal

PREP: 20 MINUTES • **BAKE:** 35 MINUTES • **YIELD:** 9 SERVINGS

This oatmeal bake is a staple in our home. It's very easy to prepare the night before, just keep the dry and wet ingredients separate until ready to bake. I've tried a variety of fruits, but the blueberry and peach is our favorite.

—*Rosemarie Weleski, Natrona Heights, Pennsylvania*

3 cups old-fashioned oats
½ cup packed brown sugar
2 teaspoons baking powder
½ teaspoon salt
2 large egg whites
1 large egg
1¼ cups fat-free milk

¼ cup canola oil
1 teaspoon vanilla extract
1 can (15 ounces) sliced peaches in juice, drained and chopped
1 cup fresh or frozen blueberries
⅓ cup chopped walnuts
Additional fat-free milk, optional

1. Preheat oven to 350°. In a large bowl, combine the oats, brown sugar, baking powder and salt. In a medium bowl, whisk the egg whites, egg, milk, oil and vanilla; add to dry ingredients and stir until blended. Let stand for 5 minutes. Stir in peaches and blueberries.

2. Transfer to an 11x7-inch baking dish coated with cooking spray. Sprinkle with walnuts. Bake, uncovered, for 35–40 minutes or until top is lightly browned and a thermometer reads 160°. Serve with additional milk if desired.

NUTRITIONAL FACTS
1 SERVING (CALCULATED WITHOUT ADDITIONAL MILK): 277 calories, 11 g fat (1 g saturated fat), 24 mg cholesterol, 263 mg sodium, 38 g carbohydrate (19 g sugars, 3 g fiber), 8 g protein

Apple Walnut Pancakes

PREP/TOTAL TIME: 30 MINUTES ● **YIELD:** 18 PANCAKES

The whole wheat flavor really comes through in these hearty pancakes. They taste great with a light touch of maple syrup.

—Kerry Blondheim, Denmark, Wisconsin

1 cup all-purpose flour	1 large egg, lightly beaten
1 cup whole wheat flour	2 cups fat-free milk
1 tablespoon brown sugar	2 tablespoons canola oil
2 teaspoons baking powder	1 medium apple, peeled and chopped
1 teaspoon salt	$\frac{1}{2}$ cup chopped walnuts
2 large egg whites	Maple syrup

1. In a large bowl, whisk flours, brown sugar, baking powder and salt. In another bowl, whisk egg whites, egg, milk and oil until blended. Add to dry ingredients, stirring just until moistened. Fold in apple and walnuts.

2. Heat a griddle coated with cooking spray on medium heat. Pour batter by $\frac{1}{4}$ cupfuls onto griddle. Cook until bubbles on top begin to pop and bottoms are golden brown. Turn; cook until second side is golden brown. Serve with syrup.

NUTRITIONAL FACTS
2 PANCAKES (CALCULATED WITHOUT SYRUP): 208 calories, 8 g fat (1 g saturated fat), 25 mg cholesterol, 396 mg sodium, 27 g carbohydrate (6 g sugars, 3 g fiber), 8 g protein

Freeze It

Freeze cooled pancakes between layers of waxed paper in a resealable plastic freezer bag. To use, place pancakes on an ungreased baking sheet, cover with foil and reheat in a preheated 375° oven for 6–10 minutes. Or, place a stack of three pancakes on a microwave-safe plate and microwave on high for $1\frac{1}{4}$ to $1\frac{1}{2}$ minutes or until heated through.

Sweet Potato Pancakes with Cinnamon Cream

PREP: 25 MINUTES • **COOK:** 5 MINUTES/BATCH • **YIELD:** 12 SERVINGS (1½ CUPS TOPPING)

Topped with a rich cinnamon cream, these pancakes are an ideal side dish for celebrating the tastes and aromas of fall.

—*Tammy Rex, New Tripoli, Pennsylvania*

- 1 package (8 ounces) cream cheese, softened
- ¼ cup packed brown sugar
- ½ teaspoon ground cinnamon
- ½ cup sour cream
- 6 large eggs
- ¾ cup all-purpose flour
- ½ teaspoon ground nutmeg
- ½ teaspoon salt
- ¼ teaspoon pepper
- 6 cups shredded peeled sweet potatoes (about 3 large)
- 3 cups shredded peeled apples (about 3 large)
- ⅓ cup grated onion
- ½ cup canola oil

1. In a small bowl, beat the cream cheese, brown sugar and cinnamon until blended; beat in sour cream. Set aside.

2. In a large bowl, whisk the eggs, flour, nutmeg, salt and pepper. Add the sweet potatoes, apples and onion; toss to coat.

3. In a large nonstick skillet, heat 2 tablespoons oil over medium heat. Working in batches, drop sweet potato mixture by ⅓ cupfuls into oil; press slightly to flatten. Fry for 2–3 minutes on each side until golden brown, using remaining oil as needed. Drain on paper towels. Serve with cinnamon topping.

NUTRITIONAL FACTS
2 PANCAKES WITH 2 TABLESPOONS TOPPING: 325 calories, 21 g fat (7 g saturated fat), 114 mg cholesterol, 203 mg sodium, 30 g carbohydrate (15 g sugars, 3 g fiber), 6 g protein

Dutch Baby Pancake with Strawberry-Almond Compote

PREP: 15 MINUTES • **BAKE:** 20 MINUTES • **YIELD:** 6 SERVINGS (3 CUPS TOPPING)

Pannekoeken, or Dutch baked pancakes, are a treat in my husband's family. You can also try this recipe with vanilla extract, blueberries and lemon peel.

—*Jennifer Beckman, Falls Church, Virginia*

2 tablespoons butter
4 large eggs
$\frac{2}{3}$ cup 2% milk
2 tablespoons grated orange peel
$\frac{1}{2}$ teaspoon almond extract
$\frac{2}{3}$ cup all-purpose flour
2 tablespoons sugar
$\frac{1}{2}$ teaspoon kosher salt

TOPPING:

1 pound fresh strawberries, hulled and quartered
$\frac{1}{2}$ cup slivered almonds, toasted
2 tablespoons orange juice
1 tablespoon sugar

1. Preheat oven to 400°. Place butter in a 9-inch pie plate. Place in oven for 4–5 minutes or until butter is melted; carefully swirl to coat evenly.

2. Meanwhile, in a large bowl, whisk eggs, milk, orange peel and extract until blended. Whisk in flour, sugar and salt. Pour into hot pie plate. Bake 20–25 minutes or until puffed and sides are golden brown and crisp.

3. In a small bowl, combine topping ingredients. Remove pancake from oven; serve immediately with topping.

NOTE: To toast nuts, bake in a shallow pan in a 350° oven for 5–10 minutes or cook in a skillet over low heat until lightly browned, stirring occasionally.

NUTRITIONAL FACTS
1 SLICE WITH $\frac{1}{2}$ CUP TOPPING: 252 calories, 13 g fat (4 g saturated fat), 153 mg cholesterol, 245 mg sodium, 27 g carbohydrate (13 g sugars, 3 g fiber), 9 g protein

Quick Tip

Almonds are versatile nuts. They blend well with other items, savory and sweet, and they're delicious eaten as a nutritious snack. They offer a great crunch in recipes.

Savory Sausage French Toast

PREP: 15 MINUTES • **COOK:** 20 MINUTES • **YIELD:** 6 SERVINGS

I first made French toast with sausage to use up leftovers. Now I make it because it's a heavenly way to start the day.

—*Suzanne Earl, Spring, Texas*

2 packages (12 ounces each) reduced-fat bulk pork sausage
2 tablespoons butter
2 tablespoons all-purpose flour
2 cups heavy whipping cream
1 cup 2% milk, divided

$\frac{1}{2}$ cup grated Parmesan cheese
1 teaspoon pepper
$\frac{1}{4}$ teaspoon salt
3 large eggs
6 slices French bread (1 inch thick)

1. In a large skillet, cook sausage over medium heat 6–8 minutes or until no longer pink, breaking into crumbles; remove with a slotted spoon. Discard drippings. In same skillet, heat butter over medium heat. Stir in flour until blended; gradually stir in cream and $\frac{1}{2}$ cup milk. Bring to a boil, stirring constantly; cook and stir 4–6 minutes or until sauce is thickened. Stir in sausage, cheese, pepper and salt; keep warm.

2. Lightly grease a griddle; heat over medium heat. Meanwhile, in a shallow bowl, whisk eggs and remaining milk until blended. Dip both sides of bread in egg mixture. Cook 2–3 minutes on each side or until golden brown. Serve with gravy.

NUTRITIONAL FACTS
1 SLICE FRENCH TOAST WITH $\frac{2}{3}$ CUP GRAVY: 723 calories, 59 g fat (30 g saturated fat), 259 mg cholesterol, 1171 mg sodium, 21 g carbohydrate (4 g sugars, 1 g fiber), 29 g protein

Orange-Cinnamon French Toast

PREP/TOTAL TIME: 30 MINUTES ● **YIELD:** 6 SLICES

Everyone eats at the same time when you fix this tasty oven-baked French toast.
—Bernice Smith, Sturgeon Lake, Minnesota

2 to 4   tablespoons butter, melted
   2   tablespoons honey
  $\frac{1}{2}$ teaspoon ground cinnamon
   3   large eggs

$\frac{1}{2}$ cup orange juice
$\frac{1}{8}$ teaspoon salt, optional
 6   slices bread
   Additional honey, optional

1. Preheat oven to 400°. In a small bowl, mix the butter, honey and cinnamon. Pour into a greased 13x9-inch baking pan; spread to coat bottom of pan.

2. In a shallow bowl, whisk the eggs, orange juice and, if desired, salt. Dip both sides of bread in egg mixture. Place in prepared pan.

3. Bake for 15–20 minutes or until golden brown. Invert onto a serving platter; serve with honey if desired.

NUTRITIONAL FACTS
1 SLICE: 158 calories, 5 g fat (0 saturated fat), 1 mg cholesterol, 231 mg sodium, 23 g carbohydrate (0 sugars, 0 fiber), 6 g protein

Bananas Foster Baked French Toast

PREP: 20 MINUTES + CHILLING ● **BAKE:** 35 MINUTES + STANDING ● **YIELD:** 6 SERVINGS

Mmm . . . bananas Foster for breakfast! This yummy baked French toast serves up all the taste of the spectacular dessert in fine fashion.

—L G Nasson, Quincy, Massachusetts

½ cup butter, cubed
⅔ cup packed brown sugar
½ cup heavy whipping cream
½ teaspoon ground cinnamon
½ teaspoon ground allspice
¼ cup chopped pecans, optional

3 large bananas, sliced
12 slices egg bread or challah (about ¾ pound)
1½ cups 2% milk
3 large eggs
1 tablespoon sugar
1 teaspoon vanilla extract

1. Place butter in a microwave-safe bowl; microwave, covered, 30–45 seconds or until melted. Stir in brown sugar, cream, cinnamon, allspice and, if desired, pecans. Add bananas; toss gently to coat.

2. Transfer to a greased 13x9-inch baking dish. Arrange bread over top, trimming to fit as necessary.

3. Place remaining ingredients in a blender; process just until blended. Pour over bread. Refrigerate, covered, 8 hours or overnight.

4. Preheat oven to 375°. Remove French toast from refrigerator while oven heats. Bake, uncovered, 35–40 minutes or until a knife inserted near the center comes out clean. Let stand 5–10 minutes. Invert to serve.

NUTRITIONAL FACTS
1 PIECE (CALCULATED WITHOUT PECANS): 658 calories, 31 g fat (17 g saturated fat), 218 mg cholesterol, 584 mg sodium, 84 g carbohydrate (39 g sugars, 4 g fiber), 14 g protein

Overnight Apple French Toast

PREP: 25 MINUTES + CHILLING ● **BAKE:** 35 MINUTES ● **YIELD:** 9 SERVINGS

My in-laws own and operate an orchard, so we have an abundance of fruit fresh from the trees. This dish includes fresh apples, apple jelly and applesauce all in one recipe. It's a warm, hearty breakfast for busy days.
—Debra Blazer, Hegins, Pennsylvania

1 cup packed brown sugar	**SYRUP:**
½ cup butter, cubed	1 jar (10 ounces) apple jelly
2 tablespoons light corn syrup	1 cup applesauce
2 large tart apples, peeled and cut into ¼-inch slices	½ teaspoon ground cinnamon
3 large eggs	⅛ teaspoon ground cloves
1 cup whole milk	
1 teaspoon vanilla extract	
9 slices day-old French bread (¾ inch thick)	

1. In a small saucepan, combine the brown sugar, butter and syrup. Cook over medium heat for 5–7 minutes or until thickened. Pour into an ungreased 13x9-inch baking dish. Arrange apples over top.

2. In a large bowl, beat eggs, milk and vanilla. Dip bread slices into the egg mixture 1 minute; place over apples. Cover and refrigerate overnight.

3. Remove from the refrigerator 30 minutes before baking. Preheat oven to 350°. Bake, uncovered, 35–40 minutes. Meanwhile, in a small saucepan, combine syrup ingredients; heat through. Serve with French toast.

NUTRITIONAL FACTS
1 EACH: 394 calories, 13 g fat (7 g saturated fat), 102 mg cholesterol, 259 mg sodium, 67 g carbohydrate (53 g sugars, 1 g fiber), 5 g protein

Quick Tip
When making French toast, try giving it a boost by using a flavored nondairy coffee creamer instead of milk in the egg-milk mixture. French vanilla is especially yummy.

Breakfast Praline Bread Pudding

PREP: 20 MINUTES + CHILLING • **BAKE:** 40 MINUTES • **YIELD:** 12 SERVINGS

Baked French toast inspired this simple make-ahead dish that's perfect for a large holiday meal in the morning. It also travels well.

—Erin Furby, Anchorage, Alaska

8 large eggs, lightly beaten
2 cups half-and-half cream
1 cup 2% milk
2 tablespoons brown sugar
3 teaspoons vanilla extract
1 teaspoon ground cinnamon
$\frac{3}{4}$ teaspoon ground nutmeg

$\frac{1}{2}$ teaspoon salt
1 loaf (1 pound) French bread, cut into 1-inch cubes
1 cup chopped pecans
$\frac{1}{2}$ cup packed brown sugar
$\frac{1}{2}$ cup butter, melted

1. In a large bowl, whisk the first eight ingredients until blended. Stir in bread. Transfer to a greased 13x9-inch baking dish. Sprinkle with pecans and brown sugar; drizzle with butter. Refrigerate, covered, several hours or overnight.

2. Preheat oven to 350°. Remove bread pudding from refrigerator; uncover and let stand while oven heats. Bake 40–50 minutes or until puffed, golden and a knife inserted near the center comes out clean. Serve warm.

NUTRITIONAL FACTS
1 SERVING: 403 calories, 23 g fat (10 g saturated fat), 183 mg cholesterol, 479 mg sodium, 37 g carbohydrate (15 g sugars, 2 g fiber), 12 g protein

Chocolate-Peanut Granola Bars

PREP/TOTAL TIME: 30 MINUTES • **YIELD:** 2 DOZEN

Nutella and peanut butter meet to make some amazing granola bars. Everyone always thinks they're eating something naughty when I serve these, but they're full of oats and healthy fats.

—*Brenda Caughell, Durham, North Carolina*

2½ cups old-fashioned oats	½ cup honey
¾ cup lightly salted dry roasted peanuts, coarsely chopped	¼ cup packed brown sugar
	3 tablespoons butter
¾ cup wheat germ	⅓ cup creamy peanut butter
¾ cup sunflower kernels	⅓ cup Nutella

1. Preheat oven to 400°. In an ungreased 15x10x1-inch baking pan, combine oats, peanuts, wheat germ and sunflower kernels. Bake 8–12 minutes or until toasted, stirring occasionally. Cool on a wire rack.

2. In a small saucepan, combine honey, brown sugar and butter. Cook and stir over medium heat until mixture comes to a boil; cook 2 minutes longer. Remove from heat; stir in peanut butter and Nutella until blended.

3. Transfer oat mixture to a large bowl; add honey mixture and toss to coat. Press into a greased 13x9-inch pan. Cool. Cut into bars.

NUTRITIONAL FACTS
1 BAR: 178 calories, 10 g fat (2 g saturated fat), 4 mg cholesterol, 75 mg sodium, 20 g carbohydrate (11 g sugars, 2 g fiber), 5 g protein

Morning Maple Muffins

PREP/TOTAL TIME: 30 MINUTES ● **YIELD:** 16 MUFFINS

Maple combines with a subtle touch of cinnamon and nuts to give these muffins the flavor of a hearty pancake breakfast. But you don't have to sit down to enjoy them. Our 2-year-old comes back for seconds, and even my husband, who's not a muffin eater, likes these.

—*Elizabeth Talbot, Lexington, Kentucky*

2 cups all-purpose flour
½ cup packed brown sugar
2 teaspoons baking powder
½ teaspoon salt
¾ cup whole milk
½ cup butter, melted
½ cup maple syrup
¼ cup sour cream
1 large egg
½ teaspoon vanilla extract

TOPPING:
3 tablespoons all-purpose flour
3 tablespoons sugar
2 tablespoons chopped nuts
½ teaspoon ground cinnamon
2 tablespoons cold butter

1. Preheat oven to 400°. In a large bowl, combine flour, brown sugar, baking powder and salt. In another bowl, combine milk, butter, syrup, sour cream, egg and vanilla. Stir into dry ingredients just until moistened.

2. Fill greased or paper-lined muffin cups two-thirds full. For topping, combine flour, sugar, nuts and cinnamon; cut in butter until crumbly. Sprinkle over batter.

3. Bake 16–20 minutes or until a toothpick inserted in center comes out clean. Cool 5 minutes before removing from pans to wire racks. Serve warm.

NUTRITIONAL FACTS
1 EACH: 212 calories, 9 g fat (5 g saturated fat), 36 mg cholesterol, 211 mg sodium, 30 g carbohydrate (16 g sugars, 1 g fiber), 3 g protein

Freeze It **Freeze cooled muffins in resealable plastic freezer bags. To use, thaw at room temperature or, if desired, microwave each muffin on high for 20–30 seconds or until heated through.**

Berry Cream Muffins

PREP: 15 MINUTES ● **BAKE:** 20 MINUTES ● **YIELD:** ABOUT 2 DOZEN

If you can't decide which berries to use in these muffins, you can't go wrong using half raspberries and half blueberries!

—Linda Gilmore, Hampstead, Maryland

4 cups all-purpose flour	4 large eggs, lightly beaten
2 cups sugar	2 cups (16 ounces) sour cream
1¼ teaspoons baking powder	1 cup canola oil
1 teaspoon baking soda	1 teaspoon vanilla extract
1 teaspoon salt	
3 cups fresh or frozen raspberries or blueberries	

1. Preheat oven to 400°. In a large bowl, combine the flour, sugar, baking powder, baking soda and salt; add berries and toss gently. In a medium bowl, combine the eggs, sour cream, oil and vanilla; mix well. Stir into dry ingredients just until moistened.

2. Fill greased muffin cups two-thirds full. Bake for 20–25 minutes or until a toothpick inserted near the center comes out clean. Cool for 5 minutes before removing from pans to a wire rack. Serve warm.

NUTRITIONAL FACTS
1 EACH: 481 calories, 23 g fat (6 g saturated fat), 84 mg cholesterol, 330 mg sodium, 60 g carbohydrate (31 g sugars, 3 g fiber), 7 g protein

Blueberry Brunch Loaf

PREP: 15 MINUTES ● **BAKE:** 55 MINUTES + COOLING ● **YIELD:** 1 LOAF

I like to make special breakfasts on the weekend for my husband and children. This recipe's sweet frosting really makes the already delicious blueberry bread even tastier.

—*Jean Nietert, Claremont, South Dakota*

¼ cup butter, softened	**GLAZE:**
¾ cup packed brown sugar	½ cup confectioners' sugar
1 large egg	2 teaspoons butter, softened
1 tablespoon grated orange peel	½ teaspoon grated orange peel
2¼ cups all-purpose flour	1 to 1½ tablespoons whole milk
1 tablespoon baking powder	
½ teaspoon salt	
½ cup whole milk	
¼ cup orange juice	
1 cup fresh or frozen blueberries	

1. Preheat oven to 350°. In a large bowl, cream butter and brown sugar. Stir in egg and orange peel. In a medium bowl, combine flour, baking powder and salt; add to creamed mixture alternately with milk and juice, mixing thoroughly after each addition. Fold in blueberries. Pour into a greased 9x5-inch loaf pan.

2. Bake for 50–55 minutes or until bread tests done. Cool in pan 10 minutes before removing to a wire rack.

3. For glaze, combine sugar, butter and orange peel. Gradually add milk until glaze is of spreading consistency; drizzle over warm bread.

NUTRITIONAL FACTS
1 SLICE: 164 calories, 4 g fat (2 g saturated fat), 23 mg cholesterol, 195 mg sodium, 29 g carbohydrate (16 g sugars, 1 g fiber), 3 g protein

Petite Sticky Buns

PREP: 30 MINUTES + RISING ● BAKE: 15 MINUTES ● YIELD: 2 DOZEN

Start your morning on a sweet note with these tender, maple sticky buns. They are fantastically light and airy. But be careful not to overbake, or they're difficult to get out of the pan!

—*Lisa Naugle, Fayetteville, Pennsylvania*

3 to 3¼ cups all-purpose flour
   ¼ cup sugar
   1 package (¼ ounce) active dry yeast
   1 teaspoon salt
 1¼ cups whole milk
   ¼ cup butter, cubed
   1 large egg

TOPPING:
   1 cup packed brown sugar
   ¾ cup butter, cubed
   ¾ cup chopped pecans, toasted
   2 tablespoons honey
   1 teaspoon ground cinnamon
   ½ teaspoon maple flavoring

1. In a large bowl, combine 2 cups flour, sugar, yeast and salt. In a small saucepan, heat the milk and butter to 120°–130°. Add to dry ingredients; beat just until moistened. Add egg; beat until smooth. Stir in enough remaining flour to form a soft dough (dough will be sticky). Do not knead. Cover and let rise in a warm place until doubled, about an hour.

2. In a small saucepan over low heat, cook and stir topping ingredients until butter is melted. Drop by rounded teaspoonfuls into 24 well-greased muffin cups.

3. Stir dough down. Fill prepared muffin cups half full. Cover and let rise in a warm place until doubled, about 30 minutes.

4. Preheat oven to 375°. Place muffin cups on foil-lined baking sheets. Bake for 12–15 minutes or until golden brown. Cool for 2 minutes before inverting onto baking sheets. Transfer to serving platters. Serve warm.

NUTRITIONAL FACTS
1 EACH: 210 calories, 11 g fat (5 g saturated fat), 30 mg cholesterol, 164 mg sodium, 26 g carbohydrate (13 g sugars, 1 g fiber), 3 g protein.

Orange Cheesecake Breakfast Rolls

PREP: 50 MINUTES + RISING • **BAKE:** 25 MINUTES • **YIELD:** 2 DOZEN

These yummy rolls are a nice change of pace from the typical brown sugar and cinnamon kind. They make a nice treat for breakfast or brunch.

—*Hannah Cobb, Owings Mills, Maryland*

2 packages ($\frac{1}{4}$ ounce each) active dry yeast
$\frac{3}{4}$ cup warm water (110° to 115°)
$1\frac{3}{4}$ cups warm 2% milk (110° to 115°)
1 cup sugar
2 large eggs
3 tablespoons butter, melted
$1\frac{1}{2}$ teaspoons salt
7 to 8 cups all-purpose flour

FILLING:
1 package (8 ounces) cream cheese, softened
$\frac{1}{2}$ cup sugar
1 tablespoon thawed orange juice concentrate
$\frac{1}{2}$ teaspoon vanilla extract

GLAZE:
2 cups confectioners' sugar
3 tablespoons orange juice
1 teaspoon grated orange peel

1. In a large bowl, dissolve yeast in warm water. Add milk, sugar, eggs, butter, salt and 5 cups flour. Beat until smooth. Stir in enough remaining flour to form a firm dough.

2. Turn onto a floured surface; knead until smooth and elastic, about 6–8 minutes. Place in a greased bowl, turning once to grease the top. Cover and let rise in a warm place until doubled, about 1 hour.

3. In a small bowl, beat cream cheese, sugar, orange juice concentrate and vanilla until smooth. Punch dough down. Turn onto a lightly floured surface; divide in half. Roll one portion into an 18x7-inch rectangle. Spread half of the filling to within $\frac{1}{2}$ inch of edges.

4. Roll up jelly-roll style, starting with a long side; pinch seam to seal. Cut into 12 slices; place cut side down in a greased 13x9-inch baking pan. Repeat with remaining dough and filling. Cover and let rise until doubled, about 30 minutes.

5. Meanwhile, preheat oven to 350°. Bake 25–30 minutes or until golden brown. Combine confectioners' sugar, orange juice and peel; drizzle over warm rolls. Refrigerate leftovers.

NUTRITIONAL FACTS
1 EACH: 284 calories, 6 g fat (3 g saturated fat), 33 mg cholesterol, 201 mg sodium, 52 g carbohydrate (24 g sugars, 1 g fiber), 6 g protein

Make It Ahead
Prepare, shape and place rolls in baking pans as directed. Cover and refrigerate overnight. Remove rolls from the refrigerator and let stand for 30 minutes. Bake and glaze as directed.

Lovely Lunches and Light Meals

Hearty Beef & Bean Soup

PREP: 15 MINUTES ● **COOK:** 30 MINUTES ● **YIELD:** 10 SERVINGS (4 QUARTS)

I love cooking, and often share my soups with my co-workers—and they're happy I do. This one is perfect for late summer, because it has a lot of zippy flavor but isn't as heavy as chili. I use my homegrown cayenne peppers in the recipe.

—Lori Steiner, Maquoketa, Iowa

- 1 pound lean ground beef (90% lean)
- 1 large onion, chopped
- 1 small green pepper, chopped
- 1 can (28 ounces) petite diced tomatoes, undrained
- 1 can (16 ounces) chili beans, undrained
- 1 can (15½ ounces) white kidney or cannellini beans, rinsed and drained
- 1 can (15 ounces) black beans, rinsed and drained

- 1 package (13½ ounces) beef smoked sausage, sliced
- 2 serrano peppers, seeded and chopped
- 2 teaspoons chili powder
- 1 teaspoon salt
- 1 carton (32 ounces) beef broth
- 2 cups water

1. In a Dutch oven, cook beef, onion and green pepper over medium heat 8–10 minutes or until meat is no longer pink, breaking up beef into crumbles. Drain.

2. Stir in remaining ingredients; bring to a boil. Reduce heat; simmer, uncovered, 15–20 minutes or until flavors are blended.

NOTE: Wear disposable gloves when cutting hot peppers; the oils can burn skin. Avoid touching your face.

NUTRITIONAL FACTS

1½ CUPS: 332 calories, 15 g fat (6 g saturated fat), 54 mg cholesterol, 1507 mg sodium, 28 g carbohydrate (6 g sugars, 8 g fiber), 22 g protein

Freeze It

Freeze cooled soup in freezer containers. To use, partially thaw in refrigerator overnight. Heat through in a saucepan, stirring occasionally.

Cabbage and Beef Soup

PREP: 10 MINUTES ● **COOK:** 70 MINUTES ● **YIELD:** 12 SERVINGS (3 QUARTS)

When I was a little girl, I helped my parents work the fields of their small farm. Lunchtime was always a treat when Mother picked fresh vegetables from her garden and simmered them in her big soup pot. We loved making this delicious soup.

—Ethel Ledbetter, Canton, North Carolina

1 pound lean ground beef (90% lean)
$\frac{1}{2}$ teaspoon garlic salt
$\frac{1}{4}$ teaspoon garlic powder
$\frac{1}{4}$ teaspoon pepper
2 celery ribs, chopped
1 can (16 ounces) kidney beans, rinsed and drained

$\frac{1}{2}$ medium head cabbage, chopped
1 can (28 ounces) diced tomatoes, undrained
$3\frac{1}{2}$ cups water
4 teaspoons beef bouillon granules
Minced fresh parsley

1. In a Dutch oven, cook beef over medium heat until no longer pink; drain. Stir in the remaining ingredients except parsley.

2. Bring to a boil. Reduce heat; cover and simmer for 1 hour. Garnish with parsley. If you are cooking for two, the soup can be frozen in serving-size portions to enjoy months later.

NUTRITIONAL FACTS
1 CUP: 116 calories, 3 g fat (1 g saturated fat), 19 mg cholesterol, 582 mg sodium, 11 g carbohydrate (3 g sugars, 3 g fiber), 11 g protein

Take-It Tip
If I decide to take a slow cooker dish to a party, I line a clean milk crate with a towel, take the cover off the slow cooker and put foil over the top. Then I set the cooker in the crate, along with my serving utensil. The crate keeps the cooker from tipping and also catches any drips.—Helen P., Horse Heads, NY

Chili con Carne

PREP: 20 MINUTES ● **COOK:** 1½ HOURS ● **YIELD:** 10 SERVINGS (ABOUT 2½ QUARTS)

At chili suppers, this one always disappears first! It's nice at home, too, since the longer it sits in the refrigerator, the better the taste seems to get.

—Janie Turner, Tuttle, Oklahoma

- 2 pounds ground beef
- 2 tablespoons olive oil
- 2 medium onions, chopped
- 2 garlic cloves, minced
- 1 medium green pepper, chopped
- 1½ teaspoons salt
- 2 tablespoons chili powder
- ⅛ teaspoon cayenne pepper
- ¼ teaspoon ground cinnamon
- 1 teaspoon ground cumin
- 1 teaspoon dried oregano
- 2 cans (14½ ounces each) diced tomatoes, undrained
- 3 teaspoons beef bouillon granules
- 1 cup water
- 1 can (16 ounces) kidney beans, rinsed and drained

1. In a Dutch oven, cook beef over medium heat until no longer pink; drain and set aside.

2. In the same pot, heat oil; saute onions until tender. Add garlic; cook 1 minute longer. Stir in the green pepper, salt, chili powder, cayenne, cinnamon, cumin and oregano. Cook for 2 minutes, stirring until combined.

3. Add tomatoes and browned beef. Stir in bouillon and water. Bring to a boil. Reduce heat; cover and simmer for about 1 hour. Add beans and heat through.

NUTRITIONAL FACTS
1 CUP: 268 calories, 14 g fat (4 g saturated fat), 56 mg cholesterol, 835 mg sodium, 16 g carbohydrate (6 g sugars, 5 g fiber), 20 g protein

Quick Tip   **I add a can of refried beans to each pot of chili. No one seems to notice, but they sure enjoy the thick texture.—Kara K., Kalamazoo, MI**

Southwestern Pork and Squash Soup

PREP: 20 MINUTES • **COOK:** 4 HOURS • **YIELD:** 6 SERVINGS

I adapted a pork and squash stew recipe, using tomatoes and Southwestern-style seasonings. My husband and sons loved it, and the leftovers were even better the next day! Try it with fresh corn muffins.

—Molly Newman, Portland, Oregon

1 pound pork tenderloin, cut into 1-inch cubes
1 medium onion, chopped
1 tablespoon canola oil
3 cups reduced-sodium chicken broth
1 medium butternut squash, peeled and cubed
2 medium carrots, sliced

1 can (14½ ounces) diced tomatoes with mild green chilies, undrained
1 tablespoon chili powder
1 teaspoon ground cumin
1 teaspoon dried oregano
½ teaspoon pepper
¼ teaspoon salt

In a large skillet, brown pork and onion in oil; drain. Transfer to a 4- or 5-qt. slow cooker. Stir in the remaining ingredients. Cover and cook on low for 4–5 hours or until meat is tender.

NUTRITIONAL FACTS
1½ CUPS: 220 calories, 5 g fat (1 g saturated fat), 42 mg cholesterol, 708 mg sodium, 26 g carbohydrate (10 g sugars, 7 g fiber), 19 g protein

Root Vegetable Soup with Sausage

PREP: 30 MINUTES • **COOK:** 45 MINUTES • **YIELD:** 20 SERVINGS

I had a similar soup at a restaurant and re-created it at home. To my surprise, it came out even better than the original! This soup actually won top honors in our town's annual cook-off.

—Donna Class, Keyser, West Virginia

$\frac{1}{2}$ pound bulk Italian sausage	10 cups water
1 medium butternut squash (about 3 pounds), peeled and cubed	2 cans (14$\frac{1}{2}$ ounces each) vegetable broth
4 large potatoes, peeled and cubed	2 tablespoons sugar
3 large sweet potatoes, peeled and cubed	1$\frac{1}{2}$ teaspoons salt
1 large rutabaga, peeled and cubed	1 teaspoon ground ginger
1 pound fresh baby carrots	$\frac{1}{8}$ teaspoon pepper
1 medium turnip, peeled and diced	$\frac{1}{4}$ cup heavy whipping cream

1. Crumble sausage into a stockpot. Cook over medium heat until no longer pink; drain.

2. Stir in the vegetables, water, broth, sugar and seasonings; bring to a boil. Reduce heat; cover and simmer for 35–40 minutes or until vegetables are tender. Cool slightly.

3. In a blender, process soup in batches until smooth. Return to the pan; whisk in cream. Heat through (do not boil).

NUTRITIONAL FACTS
1 CUP: 177 calories, 3 g fat (1 g saturated fat), 9 mg cholesterol, 466 mg sodium, 35 g carbohydrate (11 g sugars, 6 g fiber), 5 g protein

Slow-Cooked Loaded Potato Soup

PREP: 30 MINUTES • **COOK:** 8¼ HOURS • **YIELD:** 12 SERVINGS (4 QUARTS)

I put a twist on one of my favorite comfort foods from my grandmother's recipes. I look forward to passing this down to my kids.

—Jamie Chase, Rising Sun, Indiana

5 pounds potatoes, peeled and cubed (about 10 cups)
1 medium onion, finely chopped
5 cans (14½ ounces each) chicken broth
1 garlic clove, minced
1½ teaspoons salt
¼ teaspoon pepper
2 packages (8 ounces each) cream cheese, softened and cubed
1 cup half-and-half cream
¼ cup butter, cubed

TOPPINGS:
1 pound bacon strips, cooked and crumbled
¾ cup shredded sharp cheddar cheese
¼ cup minced chives

1. Place potatoes and onion in a 6-qt. slow cooker; add broth, garlic, salt and pepper. Cook, covered, on low 8–10 hours or until potatoes are tender.

2. Mash potatoes to desired consistency. Stir in cream cheese, cream and butter. Cook, covered, 15 minutes longer or until heated through.

3. Just before serving, whisk soup to combine. Top servings with bacon, cheese and chives.

NUTRITIONAL FACTS
1⅓ CUPS: 447 calories, 27 g fat (14 g saturated fat), 86 mg cholesterol, 1512 mg sodium, 37 g carbohydrate (5 g sugars, 4 g fiber), 14 g protein

Quick Tip   **Milk-based products may break down when cooked in a slow cooker. When practical, add those ingredients toward the end of the cooking time.**

Creamy Bacon Mushroom Soup

PREP/TOTAL TIME: 30 MINUTES ● **YIELD:** 8 SERVINGS (2 QUARTS)

I've always enjoyed cooking and recently created this rich soup. It's always a hit. You can also garnish it with chopped green onion tops or shredded Swiss cheese. For a creamier, smoother consistency, try pouring the soup through a strainer.

—*Nathan Mercer, Inman, South Carolina*

10	bacon strips, diced	$1\frac{1}{4}$	cups shredded Swiss cheese
1	pound sliced fresh mushrooms	3	tablespoons cornstarch
1	medium onion, chopped	$\frac{1}{2}$	teaspoon salt
3	garlic cloves, minced	$\frac{1}{2}$	teaspoon pepper
1	quart heavy whipping cream	3	tablespoons cold water
1	can ($14\frac{1}{2}$ ounces) chicken broth		

1. In a large saucepan, cook bacon over medium heat until crisp. Using a slotted spoon, remove to paper towels; drain, reserving 2 tablespoons drippings. In the drippings, saute mushrooms and onion until tender. Add garlic; cook 1 minute longer. Stir in cream and broth. Gradually stir in cheese until melted.

2. In a small bowl, combine the cornstarch, salt, pepper and water until smooth. Stir into soup. Bring to a boil; cook and stir for 2 minutes or until thickened. Garnish with bacon.

NUTRITIONAL FACTS
1 CUP: 592 calories, 56 g fat (33 g saturated fat), 193 mg cholesterol, 649 mg sodium, 12 g carbohydrate (3 g sugars, 1 g fiber), 13 g protein

Mulligatawny

PREP: 20 MINUTES • **COOK:** 6 HOURS • **YIELD:** 8 SERVINGS (2 QUARTS)

I learned to cook and bake from my mom and grandmother, and always try to use fresh fruits, vegetables and herbs. This is a delicious and satisfying soup that I make with leftover chicken, turkey and sometimes beef, pork or lamb. My family enjoys this on a crisp fall or winter day.

—*Mary Ann Marino, West Pittsburg, Pennsylvania*

1   carton (32 ounces) chicken broth
1   can (14½ ounces) diced tomatoes
2   cups cubed cooked chicken
1   large tart apple, peeled and chopped
¼   cup finely chopped onion
¼   cup chopped carrot
¼   cup chopped green pepper

1   tablespoon minced fresh parsley
2   teaspoons lemon juice
1   teaspoon salt
1   teaspoon curry powder
½   teaspoon sugar
¼   teaspoon pepper
2   whole cloves

In a 3- or 4-qt. slow cooker, combine all ingredients. Cover and cook on low for 6–8 hours or until vegetables are tender. Discard cloves.

NUTRITIONAL FACTS
1 CUP: 102 calories, 3 g fat (1 g saturated fat), 34 mg cholesterol, 884 mg sodium, 7 g carbohydrate (5 g sugars, 2 g fiber), 11 g protein

Ginger Chicken Noodle Soup

PREP: 15 MINUTES • **COOK:** 3½ HOURS • **YIELD:** 8 SERVINGS (2½ QUARTS)

This is one of my favorite soup recipes to serve in the winter time because it's super easy to make and fills the whole house with a wonderful aroma. My whole family loves it!

—*Brandy Stansbury, Edna, Texas*

1 pound boneless skinless chicken breasts, cubed	2 to 3 teaspoons minced fresh gingerroot
2 medium carrots, shredded	¼ teaspoon pepper
3 tablespoons sherry or reduced-sodium chicken broth	6 cups reduced-sodium chicken broth
2 tablespoons rice vinegar	1 cup water
1 tablespoon reduced-sodium soy sauce	2 cups fresh snow peas, halved
	2 ounces uncooked angel hair pasta, broken into thirds

1. In a 5-qt. slow cooker, combine the first seven ingredients; stir in broth and water. Cook, covered, on low 3–4 hours or until chicken is tender.

2. Stir in snow peas and pasta. Cook, covered, on low 30 minutes longer or until snow peas and pasta are tender.

NUTRITIONAL FACTS
1¼ CUPS: 126 calories, 2 g fat (0 saturated fat), 31 mg cholesterol, 543 mg sodium, 11 g carbohydrate (3 g sugars, 2 g fiber), 16 g protein

Minestrone with Turkey

PREP/TOTAL TIME: 30 MINUTES ● **YIELD:** 6 SERVINGS (2 QUARTS)

I remember my mom making this soup; now I make it as often as I can. It's a good way to use up leftover vegetables. Sometimes I add a can of rinsed and drained kidney or garbanzo beans.

—*Angela Goodman, Kaneohe, Hawaii*

1 tablespoon olive oil

1 medium onion, chopped

1 medium carrot, sliced

1 celery rib, sliced

1 garlic clove, minced

4 cups chicken broth or homemade turkey stock

1 can (14$\frac{1}{2}$ ounces) diced tomatoes, undrained

$\frac{2}{3}$ cup each frozen peas, corn and cut green beans, thawed

$\frac{1}{2}$ cup uncooked elbow macaroni

1 teaspoon salt

$\frac{1}{4}$ teaspoon dried basil

$\frac{1}{4}$ teaspoon dried oregano

$\frac{1}{4}$ teaspoon pepper

1 bay leaf

1 cup cubed cooked turkey

1 small zucchini, halved lengthwise and cut into $\frac{1}{4}$-inch slices

$\frac{1}{4}$ cup grated Parmesan cheese, optional

1. In a Dutch oven, heat oil over medium-high heat. Add onion, carrot and celery; cook and stir until tender. Add garlic; cook 1 minute longer. Add broth, vegetables, macaroni and seasonings. Bring to a boil.

2. Reduce heat; simmer, uncovered, 5 minutes or until macaroni is al dente. Stir in turkey and zucchini; cook until zucchini is crisp-tender. Discard bay leaf. If desired, sprinkle servings with cheese.

NUTRITIONAL FACTS
1$\frac{1}{3}$ CUPS (CALCULATED WITHOUT CHEESE): 172 calories, 5 g fat (1 g saturated fat), 24 mg cholesterol, 1251 mg sodium, 20 g carbohydrate (7 g sugars, 4 g fiber), 12 g protein

Freeze It **Transfer cooled soup to freezer container and freeze up to 3 months. To use, thaw in the refrigerator overnight. Transfer to a saucepan. Cover and cook over medium heat until heated through. Serve with cheese if desired.**

Maryland-Style Crab Soup

PREP: 20 MINUTES ● **COOK:** 6¼ HOURS ● **YIELD:** 8 SERVINGS (3 QUARTS)

Try this hearty soup that incorporates the best of vegetable soup and flavorful crab. Whole crabs and claws can be broken into pieces and dropped into the soup, which is my personal preference. I serve the soup with saltine crackers and a cold beer.

—Freelove Knott, Palm Bay, Florida

- 2 cans (14½ ounces each) diced tomatoes with green peppers and onions, undrained
- 2 cups water
- 1½ pounds potatoes, cut into ½-inch cubes (about 5 cups)
- 2 cups cubed peeled rutabaga
- 2 cups chopped cabbage
- 1 medium onion, finely chopped
- 1 medium carrot, sliced
- ½ cup frozen corn, thawed
- ½ cup frozen lima beans, thawed
- ½ cup frozen peas, thawed
- ½ cup cut fresh green beans (1-inch pieces)
- 4 teaspoons seafood seasoning
- 1 teaspoon celery seed
- 1 vegetable bouillon cube
- ¼ teaspoon salt
- ¼ teaspoon pepper
- 1 pound fresh or lump crabmeat, drained

1. In a 6-qt. slow cooker, combine the first 16 ingredients. Cook, covered, on low 6–8 hours or until vegetables are tender.

2. Stir in crab. Cook, covered, on low 15 minutes longer or until heated through.

NOTE: This recipe was prepared with Knorr vegetable bouillon.

NUTRITIONAL FACTS
1½ CUPS: 202 calories, 1 g fat (0 saturated fat), 55 mg cholesterol, 1111 mg sodium, 34 g carbohydrate (11 g sugars, 7 g fiber), 15 g protein

Lima Bean Soup

PREP: 10 MINUTES • **COOK:** 30 MINUTES • **YIELD:** 12 SERVINGS (3 QUARTS)

Each fall there's a Lima Bean Festival in nearby West Cape May to honor the many growers there and showcase different recipes using their crop. This comforting chowder was a festival recipe contest winner several years ago.

—*Kathleen Olsack, North Cape May, New Jersey*

3 cans (14½ ounces each) chicken broth
2 cans (15¼ ounces each) lima beans, rinsed and drained
3 medium carrots, thinly sliced
2 medium potatoes, peeled and diced
2 small sweet red peppers, chopped
2 small onions, chopped
2 celery ribs, thinly sliced

¼ cup butter
1½ teaspoons dried marjoram
½ teaspoon salt
½ teaspoon pepper
½ teaspoon dried oregano
1 cup half-and-half cream
3 bacon strips, cooked and crumbled

1. In a Dutch oven or soup kettle, combine the first 12 ingredients; bring to a boil over medium heat. Reduce heat; cover and simmer for 25–35 minutes or until vegetables are tender.

2. Add cream; heat through but do not boil. Sprinkle with bacon just before serving.

NUTRITIONAL FACTS
1 CUP: 110 calories, 7 g fat (4 g saturated fat), 22 mg cholesterol, 431 mg sodium, 9 g carbohydrate (3 g sugars, 2 g fiber), 3 g protein

Winning Cream of Asparagus Soup

PREP/TOTAL TIME: 30 MINUTES • **YIELD:** 6 SERVINGS

I developed this recipe myself by substituting asparagus for broccoli in cream of broccoli soup. It's a big favorite at our house!

—*Westelle Griswa, Monroe, Connecticut*

4 cups cut fresh asparagus ($\frac{1}{2}$-inch pieces)

2 cups water, divided

$\frac{1}{4}$ cup finely chopped green onions or 1 teaspoon onion powder

5 tablespoons butter

5 tablespoons all-purpose flour

$\frac{1}{2}$ to 1 teaspoon salt

$\frac{1}{4}$ teaspoon white pepper

4 cups whole milk

1 tablespoon chicken bouillon granules

1. Place asparagus in a large saucepan and cover with 1 cup water. Bring to a boil, cover and cook for 3–5 minutes or until crisp-tender. Drain, reserving liquid.

2. In another saucepan, saute onions in butter until tender. Stir in the flour, salt and pepper until blended. Gradually stir in the milk, bouillon, reserved cooking liquid and remaining water. Bring to a boil. Cook and stir for 2 minutes or until thickened and bubbly. Stir in asparagus; heat through.

NUTRITIONAL FACTS

1 CUP: 232 calories, 15 g fat (9 g saturated fat), 48 mg cholesterol, 795 mg sodium, 17 g carbohydrate (10 g sugars, 2 g fiber), 8 g protein

Quick Tip

In order to keep asparagus fresh longer, I place the cut stems in a container of cold water—similar to flowers in a vase. I keep the asparagus in the refrigerator, changing the water at least once every 3 days.—Mary S., Council Bluffs, IA

Broccoli Beer Cheese Soup

PREP: 20 MINUTES • **COOK:** 30 MINUTES • **YIELD:** 10 SERVINGS (2½ QUARTS)

This soup tastes just as wonderful without the beer, making a great broccoli cheese soup. I always make extra and pop individual servings in the freezer.

—Lori Lee, Brooksville, Florida

3 tablespoons butter
5 celery ribs, finely chopped
3 medium carrots, finely chopped
1 small onion, finely chopped
4 cups fresh broccoli florets, chopped
¼ cup chopped sweet red pepper
4 cans (14½ ounces each) chicken broth
½ teaspoon pepper
½ cup all-purpose flour
½ cup water
3 cups shredded cheddar cheese

1 package (8 ounces) cream cheese, cubed
1 bottle (12 ounces) beer or nonalcoholic beer
Additional shredded cheddar cheese, optional
Bacon strips, cooked and crumbled, optional
Chopped green onions, optional
Sour cream, optional
Salad croutons, optional

1. In a Dutch oven, melt butter over medium-high heat. Add celery, carrots and onion; saute until crisp-tender. Add broccoli and red pepper; stir in broth and pepper. Combine flour and water until smooth; gradually stir into pan. Bring to a boil. Reduce heat; simmer, uncovered, until thickened and vegetables are tender, 25–30 minutes.

2. Stir in cheeses and beer until cheeses are melted (do not boil). If desired, top with additional shredded cheese, bacon, green onions, sour cream and croutons.

NUTRITIONAL FACTS
1 CUP: 316 calories, 23 g fat (13 g saturated fat), 69 mg cholesterol, 1068 mg sodium, 13 g carbohydrate (5 g sugars, 2 g fiber), 12 g protein

Freeze It

Before adding toppings, cool soup; transfer to freezer containers. Freeze up to 3 months. To use, partially thaw in refrigerator overnight; heat through in a large saucepan over medium-low heat, stirring occasionally (do not boil). Add toppings if desired.

Taco Salad for a Large Crowd

PREP: 25 MINUTES • **COOK:** 10 MINUTES • **YIELD:** 26 SERVINGS

I made this huge taco salad to bring to a party, and people were scrambling to figure out who made it. Needless to say I only brought home an empty bowl and the guests went home with a full stomach! Everyone loves this taco salad recipe.

—Lisa Homer, Avon, New York

1½ pounds ground beef
2 envelopes taco seasoning, divided
1 medium head iceberg lettuce
1 package (10 ounces) nacho tortilla chips, coarsely crushed
2 pints grape tomatoes, halved
2 cans (16 ounces each) kidney beans, rinsed and drained

3 cans (2¼ ounces each) sliced ripe olives, drained
1½ cups shredded cheddar cheese
1 large sweet onion, chopped
2 cans (4 ounces each) chopped green chilies
1½ cups Thousand Island salad dressing
1⅓ cups salsa
⅓ cup sugar

1. In a Dutch oven over medium heat, cook beef with 1 envelope plus 2 tablespoons taco seasoning until no longer pink; drain.

2. In a very large serving bowl, combine the lettuce, chips, tomatoes, beans, olives, cheese, onion, chilies and beef mixture.

3. In a small bowl, combine the salad dressing, salsa, sugar and remaining taco seasoning; pour over salad and toss to coat.

NUTRITIONAL FACTS
1⅓ CUP: 262 calories, 15 g fat (4 g saturated fat), 24 mg cholesterol, 696 mg sodium, 23 g carbohydrate (7 g sugars, 3 g fiber), 10 g protein

Kielbasa Summer Salad

PREP: 15 MINUTES + CHILLING ● **YIELD:** 10 SERVINGS

The unexpected combination of flavors and textures in this cool salad sparks taste buds. It can be a main course for a luncheon or a side dish at a dinner or a barbecue. I've gotten many compliments sharing it as a potluck dish.

—Sara Primarolo, Sanquoit, New York

1 pound smoked kielbasa or Polish sausage, halved and cut into $\frac{1}{4}$-inch pieces

1 can (15$\frac{1}{2}$ ounces) black-eyed peas, rinsed and drained

2 medium tart apples, cut into $\frac{1}{2}$-inch chunks

1 medium green pepper, chopped

4 large green onions, thinly sliced

DRESSING:

$\frac{1}{3}$ cup vegetable oil

3 tablespoons cider vinegar

1 tablespoon Dijon mustard

2 teaspoons sugar

$\frac{1}{2}$ to 1 teaspoon pepper

1. In a nonstick skillet, brown sausage. Drain on paper towels. In a large bowl, combine peas, apples, green pepper, onions and sausage.

2. In a small bowl, combine the dressing ingredients. Pour over sausage mixture; toss to coat. Cover and refrigerate for 4 hours or overnight.

NUTRITIONAL FACTS
1 CUP: 192 calories, 12 g fat (0 saturated fat), 28 mg cholesterol, 561 mg sodium, 14 g carbohydrate (0 sugars, 0 fiber), 9 g protein

Deli-Style Pasta Salad

PREP: 20 MINUTES + CHILLING • **YIELD:** 12 SERVINGS

Pasta provides a base for this tongue-tingling make-ahead salad. It has lots of fresh and satisfying ingredients topped with a flavorful dressing. It's terrific to serve to company or take to a potluck.

—Joyce McLennan, Algonac, Michigan

- 7 ounces tricolor spiral pasta
- 6 ounces thinly sliced hard salami, julienned
- 6 ounces provolone cheese, cubed
- 1 can (2¼ ounces) sliced ripe olives, drained
- 1 small red onion, thinly sliced
- 1 small zucchini, halved and thinly sliced
- ½ cup chopped green pepper
- ½ cup chopped sweet red pepper
- ¼ cup minced fresh parsley
- ¼ cup grated Parmesan cheese
- ½ cup olive oil
- ¼ cup red wine vinegar
- 1 garlic clove, minced
- 1½ teaspoons ground mustard
- 1 teaspoon dried basil
- 1 teaspoon dried oregano
- ¼ teaspoon salt
- Dash pepper
- 2 medium tomatoes, cut into wedges

1. Cook the pasta according to package directions; rinse in cold water and drain. Place in a large bowl; add the next nine ingredients.

2. In a jar with a tight-fitting lid, combine oil, vinegar, garlic, mustard, basil, oregano, salt and pepper; shake well.

3. Pour over salad; toss to coat. Cover and chill for 8 hours or overnight. Toss before serving. Garnish with tomatoes.

NUTRITIONAL FACTS
1 CUP: 273 calories, 18 g fat (6 g saturated fat), 25 mg cholesterol, 536 mg sodium, 17 g carbohydrate (3 g sugars, 1 g fiber), 11 g protein

Barbecue Chicken Cobb Salad

PREP: 30 MINUTES • **COOK:** 3 HOURS • **YIELD:** 6 SERVINGS

I turned barbecue chicken into a major salad with romaine and carrots, sweet peppers and avocados. That's how I got my family to eat more veggies.

—Camille Beckstrand, Layton, Utah

1 bottle (18 ounces) barbecue sauce	1 medium sweet red or green pepper, chopped
2 tablespoons brown sugar	2 avocados, peeled and chopped
½ teaspoon garlic powder	3 hard-cooked large eggs, chopped
¼ teaspoon paprika	6 bacon strips, cooked and crumbled
1½ pounds boneless skinless chicken breasts	1½ cups shredded cheddar cheese
12 cups chopped romaine	Salad dressing of your choice
3 plum tomatoes, chopped	
2 small carrots, thinly sliced	

1. In a greased 3-qt. slow cooker, mix barbecue sauce, brown sugar, garlic powder and paprika. Add chicken; turn to coat. Cook, covered, on low 3–4 hours or until chicken is tender (a thermometer should read at least 165°).

2. Remove chicken from slow cooker; cut into bite-size pieces. In a bowl, toss chicken with 1 cup barbecue sauce mixture. Place romaine on a large serving platter; arrange chicken, vegetables, avocados, eggs, bacon and cheese over romaine. Drizzle with dressing.

NUTRITIONAL FACTS
1 SERVING (CALCULATED WITHOUT DRESSING): 571 calories, 26 g fat (9 g saturated fat), 192 mg cholesterol, 1314 mg sodium, 47 g carbohydrate (32 g sugars, 7 g fiber), 39 g protein

Balsamic Chicken Pasta Salad

PREP/TOTAL TIME: 25 MINUTES ● **YIELD:** 8 SERVINGS

I love all the colors and flavors of this quick and easy dish and serve it often in summer. Everyone loves it! Leftover grilled shrimp makes a tasty substitution.

—Terry McCarty, Oro Grande, California

3 cups uncooked bow tie pasta
4 cups cubed cooked chicken breasts
2 cups chopped tomatoes
$\frac{1}{2}$ cup chopped red onion
4 bacon strips, cooked and crumbled
$\frac{1}{4}$ cup crumbled Gorgonzola cheese
$\frac{1}{2}$ cup olive oil

$\frac{1}{4}$ cup minced fresh basil
$\frac{1}{4}$ cup balsamic vinegar
2 tablespoons brown sugar
1 teaspoon minced garlic
$\frac{1}{4}$ teaspoon salt
$\frac{1}{4}$ teaspoon pepper
$\frac{1}{2}$ cup grated Parmesan cheese

1. Cook pasta according to package directions. Drain and rinse in cold water; transfer to a large bowl. Add the chicken, tomatoes, onion, bacon and Gorgonzola cheese.

2. In a small bowl, whisk the oil, basil, vinegar, brown sugar, garlic, salt and pepper. Drizzle over salad and toss to coat; sprinkle with Parmesan cheese.

NUTRITIONAL FACTS
1$\frac{1}{3}$ CUPS: 408 calories, 20 g fat (5 g saturated fat), 65 mg cholesterol, 323 mg sodium, 28 g carbohydrate (7 g sugars, 2 g fiber), 28 g protein

Brown Rice Salad with Grilled Chicken

PREP/TOTAL TIME: 20 MINUTES ● **YIELD:** 9 SERVINGS

This delightful dish is nutritious, simple to fix and brightens up any buffet table. It's a terrific way to use up leftover chicken, and you can add veggies according to your family's liking.

—Glenda Harper, Cable, Ohio

3 cups cooked brown rice
2 cups cubed grilled chicken breasts
2 medium apples, chopped
1 medium sweet red pepper, chopped
2 celery ribs, finely chopped
$2/3$ cup chopped green onions
$1/2$ cup chopped pecans

3 tablespoons minced fresh parsley
$1/4$ cup cider vinegar
3 tablespoons canola oil
1 tablespoon lemon juice
1 teaspoon salt
$1/4$ teaspoon pepper
Lettuce leaves, optional

In a large bowl, combine the first eight ingredients. In a small bowl, whisk the vinegar, oil, lemon juice, salt and pepper. Pour over salad and toss to coat. Serve immediately or refrigerate. Serve in lettuce-lined bowls if desired.

NUTRITIONAL FACTS
1 CUP: 236 calories, 11 g fat (1 g saturated fat), 26 mg cholesterol, 295 mg sodium, 23 g carbohydrate (0 sugars, 3 g fiber), 12 g protein

Make It Ahead

Sometimes on a weekend, I make a good-sized pot of rice. Having the cooked rice in the refrigerator is quite a time-saver during the week.
—Grace R., Wrightwood, CA

Chicken Pita Salad

PREP: 30 MINUTES + CHILLING ● **YIELD:** 16 SERVINGS

I make this refreshing dish to take to family get-togethers. Its great Greek flavors and crispy chewiness guarantee it will be gone in a blink.

—Catherine Slussler, Tomball, Texas

3 pita breads (6 inches)	1 teaspoon salt
¼ cup olive oil	¼ teaspoon pepper
¼ cup balsamic vinegar	2 cups shredded cooked chicken
3 tablespoons lemon juice	1 can (15 ounces) garbanzo beans or chickpeas, rinsed and drained
1 tablespoon minced fresh oregano or 1 teaspoon dried oregano	1 English cucumber, halved and sliced
2 garlic cloves, minced	1 pint cherry tomatoes, halved
2 teaspoons grated lemon peel	1 small red onion, quartered and sliced
1 teaspoon sugar	½ cup crumbled feta cheese

1. Preheat oven to 350°. Cut each pita bread into eight triangles; split in half. Place on a baking sheet. Bake for 10–12 minutes or until lightly toasted.

2. For dressing, in a small bowl, whisk the oil, vinegar, lemon juice, oregano, garlic, lemon peel, sugar, salt and pepper.

3. In a large bowl, combine the chicken, garbanzo beans, cucumber, tomatoes and onion. Stir in pita triangles. Drizzle with dressing and toss to coat.

4. Cover and refrigerate for at least 30 minutes. Just before serving, sprinkle with cheese.

NUTRITIONAL FACTS
¾ CUP: 141 calories, 6 g fat (1 g saturated fat), 17 mg cholesterol, 294 mg sodium, 14 g carbohydrate (3 g sugars, 2 g fiber), 8 g protein

Cashew-Curry Chicken Salad

PREP/TOTAL TIME: 20 MINUTES ● **YIELD:** 6 SERVINGS

My husband and I fell hard for the curried chicken salad from our grocery store deli, and I knew I could find a way to make something similar. This version has become one of our favorites to take on trips to the beach.
—*Janine Cooper Moren, Portland, Oregon*

3 cups cubed cooked chicken breast	1 teaspoon curry powder
4 celery ribs, chopped	¼ teaspoon salt
2 medium carrots, chopped	¼ teaspoon garlic powder
⅔ cup golden raisins	¼ teaspoon pepper
½ cup chopped cashews	⅛ teaspoon ground ginger

DRESSING:
⅔ cup honey Greek yogurt
4 teaspoons lemon juice
4 teaspoons honey

1. In a large bowl, combine chicken, celery, carrots, raisins and cashews.

2. In a small bowl, mix yogurt, lemon juice, honey and spices. Pour over chicken mixture; toss to coat.

NUTRITIONAL FACTS
1 CUP: 287 calories, 10 g fat (3 g saturated fat), 60 mg cholesterol, 267 mg sodium, 27 g carbohydrate (20 g sugars, 2 g fiber), 24 g protein

Feta Salmon Salad

PREP/TOTAL TIME: 25 MINUTES ● **YIELD:** 4 SERVINGS

My son David always ordered the salmon sandwich at a local pub. In trying to replicate it, he came up with this salad. It's the only recipe he's ever created, and our entire family thinks it's great.

—*Susan Griffiths, Mt. Pleasant, South Carolina*

- ¼ teaspoon salt
- ¼ teaspoon garlic powder
- ¼ teaspoon ground ginger
- ¼ teaspoon dried parsley flakes
- ¼ teaspoon pepper
- 4 salmon fillets (6 ounces each)

- 1 package (5 ounces) spring mix salad greens
- 1 large cucumber, chopped
- 1 large tomato, chopped
- ½ cup crumbled feta cheese
- ¼ cup red wine vinaigrette

1. In a small bowl, mix the first five ingredients; sprinkle over salmon. Moisten a paper towel with cooking oil; using long-handled tongs, lightly coat the grill rack.

2. Place salmon on grill rack, skin side down. Grill, covered, over medium heat or broil 4 inches from heat 10–12 minutes or until fish just begins to flake easily with a fork.

3. In a large bowl, toss salad greens with cucumber, tomato and cheese; divide among four plates. Top with salmon; drizzle with vinaigrette.

NUTRITIONAL FACTS
1 SERVING: 416 calories, 25 g fat (6 g saturated fat), 108 mg cholesterol, 636 mg sodium, 7 g carbohydrate (4 g sugars, 2 g fiber), 38 g protein

Shrimp Veggie Salad

PREP/TOTAL TIME: 20 MINUTES • **YIELD:** 12 SERVINGS

My family loves to have potluck barbecues during the summer. With several backyard gardens in the family, you can be sure one of us will bring a variation of this classic salad. Add a dash of your favorite hot sauce if you like to turn up the heat!

—*Karen Goodnature, Lompoc, California*

- 1 pound peeled and deveined cooked medium shrimp
- 3 medium tomatoes, seeded and cut into $\frac{1}{2}$-inch pieces
- 2 medium cucumbers, quartered and sliced
- 1 small red onion, chopped
- $\frac{1}{2}$ cup chopped fresh cilantro
- 4 green onions, chopped
- 2 jalapeno peppers, seeded and minced
- 2 tablespoons lemon juice
- $\frac{1}{2}$ teaspoon salt
- 2 medium ripe avocados, peeled and cubed

Combine the first nine ingredients in a large bowl. Gently stir in avocado. Serve immediately.

NOTE: Wear disposable gloves when cutting hot peppers; the oils can burn skin. Avoid touching your face.

NUTRITIONAL FACTS
1 CUP: 108 calories, 5 g fat (1 g saturated fat), 57 mg cholesterol, 160 mg sodium, 7 g carbohydrate (3 g sugars, 3 g fiber), 9 g protein

Layered Summertime Salad

PREP/TOTAL TIME: 30 MINUTES • **YIELD:** 16 SERVINGS

Luscious layers of pasta and veggies make up this super summer salad that can be made ahead for warm-weather picnics and deck parties. It makes enough to feed a crowd.

—Betty Fulks, Onia, Arkansas

2 cups uncooked gemelli or spiral pasta	4 cups torn romaine
1 cup mayonnaise	1 cup fresh snow peas, trimmed and halved
2 tablespoons lemon juice	1 cup fresh cauliflowerets
1 teaspoon sugar	1 cup fresh broccoli florets
½ teaspoon garlic powder	1 large sweet red pepper, chopped
½ cup sliced green onions	½ cup shredded Swiss cheese
4 bacon strips, cooked and crumbled, divided	

1. Cook pasta according to package directions. Meanwhile, in a small bowl, combine the mayonnaise, lemon juice, sugar and garlic powder; set aside. Drain pasta and rinse in cold water; toss with onions and half of the bacon.

2. In a large salad bowl, layer half of the romaine, pasta mixture, peas, cauliflower, broccoli, red pepper, mayonnaise mixture and cheese. Repeat layers. Sprinkle with remaining bacon. Cover and refrigerate until serving.

NUTRITIONAL FACTS
¾ CUP: 186 calories, 13 g fat (2 g saturated fat), 9 mg cholesterol, 115 mg sodium, 13 g carbohydrate (2 g sugars, 2 g fiber), 4 g protein

Tortellini Caesar Salad

PREP/TOTAL TIME: 20 MINUTES ● **YIELD:** 10 SERVINGS

This salad was served at a dear friend's baby shower by a health-conscious friend, who suggested the dressing be prepared with low-fat or fat-free ingredients. Either way, the creamy dressing has plenty of garlic flavor and coats the pasta, romaine and croutons nicely.

—Tammy Steenbock, Sembach Air Base, Germany

1 package (19 ounces) frozen cheese tortellini
½ cup mayonnaise
¼ cup 2% milk
¼ cup plus ⅓ cup shredded Parmesan cheese, divided

2 tablespoons lemon juice
2 garlic cloves, minced
8 cups torn romaine
1 cup seasoned salad croutons
Halved cherry tomatoes, optional

1. Cook tortellini according to package directions. Meanwhile, in a small bowl, combine the mayonnaise, milk, ¼ cup Parmesan cheese, lemon juice and garlic.

2. Drain tortellini and rinse in cold water; transfer to a large bowl. Add romaine and remaining Parmesan. Just before serving, drizzle with dressing; toss to coat. Top with croutons and tomatoes if desired.

NUTRITIONAL FACTS
1 CUP (CALCULATED WITHOUT TOMATOES): 237 calories, 14 g fat (4 g saturated fat), 17 mg cholesterol, 327 mg sodium, 19 g carbohydrate (2 g sugars, 2 g fiber), 8 g protein

Fabulous Fajitas

PREP: 20 MINUTES ● **COOK:** 3 HOURS ● **YIELD:** 8 SERVINGS

I've enjoyed cooking since I was a girl growing up in the Southwest. When friends call to ask me for new recipes to try, I suggest these flavorful fajitas. It's wonderful to put the beef in the slow cooker before church and come home to a hot delicious main dish.

—Janie Reitz, Rochester, Minnesota

1½ pounds beef top sirloin steak,
     cut into thin strips
 2 tablespoons canola oil
 2 tablespoons lemon juice
 1 garlic clove, minced
1½ teaspoons ground cumin
 1 teaspoon seasoned salt
 ½ teaspoon chili powder
¼ to ½ teaspoon crushed red pepper flakes
 1 large green pepper, julienned
 1 large onion, julienned
 8 flour tortillas (8 inches)
    Shredded cheddar cheese, salsa, sour
    cream, lettuce and tomatoes, optional

1. In a large skillet, brown steak in oil over medium heat. Place steak and drippings in a 3-qt. slow cooker. Stir in the lemon juice, garlic, cumin, salt, chili powder and red pepper flakes.

2. Cover and cook on high for 2–3 hours or until meat is almost tender. Add green pepper and onion; cover and cook for 1 hour or until meat and vegetables are tender.

3. Warm tortillas according to package directions; spoon beef and vegetables down the center of tortillas. Top each with cheese, salsa, sour cream, lettuce and tomatoes if desired.

NUTRITIONAL FACTS
1 FAJITA: 314 calories, 11 g fat (2 g saturated fat), 34 mg cholesterol, 469 mg sodium, 31 g carbohydrate (1 g sugars, 2 g fiber), 23 g protein

Peppery Philly Steaks

PREP/TOTAL TIME: 30 MINUTES • **YIELD:** 6 SERVINGS

Since we love to cook and eat, my husband and I are always developing new recipes. This is one we especially enjoy when we have fresh peppers. Our home is a small mountain cabin that's 3 hours from town. We have no electricity or phone . . . and we cook about half the time on a wood stove.

—Edie Fitch, Clifton, Arizona

3 tablespoons canola oil, divided
1 medium green pepper, julienned
1 medium sweet red pepper, julienned
1 large onion, halved and thinly sliced
1½ pounds beef top sirloin steak, cut into ¼-inch strips

½ teaspoon salt
2 cans (4 ounces each) whole green chilies, drained and sliced
2 tablespoons butter, softened
6 French or Italian sandwich rolls, split
6 slices Swiss cheese

1. Preheat oven to 350°. In a large skillet, heat 1 tablespoon oil over medium heat. Add peppers and onion; cook and stir until crisp-tender. Remove from pan.

2. In same pan, heat remaining oil over medium-high heat. Add beef; cook and stir 2–3 minutes or until no longer pink. Stir in salt, chilies and pepper mixture; heat through.

3. Spread butter over cut sides of rolls. On roll bottoms, layer steak mixture and cheese; replace tops. Place in a 15x10x1-inch baking pan; cover tightly with foil. Bake 10–12 minutes or until cheese is melted.

NUTRITIONAL FACTS
1 SANDWICH: 473 calories, 21 g fat (7 g saturated fat), 66 mg cholesterol, 650 mg sodium, 36 g carbohydrate (4 g sugars, 2 g fiber), 34 g protein

Machaca Beef Dip Sandwiches

PREP: 20 MINUTES • **COOK:** 8 HOURS • **YIELD:** 6 SERVINGS

The winning combination of beef, cumin, chili powder and the spicy heat of chipotle peppers makes these sandwiches game-day food at its finest!

—*Karol Chandler-Ezell, Nacogdoches, Texas*

1 boneless beef chuck roast (2 to 3 pounds)
1 large sweet onion, thinly sliced
1 can (14½ ounces) reduced-sodium beef broth
½ cup water
3 chipotle peppers in adobo sauce, chopped
1 tablespoon adobo sauce

1 envelope au jus gravy mix
1 tablespoon Creole seasoning
1 tablespoon chili powder
2 teaspoons ground cumin
6 French rolls, split
Guacamole and salsa, optional

1. Place roast in a 3- to 4-qt. slow cooker; top with onion. In a medium bowl, combine the broth, water, chipotle peppers, adobo sauce, gravy mix, Creole seasoning, chili powder and cumin; pour over meat. Cover and cook on low for 8–10 hours or until meat is tender.

2. Remove roast; cool slightly. Skim fat from cooking juices. Shred beef with two forks and return to slow cooker; heat through. Using a slotted spoon, place meat on rolls. Serve with guacamole or salsa if desired and the cooking juices.

NOTES: Wear disposable gloves when cutting hot peppers; the oils can burn skin. Avoid touching your face. The following spices may be substituted for 1 tablespoon Creole seasoning: ¾ teaspoon each salt, garlic powder and paprika; and a pinch each of dried thyme, ground cumin and cayenne pepper.

NUTRITIONAL FACTS
1 SANDWICH (CALCULATED WITHOUT OPTIONAL TOPPINGS): 476 calories, 18 g fat (6 g saturated fat), 100 mg cholesterol, 1288 mg sodium, 39 g carbohydrate (5 g sugars, 3 g fiber), 37 g protein

Freeze It

Freeze individual portions of cooled meat mixture and juices in freezer containers. To use, partially thaw in refrigerator overnight. Heat through in a saucepan, stirring occasionally. Serve on rolls with guacamole and salsa if desired.

Chicago-Style Beef Rolls

PREP: 20 MINUTES • **COOK:** 8 HOURS • **YIELD:** 16 SERVINGS

I have fond memories of eating these big, messy sandwiches at a neighbor's house when I was growing up. Freeze extras and save for another meal, too!

—*Trisha Kruse, Eagle, Idaho*

1 boneless beef chuck roast (4 to 5 pounds)	1 tablespoon Italian seasoning
1 tablespoon olive oil	½ teaspoon crushed red pepper flakes
3 cups beef broth	16 sourdough rolls, split
1 medium onion, chopped	Sliced pepperoncini and pickled red pepper rings, optional
1 package Italian salad dressing mix	
3 garlic cloves, minced	

1. Brown roast in oil on all sides in a large skillet; drain. Transfer beef to a 5-qt. slow cooker. Combine the broth, onion, dressing mix, garlic, Italian seasoning and pepper flakes in a large bowl; pour over roast.

2. Cover and cook on low for 8–10 hours or until tender. Remove meat; cool slightly.

3. Skim fat from cooking juices. Shred beef with two forks and return to slow cooker; heat through. Place ½ cup on each roll, using a slotted spoon. Serve with pepperoncini and pepper rings if desired.

NUTRITIONAL FACTS
1 SANDWICH (CALCULATED WITHOUT OPTIONAL TOPPINGS): 418 calories, 16 g fat (5 g saturated fat), 74 mg cholesterol, 771 mg sodium, 36 g carbohydrate (6 g sugars, 1 g fiber), 31 g protein

Beef Stroganoff Sandwich

PREP/TOTAL TIME: 30 MINUTES • **YIELD:** 10 SERVINGS

This filling sandwich was a winner in our local beef cook-off several years ago. It's always been one of my favorites.

—*Julie Terstriep, Industry, Illinois*

2	pounds ground beef			Butter, softened
½	cup chopped onion		2	cups (16 ounces) sour cream
1	teaspoon salt		2	tomatoes, seeded and diced
½	teaspoon garlic powder		1	large green pepper, diced
½	teaspoon pepper		3	cups shredded cheddar cheese
1	loaf French bread			

1. Preheat oven to 350°. In a skillet, brown ground beef and onion. Drain. Add salt, garlic powder and pepper.

2. Cut bread lengthwise in half; butter both halves and place on baking sheets. Remove meat mixture from heat; stir in sour cream. Spoon onto the bread. Sprinkle with tomatoes, green pepper and cheese.

3. Bake for 20 minutes or until the cheese is melted (bake longer for crispier bread).

NUTRITIONAL FACTS
1 PIECE: 573 calories, 37 g fat (19 g saturated fat), 113 mg cholesterol, 835 mg sodium, 29 g carbohydrate (5 g sugars, 2 g fiber), 31 g protein

Pork and Beef Barbecue

PREP: 15 MINUTES ● **COOK:** 6 HOURS ● **YIELD:** 12 SERVINGS

It's the combination of beef stew meat and tender pork that keeps friends and family asking about these tangy sandwiches. Add a little lettuce and tomato for a crisp contrast.

—*Corbin Detgen, Buchanan, Michigan*

1 can (6 ounces) tomato paste	1½ pounds pork chop suey meat or pork tenderloin, cut into ¾-inch cubes
½ cup packed brown sugar	3 medium green peppers, chopped
¼ cup chili powder	2 large onions, chopped
¼ cup cider vinegar	12 sandwich buns, split
2 teaspoons Worcestershire sauce	Lettuce and tomatoes, optional
1 teaspoon salt	
1½ pounds beef stew meat, cut into ¾-inch cubes	

1. In a 5-qt. slow cooker, combine the first six ingredients. Stir in beef, pork, green peppers and onions. Cover and cook on low for 6–8 hours or until meat is tender.

2. Shred meat with two forks. Serve on buns, with lettuce and tomatoes if desired.

NUTRITIONAL FACTS
1 SANDWICH: 444 calories, 12 g fat (4 g saturated fat), 69 mg cholesterol, 684 mg sodium, 52 g carbohydrate (17 g sugars, 3 g fiber), 32 g protein

Quick Tip
When preparing meat or poultry for the slow cooker, trim off excess fat. It retains heat, and large amounts of fat could raise the temperature of the cooking liquid, causing the meat to overcook.

All-American Barbecue Sandwiches

PREP/TOTAL TIME: 25 MINUTES ● **YIELD:** 18 SERVINGS

I came up with this delicious recipe on my own. It's my husband's favorite and is a big hit with family and friends who enjoyed it at our Fourth of July picnic.

—Sue Gronholz, Beaver Dam, Wisconsin

4½ pounds ground beef	2 tablespoons vinegar
1½ cups chopped onions	2 tablespoons sugar
2¼ cups ketchup	1 tablespoon salt
3 tablespoons prepared mustard	1 tablespoon pepper
3 tablespoons Worcestershire sauce	18 hamburger buns, split

In a Dutch oven, cook beef and onions until meat is no longer pink and onion is tender; drain. Stir in the ketchup, mustard, Worcestershire sauce, vinegar, sugar, salt and pepper. Heat through. Serve on buns.

NUTRITIONAL FACTS
1 EACH: 391 calories, 16 g fat (6 g saturated fat), 75 mg cholesterol, 1100 mg sodium, 33 g carbohydrate (9 g sugars, 2 g fiber), 27 g protein

Slow-Cooked Sloppy Joes

PREP: 15 MINUTES ● **COOK:** 4 HOURS ● **YIELD:** 12 SERVINGS

Slow-cook your way to a crowd-pleasing entree! Ground beef is transformed into a classic sandwich filling with just a few pantry staples.

—Joeanne Steras, Garrett, Pennsylvania

2 pounds ground beef	2 envelopes sloppy joe mix
1 cup chopped green pepper	2 tablespoons brown sugar
$2/3$ cup chopped onion	1 teaspoon prepared mustard
2 cups ketchup	12 hamburger buns, split

1. In a large skillet, cook the beef, pepper and onion over medium heat until meat is no longer pink; drain. Stir in the ketchup, sloppy joe mix, brown sugar and mustard.

2. Transfer to a 3-qt. slow cooker. Cover and cook on low for 4–5 hours or until flavors are blended. Spoon $1/2$ cup onto each bun.

NUTRITIONAL FACTS
1 SANDWICH: 337 calories, 9 g fat (4 g saturated fat), 37 mg cholesterol, 1251 mg sodium, 47 g carbohydrate (23 g sugars, 1 g fiber), 18 g protein

Quick Tip **Unless you're preparing meat loaf, it's best to brown ground beef on the stovetop before adding it to your slow cooker. Not only will it be cooked through, but it will have a rich appearance, flavor, and texture.**

Italian Meatball Subs

PREP: 25 MINUTES • **COOK:** 4 HOURS • **YIELD:** 6-7 SERVINGS

This is one of those recipes you always come back to. A flavorful tomato sauce and mildly spiced meatballs make a hearty sandwich filling, or they can be served over pasta. I broil the meatballs first to quickly brown them.

—Jean Glacken, Elkton, Maryland

- 2 large eggs, lightly beaten
- ¼ cup whole milk
- ½ cup dry bread crumbs
- 2 tablespoons grated Parmesan cheese
- 1 teaspoon salt
- ¼ teaspoon pepper
- ⅛ teaspoon garlic powder
- 1 pound ground beef
- ½ pound bulk Italian sausage

SAUCE:
- 1 can (15 ounces) tomato sauce
- 1 can (6 ounces) tomato paste
- 1 small onion, chopped
- ½ cup chopped green pepper
- ½ cup dry red wine or beef broth
- ⅓ cup water
- 2 garlic cloves, minced
- 1 teaspoon dried oregano
- 1 teaspoon salt
- ½ teaspoon sugar
- ½ teaspoon pepper
- 6 to 7 Italian rolls, split
  Shredded Parmesan cheese, optional

1. Preheat broiler. In a large bowl, combine eggs and milk; add the bread crumbs, cheese, salt, pepper and garlic powder. Add beef and sausage; mix well. Shape into 1-inch balls. Place meatballs in a 15x10x1-inch baking pan. Broil 4 inches from the heat for 4 minutes; turn and broil 3 minutes longer.

2. Transfer to a 5-qt. slow cooker. In a bowl, combine the tomato sauce and paste, onion, green pepper, wine, water and seasonings; pour over meatballs. Cover and cook on low for 4–5 hours. Serve on rolls. Sprinkle with shredded cheese if desired.

NUTRITIONAL FACTS
1 EACH: 482 calories, 21 g fat (8 g saturated fat), 131 mg cholesterol, 1545 mg sodium, 40 g carbohydrate (8 g sugars, 4 g fiber), 27 g protein

Baked Lasagna in a Bun

PREP: 20 MINUTES • **BAKE:** 25 MINUTES • **YIELD:** 8 SERVINGS

My family loves the meat sauce and cheese tucked into the hollowed-out buns. Add a crisp salad for a complete meal.

—*Cindy Morelock, Afton, Tennessee*

8 submarine or hoagie buns (8 inches)
1 pound ground beef
1 cup spaghetti sauce
1 tablespoon garlic powder
1 tablespoon Italian seasoning

1 cup ricotta cheese
¼ cup grated Parmesan cheese
1 cup shredded cheddar cheese, divided
1 cup shredded part-skim mozzarella cheese, divided

1. Preheat oven to 350°. Make a 2-inch-wide V-shaped cut in the center of each bun to within 1 inch of bottom. Remove cut portion and save for another use. Place buns on an ungreased baking sheet.

2. In a large skillet, cook beef over medium heat 6–8 minutes or until no longer pink, breaking into crumbles; drain. Stir in spaghetti sauce, garlic powder and Italian seasoning; heat through.

3. Meanwhile, in a small bowl, mix ricotta cheese, Parmesan cheese and half of the cheddar and mozzarella cheeses. Spoon meat sauce into buns; top with ricotta mixture. Cover loosely with foil.

4. Bake 20 minutes. Sprinkle tops with remaining cheddar and mozzarella cheeses; bake, uncovered, 3–5 minutes or until cheese is melted.

NUTRITIONAL FACTS
1 SANDWICH: 650 calories, 24 g fat (11 g saturated fat), 69 mg cholesterol, 1170 mg sodium, 74 g carbohydrate (9 g sugars, 4 g fiber), 33 g protein

State Fair Subs

PREP: 20 MINUTES • **BAKE:** 20 MINUTES • **YIELD:** 6 SERVINGS

My college roommate and I first ate these meaty sandwiches at the Iowa State Fair. After a little experimenting, we re-created the recipe. We ate the subs often because they were fast to fix between classes and didn't break our next-to-nothing grocery budget.

—*Christi Ross, Mill Creek, Oklahoma*

1 loaf (1 pound unsliced) French bread	$\frac{1}{4}$ teaspoon salt
2 large eggs	1 pound bulk Italian sausage
$\frac{1}{4}$ cup whole milk	$1\frac{1}{2}$ cups chopped onion
$\frac{1}{2}$ teaspoon pepper	2 cups shredded part-skim mozzarella cheese

1. Preheat oven to 400°. Cut bread in half lengthwise; carefully hollow out top and bottom of loaf, leaving a 1-inch shell. Cube removed bread. In a large bowl, beat the eggs, milk, pepper and salt. Add bread cubes and toss to coat; set aside.

2. In a skillet over medium heat, cook sausage and onion until the meat is no longer pink; drain. Add to the bread mixture. Spoon filling into bread shells; sprinkle with cheese. Wrap each in foil. Bake for 20–25 minutes or until cheese is melted. Cut into serving-size slices.

NUTRITIONAL FACTS
1 SLICE: 622 calories, 36 g fat (15 g saturated fat), 159 mg cholesterol, 1280 mg sodium, 45 g carbohydrate (5 g sugars, 3 g fiber), 28 g protein

Root Beer Pulled Pork Sandwiches

PREP: 20 MINUTES • **COOK:** 8½ HOURS • **YIELD:** 12 SERVINGS

My husband is a huge fan of pulled pork sandwiches, so my sister shared this incredibly easy recipe with me. At potlucks and family dinners, nobody can get enough of this root beer–braised version.

—*Carolyn Palm, Walton, New York*

1 boneless pork shoulder butt roast (3 to 4 pounds)

1 can (12 ounces) root beer or cola

1 bottle (18 ounces) barbecue sauce

12 kaiser rolls, split

1. Place roast in a 4- or 5-qt. slow cooker. Add root beer; cook, covered, on low 8–10 hours or until meat is tender.

2. Remove roast; cool slightly. Discard cooking juices. Shred pork with two forks; return to slow cooker. Stir in barbecue sauce. Cook, covered, until heated through, about 30 minutes. Serve on rolls.

NUTRITIONAL FACTS
1 SANDWICH: 402 calories, 15 g fat (5 g saturated fat), 67 mg cholesterol, 809 mg sodium, 40 g carbohydrate (10 g sugars, 2 g fiber), 26 g protein

[SLOW COOKER]

Slow-Cooked Spicy Portuguese Cacoila

PREP: 20 MINUTES + MARINATING • **COOK:** 6 HOURS • **YIELD:** 12 SERVINGS

You're probably used to pulled pork coated with barbecue sauce and made into sandwiches. Portuguese pulled pork is a spicy dish often served at our large family functions. Each cook generally adds his or her own touches that reflect their taste and Portuguese heritage. A mixture of beef roast and pork can be used.

—*Michele Merlino, Exeter, Rhode Island*

4 pounds boneless pork shoulder butt roast, cut into 2-inch pieces

1½ cups dry red wine or reduced-sodium chicken broth

4 garlic cloves, minced

4 bay leaves

1 tablespoon salt

1 tablespoon paprika

2 to 3 teaspoons crushed red pepper flakes

1 teaspoon ground cinnamon

1 large onion, chopped

½ cup water

12 bolillos or hoagie buns, split, optional

1. Place pork in a large resealable bag; add wine, garlic and seasonings. Seal bag and turn to coat. Refrigerate overnight.

2. Transfer pork mixture to a 5- or 6-qt. slow cooker; add onion and water. Cook, covered, on low 6–8 hours or until meat is tender.

3. Skim fat. Remove bay leaves. Shred meat with two forks. If desired, serve with a slotted spoon on bolillos.

NUTRITIONAL FACTS
1 SANDWICH: 489 calories, 20 g fat (7 g saturated fat), 90 mg cholesterol, 1075 mg sodium, 38 g carbohydrate (6 g sugars, 2 g fiber), 34 g protein

Carolina-Style Pork Barbecue

PREP: 30 MINUTES ● **COOK:** 6 HOURS ● **YIELD:** 14 SERVINGS

I am originally from North Carolina (where swine is divine), and this recipe for the slow cooker is a family favorite. My husband swears my authentic Carolina 'cue is the best BBQ he has ever eaten!

—*Kathryn Ransom Williams, Sparks, Nevada*

1 boneless pork shoulder butt roast (4 to 5 pounds)	4 teaspoons Worcestershire sauce
2 tablespoons brown sugar	1 tablespoon sugar
2 teaspoons salt	1 tablespoon crushed red pepper flakes
1 teaspoon paprika	1 teaspoon garlic salt
½ teaspoon pepper	1 teaspoon ground mustard
2 medium onions, quartered	½ teaspoon cayenne pepper
¾ cup cider vinegar	14 hamburger buns, split
	1¾ pounds deli coleslaw

1. Cut roast into quarters. In a small bowl, mix brown sugar, salt, paprika and pepper; rub over meat. Place meat and onions in a 5-qt. slow cooker.

2. In a small bowl, whisk vinegar, Worcestershire sauce, sugar and seasonings; pour over roast. Cook, covered, on low 6–8 hours or until meat is tender.

3. Remove roast; cool slightly. Reserve 1½ cups cooking juices; discard remaining juices. Skim fat from reserved juices. Shred pork with two forks. Return pork and reserved juices to slow cooker; heat through. Serve on buns with coleslaw.

NUTRITIONAL FACTS
1 SANDWICH: 453 calories, 22 g fat (6 g saturated fat), 85 mg cholesterol, 889 mg sodium, 35 g carbohydrate (14 g sugars, 3 g fiber), 27 g protein

Freeze It **Freeze cooled meat mixture in freezer containers. To use, partially thaw in refrigerator overnight. Heat through in a saucepan, stirring occasionally and adding a little water if necessary.**

Slow-Cooked Reuben Brats

PREP: 30 MINUTES ● **COOK:** 7¼ HOURS ● **YIELD:** 10 SERVINGS

Sauerkraut gives these beer-simmered brats a big flavor boost, but it's the special chili sauce and melted cheese that put them over the top. Top your favorite burger with some of the chili sauce; you won't be sorry.

—*Alana Simmons, Johnstown, Pennsylvania*

10 uncooked bratwurst links
3 bottles (12 ounces each) light beer or nonalcoholic beer
1 large sweet onion, sliced
1 can (14 ounces) sauerkraut, rinsed and well drained
¾ cup mayonnaise
¼ cup chili sauce

2 tablespoons ketchup
1 tablespoon finely chopped onion
2 teaspoons sweet pickle relish
1 garlic clove, minced
⅛ teaspoon pepper
10 hoagie buns, split
10 slices Swiss cheese

1. In a large skillet, brown bratwurst in batches; drain. In a 5-qt. slow cooker, combine beer, sliced onion and sauerkraut; add bratwurst. Cook, covered, on low 7–9 hours or until sausages are cooked through.

2. Preheat oven to 350°. In a small bowl, mix mayonnaise, chili sauce, ketchup, chopped onion, relish, garlic and pepper until blended. Spread over cut sides of buns; top with cheese, bratwurst and sauerkraut mixture. Place on an ungreased baking sheet. Bake 8–10 minutes or until cheese is melted.

NUTRITIONAL FACTS
1 SANDWICH: 733 calories, 50 g fat (16 g saturated fat), 94 mg cholesterol, 1643 mg sodium, 45 g carbohydrate (10 g sugars, 2 g fiber), 26 g protein

Chili Coney Dogs

PREP: 20 MINUTES • **COOK:** 4 HOURS • **YIELD:** 8 SERVINGS

Everyone in our family, from smallest kids to oldest adults, loves these hot dogs. They're so easy to throw together in the morning, or even the night before.

—*Michele Harris, Vicksburg, Michigan*

1 pound lean ground beef (90% lean)
1 can (15 ounces) tomato sauce
½ cup water
2 tablespoons Worcestershire sauce
1 tablespoon dried minced onion
½ teaspoon garlic powder
½ teaspoon ground mustard
½ teaspoon chili powder
½ teaspoon pepper
Dash cayenne pepper
8 hot dogs
8 hot dog buns, split
Optional toppings: shredded cheddar cheese, relish and chopped onion

1. In a large skillet, cook beef over medium heat 6–8 minutes or until no longer pink, breaking into crumbles; drain. Stir in tomato sauce, water, Worcestershire sauce, onion and seasonings.

2. Place hot dogs in a 3-qt. slow cooker; top with beef mixture. Cook, covered, on low 4–5 hours or until heated through. Serve on buns with toppings as desired.

NUTRITIONAL FACTS
1 CHILI DOG (CALCULATED WITHOUT OPTIONAL TOPPINGS): 371 calories, 20 g fat (8 g saturated fat), 53 mg cholesterol, 992 mg sodium, 26 g carbohydrate (5 g sugars, 2 g fiber), 21 g protein

Caramelized Ham & Swiss Buns

PREP: 25 MINUTES + CHILLING ● **BAKE:** 30 MINUTES ● **YIELD:** 1 DOZEN

My next-door neighbor shared her version of this recipe with me. You can make it ahead and cook it quickly when company arrives. The combo of poppy seeds, ham and cheese, horseradish and brown sugar makes it simply delicious!

—*Iris Weihemuller, Baxter, Minnesota*

- 1 package (12 ounces) Hawaiian sweet rolls, split
- ½ cup horseradish sauce
- 12 slices deli ham
- 6 slices Swiss cheese, halved
- ½ cup butter, cubed
- 2 tablespoons finely chopped onion
- 2 tablespoons brown sugar
- 1 tablespoon spicy brown mustard
- 2 teaspoons poppy seeds
- 1½ teaspoons Worcestershire sauce
- ¼ teaspoon garlic powder

1. Spread roll bottoms with horseradish sauce. Layer with ham and cheese; replace tops. Arrange in a single layer in a greased 9-inch square baking pan.

2. In a small skillet, heat butter over medium-high heat. Add onion; cook and stir 1–2 minutes or until tender. Stir in remaining ingredients. Pour over rolls. Refrigerate, covered, several hours or overnight.

3. Preheat oven to 350°. Bake, covered, 25 minutes. Bake, uncovered, 5–10 minutes longer or until golden brown.

NUTRITIONAL FACTS
1 SANDWICH: 288 calories, 17 g fat (9 g saturated fat), 67 mg cholesterol, 447 mg sodium, 21 g carbohydrate (11 g sugars, 1 g fiber), 11 g protein

Hot Ham Sandwiches

PREP: 10 MINUTES ● **COOK:** 4 HOURS ● **YIELD:** 12 SERVINGS

I came up with this crowd-pleasing recipe when trying to re-create a favorite sandwich from a restaurant near my hometown. Flavored with sweet relish, these ham sandwiches are oh-so-easy. My family likes them with coleslaw and French fries.

—Susan Rehm, Grahamsville, New York

3 pounds thinly sliced deli ham (about 40 slices)
2 cups apple juice
⅔ cup packed brown sugar
½ cup sweet pickle relish

2 teaspoons prepared mustard
1 teaspoon paprika
12 kaiser rolls, split
   Additional sweet pickle relish, optional

1. Separate ham slices and place in a 3-qt. slow cooker. In a small bowl, combine the apple juice, brown sugar, relish, mustard and paprika. Pour over ham.

2. Cover and cook on low for 4–5 hours or until heated through. Place three to four slices of ham on each roll. Serve with additional relish if desired.

NUTRITIONAL FACTS
1 EACH: 432 calories, 13 g fat (4 g saturated fat), 62 mg cholesterol, 1974 mg sodium, 52 g carbohydrate (23 g sugars, 2 g fiber), 27 g protein

Spinach Pastrami Wraps

PREP/TOTAL TIME: 20 MINUTES ● **YIELD:** 4 SERVINGS

If you're trying to avoid carbs, wrap the meat around the other ingredients and fasten with a toothpick. Either way, they can be sliced and served for appetizers or kept whole.

—Rhonda Wilkinson, Levittown, Pennsylvania

4 flour tortillas (10 inches), room temperature
4 ounces cream cheese, softened
¾ cup shredded cheddar cheese
¼ cup chopped red onion
¼ cup sliced Greek olives
½ pound thinly sliced deli pastrami
1½ cups fresh baby spinach

Spread tortillas with cream cheese; sprinkle with cheddar cheese, onion and olives. Top with pastrami and spinach. Roll up tightly; secure with toothpicks.

NUTRITIONAL FACTS
1 EACH: 482 calories, 24 g fat (13 g saturated fat), 86 mg cholesterol, 1236 mg sodium, 35 g carbohydrate (1 g sugars, 6 g fiber), 24 g protein

Italian Muffuletta

PREP/TOTAL TIME: 25 MINUTES • **YIELD:** 6 SERVINGS

I first made this hearty sandwich when friends and family were helping to build our deck. It was a big hit, and I've made it several times since then. It also makes a quick and impressive summer party entree!

—*Dana Schmitt, Ames, Iowa*

$\frac{2}{3}$ cup pimiento-stuffed olives, chopped

1 can ($4\frac{1}{4}$ ounces) chopped ripe olives

6 tablespoons shredded Parmesan cheese

$\frac{1}{4}$ cup Italian salad dressing

2 teaspoons minced garlic

1 loaf (1 pound) Italian bread

$\frac{1}{2}$ pound sliced deli turkey

$\frac{1}{4}$ pound sliced Swiss cheese

$\frac{1}{4}$ pound thinly sliced hard salami

$\frac{1}{4}$ pound sliced provolone cheese

$\frac{1}{4}$ pound thinly sliced bologna

1. In a small bowl, combine the first five ingredients; set aside.

2. Cut bread in half horizontally; carefully hollow out top and bottom, leaving a 1-inch shell (discard removed bread or save for another use).

3. Spoon half of olive mixture over bottom half of bread. Layer with turkey, Swiss cheese, salami, provolone cheese, bologna and remaining olive mixture. Replace bread top. Cut into six wedges.

NUTRITIONAL FACTS
1 SLICE: 559 calories, 34 g fat (14 g saturated fat), 84 mg cholesterol, 2241 mg sodium, 33 g carbohydrate (1 g sugars, 2 g fiber), 31 g protein

Quick Tip **To quickly slice whole pitted ripe olives, use an egg slicer. Place olives, end to end, across the slots on the base of the slicer, then press the top down. You'll end up with neat, uniform slices.**

Buffet Sandwich

PREP: 50 MINUTES • **YIELD:** 10 SERVINGS

The first time I took this beautiful sandwich "centerpiece" to a church potluck, it disappeared so fast, I was sorry I hadn't brought two. I have often added sliced tomatoes to it.

—*Margaret Rhodes, Coaldale, Alberta*

1 loaf unsliced French bread (1 pound)	5 slices pimiento loaf, halved, optional
3 to 4 tablespoons mayonnaise	10 slices salami
2 tablespoons butter, softened	5 slices Swiss cheese, halved
1 tablespoon prepared mustard	5 slices part-skim mozzarella cheese, halved
10 lettuce leaves	10 thinly sliced red or green bell pepper rings
5 thin slices deli ham, halved	

1. Cut bread into 22 slices, leaving slices attached at the bottom. Cut off and discard the end pieces. In a small bowl, combine the mayonnaise, butter and mustard until blended. Spread over every other slice of bread.

2. Between the slices spread with mayonnaise mixture, place a lettuce leaf, the meats, cheeses and one pepper ring. To serve, cut completely through the loaf, forming sandwiches.

NUTRITIONAL FACTS
1 PIECE: 274 calories, 13 g fat (6 g saturated fat), 30 mg cholesterol, 631 mg sodium, 26 g carbohydrate (3 g sugars, 2 g fiber), 13 g protein

Shredded Chicken Gyros

PREP: 20 MINUTES • **COOK:** 3 HOURS • **YIELD:** 8 SERVINGS

We go to the annual Greek Festival in Salt Lake City for the awesome food. This chicken with lemon and spices is a great way to mix up our menu, and my kids are big fans!

—*Camille Beckstrand, Layton, Utah*

2 medium onions, chopped	$\frac{1}{4}$ cup red wine vinegar
6 garlic cloves, minced	2 tablespoons olive oil
1 teaspoon lemon-pepper seasoning	2 pounds boneless skinless chicken breasts
1 teaspoon dried oregano	8 whole pita breads
$\frac{1}{2}$ teaspoon ground allspice	Toppings: tzatziki sauce, torn romaine and sliced tomato, cucumber and onion
$\frac{1}{2}$ cup water	
$\frac{1}{2}$ cup lemon juice	

1. In a 3-qt. slow cooker, combine first nine ingredients; add chicken. Cook, covered, on low 3–4 hours or until chicken is tender (a thermometer should read at least 165°).

2. Remove chicken from slow cooker. Shred with two forks; return to slow cooker. Using tongs, place chicken mixture on pita breads. Serve with toppings.

NUTRITIONAL FACTS
1 GYRO (CALCULATED WITHOUT TOPPINGS): 337 calories, 7 g fat (1 g saturated fat), 63 mg cholesterol, 418 mg sodium, 38 g carbohydrate (2 g sugars, 2 g fiber), 29 g protein

Hearty Turkey & Feta Sandwich

PREP/TOTAL TIME: 15 MINUTES ● **YIELD:** 8 SERVINGS

I've served this highly requested sandwich at get-togethers since my college days. What makes it so good is the hummus and the pickle—everyone notices if the pickle is missing.

—*Jackie Termont, Richmond, Virginia*

1 loaf (1 pound) unsliced French bread	1 pound sliced deli turkey
½ cup roasted garlic hummus	1 large sweet red pepper, sliced
¼ cup crumbled feta cheese	4 thin sandwich pickle slices
1 teaspoon dried oregano	

1. Cut French bread lengthwise in half; hollow out each half, leaving a ¼-inch shell (save removed bread for another use).

2. Spread hummus over cut side of bread top. In a small bowl, combine cheese and oregano; sprinkle over bread bottom. Top with turkey, red pepper and pickles. Replace top; cut into slices.

NUTRITIONAL FACTS
1 SLICE: 199 calories, 4 g fat (1 g saturated fat), 22 mg cholesterol, 933 mg sodium, 24 g carbohydrate (2 g sugars, 2 g fiber), 16 g protein

Gourmet Deli Turkey Wraps

PREP/TOTAL TIME: 15 MINUTES • **YIELD:** 6 SERVINGS

These wraps are a staple for my family. They are easy and incredibly delicious and can be served for dinner, lunch or sliced to make appetizers.

—*Tamara Hanson, Big Lake, Minnesota*

2 tablespoons water
2 tablespoons red wine vinegar
1 tablespoon olive oil
$\frac{1}{8}$ teaspoon pepper
$\frac{3}{4}$ pound sliced deli turkey
6 flour tortillas (8 inches), room temperature

4 cups spring mix salad greens
2 medium pears, peeled and sliced
6 tablespoons crumbled blue cheese
6 tablespoons dried cranberries
$\frac{1}{4}$ cup chopped walnuts

In a small bowl, whisk the water, vinegar, oil and pepper. Divide turkey among tortillas; top with salad greens, pears, cheese, cranberries and walnuts. Drizzle with dressing. Roll up tightly. Secure with toothpicks.

NUTRITIONAL FACTS
1 EACH: 330 calories, 11 g fat (2 g saturated fat), 25 mg cholesterol, 819 mg sodium, 44 g carbohydrate (10 g sugars, 3 g fiber), 17 g protein

Spinach Po' Boy

PREP: 10 MINUTES ● **BAKE:** 25 MINUTES ● **YIELD:** 6 SERVINGS

I like to make this warm and cheesy sandwich for a simple dinner, served with fresh fruit on the side.

—*Jan Briggs, Greenfield, Wisconsin*

1 loaf (8 ounces) unsliced French bread	½ teaspoon garlic powder
½ cup butter, divided	⅛ teaspoon hot pepper sauce
⅓ cup chopped green onions	½ cup shredded sharp cheddar cheese
6 cups fresh spinach, coarsely chopped	½ cup shredded mozzarella cheese

1. Preheat oven to 375°. Cut bread in half lengthwise; spread cut sides with half of the butter. Set aside.

2. In a large skillet, cook onions in remaining butter over medium heat for 4–5 minutes or until tender. Add the spinach, garlic powder and hot pepper sauce; cook and stir 3 minutes longer or until spinach is tender.

3. Spread over bottom half of loaf; sprinkle with cheeses. Replace bread top. Wrap in foil; place on a baking sheet. Bake for 20 minutes. Open foil; bake 5 minutes longer or until golden brown.

NOTE: French bread rolls can be used in place of the loaf of bread.

NUTRITIONAL FACTS
1 EACH: 314 calories, 21 g fat (13 g saturated fat), 58 mg cholesterol, 494 mg sodium, 24 g carbohydrate (1 g sugars, 2 g fiber), 10 g protein

Loaded Mexican Pizza

PREP/TOTAL TIME: 30 MINUTES • **YIELD:** 6 SLICES

My husband is a picky eater, but this healthy pizza has lots of flavor, and he actually looks forward to it. Leftovers are no problem, because this meal tastes better the next day.

—Mary Barker, Knoxville, Tennessee

1 can (15 ounces) black beans, rinsed and drained
1 medium red onion, chopped
1 small sweet yellow pepper, chopped
3 teaspoons chili powder
¾ teaspoon ground cumin
3 medium tomatoes, chopped
1 jalapeno pepper, seeded and finely chopped
1 garlic clove, minced
1 prebaked 12-inch thin pizza crust
2 cups chopped fresh spinach
2 tablespoons minced fresh cilantro
 Hot pepper sauce to taste
½ cup shredded reduced-fat cheddar cheese
½ cup shredded pepper jack cheese

1. Preheat oven to 400°. In a small bowl, mash black beans. Stir in the onion, yellow pepper, chili powder and cumin. In another bowl, combine the tomatoes, jalapeno and garlic.

2. Place crust on an ungreased 12-inch pizza pan; spread with bean mixture. Top with tomato mixture and spinach. Sprinkle with cilantro, pepper sauce and cheeses.

3. Bake for 12–15 minutes or until cheese is melted.

NOTE: Wear disposable gloves when cutting hot peppers; the oils can burn skin. Avoid touching your face.

NUTRITIONAL FACTS
1 SLICE: 297 calories, 9 g fat (4 g saturated fat), 17 mg cholesterol, 566 mg sodium, 41 g carbohydrate (5 g sugars, 6 g fiber), 15 g protein

Peppery Pizza Loaves

PREP: 20 MINUTES ● **BAKE:** 20 MINUTES ● **YIELD:** 12 SERVINGS

I often take these French bread pizzas to church picnics or potluck suppers, and there is never any left. When I fix them for the two of us, I freeze two halves in foil to enjoy later.

—Lou Stasny, Poplarville, Mississippi

1½ pounds ground beef

½ teaspoon garlic powder

½ teaspoon salt

2 loaves (8 ounces each) French bread, halved lengthwise

1 jar (8 ounces) process cheese sauce

1 can (4 ounces) mushroom stems and pieces, drained

1 cup chopped green onions

1 can (4 ounces) sliced jalapenos, drained

1 can (8 ounces) tomato sauce

½ cup grated Parmesan cheese

4 cups shredded part-skim mozzarella cheese

1. In a large skillet, cook beef over medium heat until no longer pink; drain. Stir in garlic powder and salt.

2. Place each bread half on a large piece of heavy-duty foil. Spread with cheese sauce. Top with beef mixture, mushrooms, onions and jalapenos. Drizzle with tomato sauce. Top with Parmesan and mozzarella cheeses. Wrap and freeze. May be frozen for up to 3 months.

3. To bake: Unwrap loaves and thaw on baking sheets in the refrigerator. Bake at 350° for 18 minutes or until cheese is melted.

NUTRITIONAL FACTS
1 PIECE: 323 calories, 19 g fat (11 g saturated fat), 71 mg cholesterol, 907 mg sodium, 15 g carbohydrate (2 g sugars, 1 g fiber), 23 g protein

French Bread Pizza

PREP/TOTAL TIME: 25 MINUTES • **YIELD:** 8 SERVINGS

Slices of this hearty French bread are guaranteed to please. I sometimes substitute spaghetti sauce for the pizza sauce . . . or add our favorite veggies to the toppings.

—*Sue McLaughlin, Onawa, Iowa*

½ pound ground beef
1 can (15 ounces) pizza sauce
8 ounces canned sliced mushrooms, drained

1 loaf (1 pound) French bread
2 cups shredded part-skim mozzarella cheese

1. Preheat oven to 400°. In a large skillet, cook beef over medium heat until no longer pink; drain. Stir in pizza sauce and mushrooms; set aside.

2. Cut bread in half lengthwise, then into eight pieces. Spread meat sauce on bread; place on a greased baking sheet. Sprinkle with mozzarella. Bake, uncovered, 10 minutes or until cheese is melted and bubbly.

NUTRITIONAL FACTS
2 PIECES: 296 calories, 9 g fat (4 g saturated fat), 30 mg cholesterol, 764 mg sodium, 35 g carbohydrate (3 g sugars, 3 g fiber), 18 g protein

Pepperoni-Sausage Stuffed Pizza

PREP: 45 MINUTES + RISING • **BAKE:** 40 MINUTES + STANDING • **YIELD:** 12 SERVINGS

For 30 years, friends have been telling me to open a pizzeria using this recipe. It even freezes well.

—Elizabeth Wolff, Carmel, Indiana

1 package ($\frac{1}{4}$ ounce) active dry yeast
1$\frac{1}{4}$ cups warm water (110° to 115°)
2 tablespoons olive oil
1$\frac{1}{2}$ teaspoons salt
1 teaspoon sugar
3$\frac{1}{2}$ to 4 cups all-purpose flour

FILLING:
2$\frac{1}{2}$ cups shredded part-skim mozzarella cheese, divided
2$\frac{1}{2}$ cups shredded white cheddar cheese, divided

2 tablespoons all-purpose flour
2 teaspoons dried oregano
2 teaspoons dried basil
$\frac{1}{2}$ teaspoon crushed red pepper flakes
1 pound bulk Italian sausage, cooked and crumbled
$\frac{1}{2}$ pound sliced fresh mushrooms
1 package (3$\frac{1}{2}$ ounces) sliced pepperoni
1 can (15 ounces) pizza sauce
Grated Parmesan cheese, optional

1. In a small bowl, dissolve yeast in warm water. In a large bowl, combine oil, salt, sugar, yeast mixture and 1 cup flour; beat on medium speed until smooth. Stir in enough remaining flour to form a stiff dough.

2. Turn dough onto a floured surface; knead until smooth and elastic, about 6–8 minutes. Place in a greased bowl, turning once to grease the top. Cover with plastic wrap and let rise in a warm place until doubled, about 1 hour.

3. Preheat oven to 425°. Grease a 13x9-inch baking pan. Punch down dough; divide into three portions. On a lightly floured surface, combine two portions of dough and roll into a 15x11-inch rectangle. Transfer to prepared pan, pressing onto bottom and up sides of pan. Top with 2 cups mozzarella cheese and 2 cups cheddar cheese. Sprinkle with flour, seasonings, cooked sausage, mushrooms and pepperoni.

4. Roll out remaining dough into a 13x9-inch rectangle. Place dough over filling, crimping edges to seal; prick top with a fork. Sprinkle with remaining cheeses. Bake on a lower oven rack 10 minutes.

5. Reduce oven setting to 375°. Spread pizza sauce over cheese. Bake 30–35 minutes longer or until edges are lightly browned. Let stand 10 minutes before cutting. If desired, sprinkle with Parmesan cheese.

NUTRITIONAL FACTS
1 PIECE: 481 calories, 27 g fat (13 g saturated fat), 72 mg cholesterol, 1115 mg sodium, 36 g carbohydrate (4 g sugars, 2 g fiber), 24 g protein

Crowd-Pleasing Appetizers

Antipasto Appetizer Salad

PREP: 10 MINUTES + CHILLING • **YIELD:** 6 CUPS

Serve this with a slotted spoon as an appetizer or over torn romaine lettuce to enjoy as a salad. I like it with toasted baguette slices on the side.

—Tamra Duncan, Decatur, Arkansas

- 1 jar (16 ounces) roasted sweet red pepper strips, drained
- ½ pound part-skim mozzarella cheese, cubed
- 1 cup grape tomatoes
- 1 jar (7½ ounces) marinated quartered artichoke hearts, undrained
- 1 jar (7 ounces) pimiento-stuffed olives, drained

- 1 can (6 ounces) pitted ripe olives, drained
- 1 teaspoon dried basil
- 1 teaspoon dried parsley flakes
  Pepper to taste
  Toasted baguette slices or romaine lettuce, torn

1. In a large bowl, combine the first nine ingredients; toss to coat. Cover and refrigerate for at least 4 hours before serving.

2. Serve with baguette slices or over lettuce.

NUTRITIONAL FACTS
½ CUP: 132 calories, 11 g fat (3 g saturated fat), 15 mg cholesterol, 651 mg sodium, 6 g carbohydrate (2 g sugars, 1 g fiber), 4 g protein

Quick Tip
If you are hosting an appetizer party, arrange a few groupings of two or three chairs where several people can converse. Position extra end tables throughout the house so guests are able to set down their beverages.—Taste of Home Test Kitchen

Sweet and Spicy Asian Meatballs

PREP: 1 HOUR • **COOK:** 3 HOURS • **YIELD:** ABOUT 5 DOZEN

For my niece's annual Halloween party, I make glazed meatballs and deliver them in the slow cooker so they're spicy, sweet and ready to eat.

—*Gail Borczyk, Boca Raton, Florida*

1 large egg, lightly beaten
½ medium onion, finely chopped
⅓ cup sliced water chestnuts, minced
3 tablespoons minced fresh cilantro
1 jalapeno pepper, seeded and finely chopped
3 tablespoons reduced-sodium soy sauce
4 garlic cloves, minced
1 tablespoon minced fresh gingerroot
⅔ cup panko (Japanese) bread crumbs
2 pounds ground pork

SAUCE:

2 cups sweet-and-sour sauce
¼ cup barbecue sauce
¼ cup duck sauce
2 tablespoons chicken broth
1 tablespoon minced fresh cilantro
1 tablespoon reduced-sodium soy sauce
2 garlic cloves, minced
1½ teaspoons minced fresh gingerroot
Thinly sliced green onions, optional

1. Preheat oven to 375°. In a large bowl, combine the first eight ingredients; stir in bread crumbs. Add pork; mix lightly but thoroughly. Shape into 1¼-inch balls. Place meatballs on a greased rack in a 15x10x1-inch baking pan. Bake 18–22 minutes or until lightly browned.

2. Transfer meatballs to a 4-qt. slow cooker. In small bowl, mix the first eight sauce ingredients. Pour over meatballs. Cook, covered, on low 3–4 hours or until meatballs are cooked through. If desired, sprinkle with green onions.

NOTE: Wear disposable gloves when cutting hot peppers; the oils can burn skin. Avoid touching your face.

NUTRITIONAL FACTS
1 MEATBALL: 52 calories, 2 g fat (1 g saturated fat), 13 mg cholesterol, 119 mg sodium, 4 g carbohydrate (3 g sugars, 0 fiber), 3 g protein

Freeze It

Freeze cooled meatball mixture in freezer containers. To use, partially thaw in refrigerator overnight. Heat through in a covered saucepan, gently stirring and adding a little broth or water if necessary. Sprinkle with green onions.

Party Shrimp

PREP: 15 MINUTES + MARINATING • **BROIL:** 10 MINUTES • **YIELD:** ABOUT 2½ DOZEN

The marinade for this dish makes the shrimp so flavorful, you won't even need a dipping sauce. Even those who claim they don't like shellfish really dig this appetizer.

—*Kendra Doss, Colorado Springs, Colorado*

1 tablespoon olive oil	½ teaspoon Italian seasoning
1½ teaspoons brown sugar	½ teaspoon dried basil
1½ teaspoons lemon juice	¼ teaspoon pepper
1 garlic clove, thinly sliced	1 pound uncooked large shrimp, peeled and deveined
½ teaspoon paprika	

1. In a large resealable plastic bag, combine the first eight ingredients. Add shrimp; seal bag and turn to coat. Refrigerate 2 hours.

2. Drain shrimp, discarding marinade. Place shrimp on an ungreased baking sheet. Broil 4 inches from heat 3–4 minutes on each side or until shrimp turn pink.

NUTRITIONAL FACTS
1 SHRIMP: 14 calories, 0 fat (0 saturated fat), 18 mg cholesterol, 18 mg sodium, 0 carbohydrate (0 sugars, 0 fiber), 2 g protein

Mark's Marinated Mushrooms

PREP: 15 MINUTES + MARINATING • **YIELD:** 3 CUPS

Add these flavorful mushrooms to an antipasto platter, toss in a salad or just serve by themselves.

—*Mark Curry, Buena Vista, Colorado*

1 pound small fresh mushrooms

1 small onion, thinly sliced

⅓ cup white wine vinegar

⅓ cup canola oil

1 teaspoon salt

1 teaspoon ground mustard

In a large saucepan, combine all ingredients. Bring to a boil over medium-high heat. Cook, uncovered, for 6 minutes, stirring once. Cool to room temperature. Transfer to a large bowl; cover and refrigerate overnight.

NUTRITIONAL FACTS
¼ CUP: 69 calories, 6 g fat (1 g saturated fat), 0 cholesterol, 198 mg sodium, 3 g carbohydrate (1 g sugars, 1 g fiber), 1 g protein

Cherry-Brandy Baked Brie

PREP/TOTAL TIME: 20 MINUTES • **YIELD:** 8 SERVINGS

No one will believe this impressive appetizer is so easy to make. You can substitute dried cranberries or apricots for the cherries and apple juice for the brandy.

—Kevin Phebus, Katy, Texas

1 round (8 ounces) Brie cheese	$\frac{1}{4}$ cup brandy or unsweetened apple juice
$\frac{1}{2}$ cup dried cherries	French bread baguette, sliced and
$\frac{1}{2}$ cup chopped walnuts	toasted, or assorted crackers
$\frac{1}{4}$ cup packed brown sugar	

1. Preheat oven to 350°. Place cheese in a 9-inch pie plate. In a small bowl, combine cherries, walnuts, brown sugar and brandy; spoon over cheese.

2. Bake 15–20 minutes or until cheese is softened. Serve with baguette.

NUTRITIONAL FACTS
1 EACH: 210 calories, 13 g fat (5 g saturated fat), 28 mg cholesterol, 182 mg sodium, 14 g carbohydrate (12 g sugars, 1 g fiber), 7 g protein

Cheeseburger Mini Muffins

PREP: 20 MINUTES • **BAKE:** 15 MINUTES • **YIELD:** 5 DOZEN

I invented these cute little muffins so I could enjoy the flavor of cheeseburgers without resorting to fast food. I often freeze a batch and reheat however many I need. They're also great as appetizers.

—*Teresa Kraus, Cortez, Colorado*

½ pound ground beef	¾ cup ketchup
1 small onion, finely chopped	¾ cup 2% milk
2½ cups all-purpose flour	½ cup butter, melted
1 tablespoon sugar	2 large eggs
2 teaspoons baking powder	1 teaspoon prepared mustard
1 teaspoon salt	2 cups shredded cheddar cheese

1. Preheat oven to 425°. In a large skillet, cook beef and onion over medium heat until meat is no longer pink; drain.

2. In a small bowl, combine the flour, sugar, baking powder and salt. In another bowl, combine the ketchup, milk, butter, eggs and mustard; stir into the dry ingredients just until moistened. Fold in the beef mixture and cheese.

3. Fill greased miniature muffin cups three-fourths full. Bake for 15–18 minutes or until a toothpick comes out clean. Cool for 5 minutes before removing from pans to wire racks. Serve warm. Refrigerate leftovers.

NOTE: Muffins may be baked in regular-size muffin cups for 20–25 minutes; recipe makes 2 dozen.

NUTRITIONAL FACTS
2 EACH: 121 calories, 7 g fat (4 g saturated fat), 35 mg cholesterol, 267 mg sodium, 11 g carbohydrate (2 g sugars, 0 fiber), 5 g protein

Mini Mac & Cheese Bites

PREP: 35 MINUTES • **BAKE:** 10 MINUTES • **YIELD:** 3 DOZEN

Young relatives were coming for a Christmas party, so I wanted something fun for them to eat. Instead, the adults devoured my mini mac and cheese.

—*Katherine Mainiero, Poughkeepsie, New York*

- 2 cups uncooked elbow macaroni
- 1 cup seasoned bread crumbs, divided
- 2 tablespoons butter
- 2 tablespoons all-purpose flour
- $\frac{1}{2}$ teaspoon onion powder
- $\frac{1}{2}$ teaspoon garlic powder
- $\frac{1}{2}$ teaspoon seasoned salt
- $1\frac{3}{4}$ cups 2% milk
- 2 cups shredded sharp cheddar cheese, divided
- 1 cup shredded Swiss cheese
- $\frac{3}{4}$ cup biscuit/baking mix
- 2 large eggs, lightly beaten

1. Preheat oven to 425°. Cook macaroni according to package directions; drain.

2. Meanwhile, sprinkle $\frac{1}{4}$ cup bread crumbs into 36 greased mini-muffin cups. In a large saucepan, melt butter over medium heat. Stir in flour and seasonings until smooth; gradually whisk in milk. Bring to a boil, stirring constantly; cook and stir 1–2 minutes or until thickened. Stir in 1 cup cheddar cheese and Swiss cheese until melted.

3. Remove from heat; stir in biscuit mix, eggs and $\frac{1}{2}$ cup bread crumbs. Add macaroni; toss to coat. Spoon about 2 tablespoons macaroni mixture into prepared mini-muffin cups; sprinkle with remaining cheddar cheese and bread crumbs.

4. Bake 8–10 minutes or until golden brown. Cool in pans 5 minutes before serving.

NUTRITIONAL FACTS
1 APPETIZER: 91 calories, 5 g fat (3 g saturated fat), 22 mg cholesterol, 162 mg sodium, 8 g carbohydrate (1 g sugars, 0 fiber), 4 g protein

Mushroom Bacon Bites

PREP/TOTAL TIME: 20 MINUTES ● **YIELD:** 2 DOZEN

This is the perfect appetizer for most any occasion. The tasty bites are easy to assemble and brush with prepared barbecue sauce. When we have a big cookout, they're always a hit . . . but they make a nice little "extra" for a family dinner, too.

—Gina Roesner, Ashland, Missouri

24 medium fresh mushrooms

12 bacon strips, halved

1 cup barbecue sauce

1. Wrap each mushroom with a piece of bacon; secure with a toothpick. Thread onto metal or soaked wooden skewers; brush with barbecue sauce.

2. Grill, uncovered, over indirect medium heat for 10–15 minutes or until the bacon is crisp and the mushrooms are tender, turning and basting occasionally with remaining barbecue sauce.

NUTRITIONAL FACTS
3 EACH: 226 calories, 20 g fat (7 g saturated fat), 23 mg cholesterol, 505 mg sodium, 6 g carbohydrate (4 g sugars, 1 g fiber), 5 g protein

Bacon-Cheddar Deviled Eggs

PREP/TOTAL TIME: 30 MINUTES • **YIELD:** 2 DOZEN

I created this recipe a few years ago when I was craving something different to do with hard-cooked eggs. I combined three of my favorite foods—bacon, eggs and cheese—in these deviled eggs. I've shared them at parties and have received many compliments on their eggstra-special taste.

—*Laura LeMay, Deerfield Beach, Florida*

12 hard-cooked large eggs
½ cup mayonnaise
4 bacon strips, cooked and crumbled
2 tablespoons finely shredded cheddar cheese

1 tablespoon honey mustard
¼ teaspoon pepper

Slice eggs in half lengthwise; remove yolks and set whites aside. In a small bowl, mash yolks. Stir in the mayonnaise, bacon, cheese, mustard and pepper. Stuff or pipe into egg whites. Refrigerate until serving.

NOTE: As a substitute for honey mustard, combine 1½ teaspoons Dijon mustard and 1½ teaspoons honey.

NUTRITIONAL FACTS
2 EACH: 163 calories, 14 g fat (3 g saturated fat), 218 mg cholesterol, 163 mg sodium, 1 g carbohydrate (1 g sugars, 0 fiber), 7 g protein

Rye Party Puffs

PREP: 30 MINUTES • **BAKE:** 20 MINUTES + COOLING • **YIELD:** 4$\frac{1}{2}$ DOZEN

I can't go anywhere without taking along my puffs. They're pretty enough for a wedding reception yet also hearty enough to snack on while watching football on television. A platterful of these will disappear even with a small group.

—Kelly Williams, La Porte, Indiana

1 cup water
$\frac{1}{2}$ cup butter, cubed
$\frac{1}{2}$ cup all-purpose flour
$\frac{1}{2}$ cup rye flour
2 teaspoons dried parsley flakes
$\frac{1}{2}$ teaspoon garlic powder
$\frac{1}{4}$ teaspoon salt
4 large eggs
Caraway seeds

CORNED BEEF FILLING:

2 packages (8 ounces each) cream cheese, softened
2 packages (2 ounces each) thinly sliced deli corned beef, chopped
$\frac{1}{2}$ cup mayonnaise
$\frac{1}{4}$ cup sour cream
2 tablespoons minced chives
2 tablespoons diced onion
1 teaspoon spicy brown or horseradish mustard
$\frac{1}{8}$ teaspoon garlic powder
10 small pimiento-stuffed olives, chopped

1. Preheat oven to 400°. In a large saucepan over medium heat, bring water and butter to a boil. Add the flours, parsley, garlic powder and salt all at once; stir until a smooth balls forms. Remove from the heat; let stand for 5 minutes. Beat in eggs, one at a time. Beat until smooth.

2. Drop batter by rounded teaspoonfuls 2 inches apart onto greased baking sheets. Sprinkle with caraway. Bake for 18–20 minutes or until golden. Remove to wire racks. Immediately cut a slit in each puff to allow steam to escape; cool.

3. In a large bowl, combine the first eight filling ingredients. Stir in olives. Split puffs; add filling. Refrigerate.

NUTRITIONAL FACTS
1 APPETIZER: 121 calories, 7 g fat (2 g saturated fat), 19 mg cholesterol, 362 mg sodium, 9 g carbohydrate (3 g sugars, 1 g fiber), 6 g protein

Salmon Mousse Cups

PREP: 25 MINUTES + CHILLING • **BAKE:** 10 MINUTES + COOLING • **YIELD:** 2 DOZEN

I make these tempting little tarts frequently for parties. They disappear at an astonishing speed, so I usually double or triple the recipe. The salmon–cream cheese filling and flaky crust will melt in your mouth.

—*Fran Rowland, Phoenix, Arizona*

- 3 ounces cream cheese, softened
- $\frac{1}{2}$ cup butter, softened
- 1 cup all-purpose flour

FILLING:

- 1 package (8 ounces) cream cheese, softened
- 1 cup fully cooked salmon chunks or 1 can (7$\frac{1}{2}$ ounces) salmon, drained, bones and skin removed

- 2 tablespoons chicken broth
- 2 tablespoons sour cream
- 1 tablespoon finely chopped onion
- 1 teaspoon lemon juice
- $\frac{1}{2}$ teaspoon salt
- 2 tablespoons minced fresh dill

1. Preheat oven to 350°. In a small bowl, beat the cream cheese and butter until smooth. Add flour and mix well. Shape into 24 balls; press onto the bottom and up the sides of greased miniature muffin cups.

2. Bake for 10–15 minutes or until golden brown. Cool for 5 minutes before removing from pans to wire racks to cool completely.

3. For filling, in a large bowl, beat cream cheese until smooth. Add the salmon, broth, sour cream, onion, lemon juice and salt until blended. Spoon into the shells. Refrigerate for at least 2 hours. Sprinkle with dill.

NUTRITIONAL FACTS
2 EACH: 228 calories, 18 g fat (11 g saturated fat), 58 mg cholesterol, 359 mg sodium, 9 g carbohydrate (1 g sugars, 0 fiber), 7 g protein

Cucumber Shrimp Appetizers

PREP/TOTAL TIME: 10 MINUTES • **YIELD:** 32 APPETIZERS

When my friend's husband needed lower-fat snacks, she served him this fresh-tasting shrimp spread. Cucumber slices are a fun and healthy alternative to crackers.

—*Patricia Kile, Elizabethtown, Pennsylvania*

1 can (8 ounces) unsweetened crushed pineapple, drained

1 can (4 ounces) tiny shrimp, rinsed and drained

¼ cup reduced-fat mayonnaise

1 tablespoon finely chopped green onion

2 teaspoons Dijon mustard

1½ teaspoons minced fresh dill

1 medium cucumber (8 inches), cut into ¼-inch slices

Fresh dill sprigs, optional

In a bowl, combine the pineapple, shrimp, mayonnaise, onion, mustard and dill. Spoon onto cucumber slices. Garnish with dill sprigs if desired.

NUTRITIONAL FACTS
1 EACH: 16 calories, 1 g fat (0 saturated fat), 7 mg cholesterol, 29 mg sodium, 2 g carbohydrate (0 sugars, 0 fiber), 1 g protein

Take-It Tip

To keep multiple dishes cold at cookouts and other warm-weather gatherings, I use a large, flat plastic storage container—the kind you can fit under a bed. I fill it with ice and nestle in the dishes that would otherwise spoil sitting out in the warm air. This keeps the food safe and tasting its best, too.—Joyce A., Oelwein, IA

Hot Pepper Pleasers

PREP: 20 MINUTES ● **BAKE:** 25 MINUTES ● **YIELD:** 20 APPETIZERS

Here's a real crowd-pleaser! The banana peppers pack a subtle punch, and the pepperoni adds spice. Have knives, forks and napkins ready so folks can eat them up neatly.

—*Darius Kovacina, Acme, Pennsylvania*

10 banana peppers
1 package (8 ounces) cream cheese, softened
1 large egg
1 cup shredded cheddar cheese

$\frac{1}{2}$ cup shredded part-skim mozzarella cheese
1 small onion, finely chopped
$\frac{1}{2}$ cup finely chopped pepperoni
2 tablespoons olive oil

1. Preheat oven to 350°. Cut peppers in half lengthwise; open and lay flat. Remove seeds if desired. In a small bowl, beat cream cheese and egg until blended. Stir in the cheddar, mozzarella, onion and pepperoni. Spoon into peppers.

2. Place in two 15x10x1-inch baking pans and drizzle with oil. Bake for 25–30 minutes or until lightly browned.

NOTE: Wear disposable gloves when cutting hot peppers; the oils can burn skin. Avoid touching your face.

NUTRITIONAL FACTS
1 EACH: 112 calories, 9 g fat (5 g saturated fat), 34 mg cholesterol, 158 mg sodium, 3 g carbohydrate (1 g sugars, 1 g fiber), 4 g protein

Garbanzo-Stuffed Mini Peppers

PREP/TOTAL TIME: 20 MINUTES ● **YIELD:** 32 APPETIZERS

Mini peppers are so colorful, and they're the perfect size for a two-bite appetizer. They have all the crunch of a pita chip, without the extra calories.

—*Christine Hanover, Lewiston, California*

1 teaspoon cumin seeds	3 tablespoons cider vinegar
1 can (15 ounces) garbanzo beans or chickpeas, rinsed and drained	1/4 teaspoon salt
1/4 cup fresh cilantro leaves	16 miniature sweet peppers, halved lengthwise
3 tablespoons water	Additional fresh cilantro leaves

1. In a dry small skillet, toast cumin seeds over medium heat 1–2 minutes or until aromatic, stirring frequently. Transfer to a food processor. Add garbanzo beans, cilantro, water, vinegar and salt; pulse until blended.

2. Spoon into pepper halves. Top with additional cilantro. Refrigerate until serving.

NUTRITIONAL FACTS
1 APPETIZER: 15 calories, 0 fat (0 saturated fat), 0 cholesterol, 36 mg sodium, 3 g carbohydrate (1 g sugars, 1 g fiber), 1 g protein

Blue Cheese Date Wraps

PREP: 25 MINUTES • **BAKE:** 10 MINUTES • **YIELD:** 3 DOZEN

My friends and I used to make the traditional bacon-wrapped jalapenos at cookouts. I decided to sweeten them up a bit with dates and apricots, which are also more kid-friendly.

—*Susan Hinton, Apex, North Carolina*

12 bacon strips
36 pitted dates

²⁄₃ cup crumbled blue cheese

1. Preheat oven to 375°. Cut each bacon strip into thirds. In a large skillet, cook bacon in batches over medium heat until partially cooked but not crisp. Remove to paper towels to drain; keep warm.

2. Carefully cut a slit in the center of each date; fill with blue cheese. Wrap a bacon piece around each stuffed date; secure with wooden toothpicks.

3. Place on ungreased baking sheets. Bake for 10–12 minutes or until bacon is crisp.

NUTRITIONAL FACTS
1 EACH: 44 calories, 2 g fat (1 g saturated fat), 4 mg cholesterol, 84 mg sodium, 6 g carbohydrate (5 g sugars, 1 g fiber), 2 g protein

Take-It Tip
When organizing a potluck, set out smaller plates of perishable foods. Storing the extras in a cooler or refrigerator and replenishing as needed keeps them at room temperature.

Potluck Sausage-Stuffed Mushrooms

PREP: 25 MINUTES • **BAKE:** 20 MINUTES • **YIELD:** 12–15 SERVINGS

Pennsylvania is often referred to as the "Mushroom Capital of the World." This recipe's a delicious appetizer and is always the hit of the party.

—*Beatrice Vetrano, Landenberg, Pennsylvania*

12 to 15 large fresh mushrooms
2 tablespoons butter, divided
2 tablespoons chopped onion
1 tablespoon lemon juice
¼ teaspoon dried basil

Salt and pepper to taste
4 ounces bulk Italian sausage
1 tablespoon chopped fresh parsley
2 tablespoons dry bread crumbs
2 tablespoons grated Parmesan cheese

1. Preheat oven to 400°. Remove stems from the mushrooms. Chop stems finely; set mushroom caps aside. Place stems in paper towels and squeeze to remove any liquid.

2. In a large skillet, heat 1½ tablespoons butter. Cook stems and onion until tender. Add the lemon juice, basil, salt and pepper; cook until almost all the liquid has evaporated. Cool.

3. In a large bowl, combine the mushroom mixture, sausage and parsley; stuff reserved mushroom caps. Combine crumbs and cheese; sprinkle over tops. Dot each with remaining butter.

4. Place in a greased baking pan. Bake for 20 minutes or until sausage is no longer pink, basting occasionally with pan juices. Serve hot.

NUTRITIONAL FACTS
1 EACH: 52 calories, 4 g fat (2 g saturated fat), 10 mg cholesterol, 92 mg sodium, 2 g carbohydrate (0 sugars, 0 fiber), 2 g protein

Stuffed Baby Red Potatoes

PREP: 45 MINUTES ● **BAKE:** 15 MINUTES ● **YIELD:** 2 DOZEN

This recipe just says "party!" The ingredients are basic, but the finished appetizer looks like you worked a lot harder than you did.

—*Carol Bess White, Portland, Oregon*

24 small red potatoes (about 2½ pounds)	1 large egg, beaten
¼ cup butter, cubed	½ teaspoon salt
½ cup shredded Parmesan cheese, divided	⅛ teaspoon pepper
½ cup crumbled cooked bacon, divided	⅛ teaspoon paprika
⅔ cup sour cream	

1. Preheat oven to 375°. Scrub potatoes; place in a large saucepan and cover with water. Bring to a boil. Reduce heat; cover and cook for 15-20 minutes or until tender. Drain. When cool enough to handle, cut a thin slice off the top of each potato. Scoop out pulp, leaving a thin shell. (Cut thin slices from potato bottoms to level if necessary.)

2. In a large bowl, mash the potato tops and pulp with butter. Set aside 2 tablespoons each of cheese and bacon for garnish; add remaining cheese and bacon to potatoes. Stir in the sour cream, egg, salt and pepper. Spoon mixture into potato shells. Top with remaining cheese and bacon; sprinkle with paprika.

3. Place in an ungreased 15x10x1-inch baking pan. Bake for 12–18 minutes or until a thermometer reads 160°.

NUTRITIONAL FACTS
1 EACH: 82 calories, 4 g fat (3 g saturated fat), 21 mg cholesterol, 135 mg sodium, 8 g carbohydrate (1 g sugars, 1 g fiber), 3 g protein

Bacon Cheddar Potato Skins

PREP/TOTAL TIME: 20 MINUTES ● **YIELD:** 8 SERVINGS

I fill my restaurant-worthy baked potato boats with cheese, bacon and a dollop of sour cream. Have them at lunch, snack time or cocktail hour.
—*Trish Perrin, Keizer, Oregon*

4 large baking potatoes, baked	$\frac{1}{8}$ teaspoon pepper
3 tablespoons canola oil	8 bacon strips, cooked and crumbled
1 tablespoon grated Parmesan cheese	$1\frac{1}{2}$ cups shredded cheddar cheese
$\frac{1}{2}$ teaspoon salt	$\frac{1}{2}$ cup sour cream
$\frac{1}{4}$ teaspoon garlic powder	4 green onions, sliced
$\frac{1}{4}$ teaspoon paprika	

1. Preheat oven to 475°. Cut potatoes in half lengthwise; scoop out pulp, leaving a $\frac{1}{4}$-inch shell (save pulp for another use). Place potato skins on a greased baking sheet.

2. In a small bowl, combine the oil, Parmesan cheese, salt, garlic powder, paprika and pepper; brush over both sides of skins.

3. Bake for 7 minutes on each side or until crisp. Sprinkle bacon and cheddar cheese inside skins. Bake 2 minutes longer or until the cheese is melted. Top with sour cream and onions. Serve immediately.

NUTRITIONAL FACTS
1 EACH: 338 calories, 17 g fat (8 g saturated fat), 38 mg cholesterol, 408 mg sodium, 35 g carbohydrate (4 g sugars, 3 g fiber), 11 g protein

Goat Cheese Crostini

PREP/TOTAL TIME: 10 MINUTES ● **YIELD:** 32 APPETIZERS

My husband got this crostini recipe from a friend at work. At first, I thought the flavors wouldn't work well together, but they blend deliciously!

—*Rebecca Ebeling, Nevada City, California*

1 cup crumbled goat cheese
1 teaspoon minced fresh rosemary
1 French bread baguette (10$\frac{1}{2}$ ounces), cut into $\frac{1}{2}$-inch slices and toasted

3 tablespoons honey
$\frac{1}{4}$ cup slivered almonds, toasted

In a small bowl, combine cheese and rosemary; spoon over toast slices. Drizzle with honey; sprinkle with almonds.

NUTRITIONAL FACTS
1 PIECE: 76 calories, 4 g fat (2 g saturated fat), 6 mg cholesterol, 92 mg sodium, 9 g carbohydrate (2 g sugars, 1 g fiber), 3 g protein

Southwestern Pulled Pork Crostini

PREP: 45 MINUTES • **COOK:** 6 HOURS • **YIELD:** 32 APPETIZERS

For a unique take on crostini, these hearty appetizers are great for tailgating and other casual parties. Everyone enjoys these spicy, sweet and salty bites, which makes the recipe even more special to me.

—*Randy Cartwright, Linden, Wisconsin*

1 boneless pork shoulder butt roast (about 2 pounds)
½ cup lime juice
2 envelopes mesquite marinade mix
¼ cup sugar
¼ cup olive oil

SALSA:

1 cup frozen corn, thawed
1 cup canned black beans, rinsed and drained
1 small tomato, finely chopped
2 tablespoons finely chopped seeded jalapeno pepper
2 tablespoons lime juice
2 tablespoons olive oil

1½ teaspoons ground cumin
1 teaspoon chili powder
½ teaspoon salt
¼ teaspoon crushed red pepper flakes

SAUCE:

1 can (4 ounces) chopped green chilies
⅓ cup apricot preserves
⅛ teaspoon salt

CROSTINI:

32 slices French bread baguette (¼ inch thick)
¼ cup olive oil
⅔ cup crumbled queso fresco or feta cheese
Lime wedges, optional

1. Place roast in a 3-qt. slow cooker. In a small bowl, whisk lime juice, marinade mix, sugar and oil until blended; pour over roast. Cook, covered, on low 6–8 hours or until meat is tender.

2. For salsa, in a small bowl, combine corn, beans, tomato and jalapeno. Stir in lime juice, oil and seasonings. In a small saucepan, combine sauce ingredients; cook and stir over low heat until blended.

3. For crostini, preheat broiler. Brush bread slices on both sides with oil; place on ungreased baking sheets. Broil 3–4 inches from heat 1–2 minutes on each side or until golden brown.

4. Remove roast from slow cooker; cool slightly. Shred pork with two forks. To serve, layer toasts with salsa, pork and cheese. Top with sauce. If desired, serve with lime wedges.

NOTE: Wear disposable gloves when cutting hot peppers; the oils can burn skin. Avoid touching your face.

NUTRITIONAL FACTS
1 APPETIZER: 121 calories, 7 g fat (2 g saturated fat), 19 mg cholesterol, 362 mg sodium, 9 g carbohydrate (3 g sugars, 1 g fiber), 6 g protein

Olive-Onion Cheese Bread

PREP/TOTAL TIME: 30 MINUTES • **YIELD:** 16 SERVINGS

This luscious cheese bread will have your guests reaching for more. The cheese, onions and olives make this bread a delicious and flavorful appetizer.

—Amy Voights, Brodhead, Wisconsin

4 cups shredded part-skim mozzarella cheese

1 cup butter, softened

1 cup mayonnaise

8 green onions, thinly sliced

1 can (8 ounces) mushroom stems and pieces, drained and chopped

1 can (4¼ ounces) chopped ripe olives

1 loaf (1 pound) unsliced French bread

1. Preheat oven to 350°. In a large bowl, combine the first six ingredients. Cut bread in half lengthwise; place on an ungreased baking sheet. Spread with cheese mixture.

2. Bake for 15–20 minutes or until cheese is melted. Cut each half into eight slices.

NUTRITIONAL FACTS
1 SLICE: 369 calories, 28 g fat (12 g saturated fat), 51 mg cholesterol, 590 mg sodium, 18 g carbohydrate (2 g sugars, 1 g fiber), 11 g protein

Savory Party Bread

PREP: 10 MINUTES ● **BAKE:** 25 MINUTES ● **YIELD:** 8 SERVINGS

It's impossible to stop nibbling on warm pieces of this cheesy, oniony bread. The sliced loaf fans out for a fun presentation.

—Kay Daly, Raleigh, North Carolina

1 unsliced round loaf sourdough bread (1 pound)	$\frac{1}{2}$ cup butter, melted
	$\frac{1}{2}$ cup chopped green onions
1 pound Monterey Jack cheese	2 to 3 teaspoons poppy seeds

1. Preheat oven to 350°. Cut bread widthwise into 1-inch slices to within $\frac{1}{2}$ inch of bottom of loaf. Repeat cuts in opposite direction. Cut cheese into $\frac{1}{4}$-inch slices; cut slices into small pieces. Place cheese in cuts.

2. In a small bowl, mix butter, green onions and poppy seeds; drizzle over bread. Wrap in foil; place on a baking sheet. Bake 15 minutes. Unwrap; bake 10 minutes longer or until cheese is melted.

NUTRITIONAL FACTS
1 SERVING: 481 calories, 31 g fat (17 g saturated fat), 91 mg cholesterol, 782 mg sodium, 32 g carbohydrate (1 g sugars, 2 g fiber), 17 g protein

Almond Cheddar Appetizers

PREP/TOTAL TIME: 25 MINUTES • **YIELD:** ABOUT 4 DOZEN

I always try to have a supply of these appetizers on hand in the freezer. If guests drop in, I just pull some out and reheat to serve. They work great as a snack, for brunch or along with a lighter lunch.

—*Linda Thompson, Southampton, Ontario*

1 cup mayonnaise	$^3/_4$ cup slivered almonds, chopped
2 teaspoons Worcestershire sauce	6 bacon strips, cooked and crumbled
1 cup shredded sharp cheddar cheese	1 loaf (1 pound) French bread
1 medium onion, chopped	

1. Preheat oven to 400°. In a bowl, combine the mayonnaise and Worcestershire sauce; stir in cheese, onion, almonds and bacon.

2. Cut bread into $^1/_2$-inch slices; spread with cheese mixture. Cut slices in half; place on a greased baking sheet. Bake for 8–10 minutes or until bubbly.

NUTRITIONAL FACTS
3 EACH: 250 calories, 18 g fat (4 g saturated fat), 15 mg cholesterol, 335 mg sodium, 17 g carbohydrate (1 g sugars, 2 g fiber), 6 g protein

Freeze It **Place unbaked appetizers in a single layer on a baking sheet; freeze for 1 hour. Remove from pan and store in an airtight container for up to 2 months. When ready to use, place thawed appetizers on a greased baking sheet. Bake at 400° for 10 minutes or until bubbly.**

Focaccia Sandwiches

PREP/TOTAL TIME: 15 MINUTES • **YIELD:** 24 SERVINGS

Slices of this pretty sandwich are great for any casual get-together. Add or change ingredients to your taste.

—*Peggy Woodward, East Troy, Wisconsin*

$\frac{1}{3}$ cup mayonnaise

1 can (4$\frac{1}{4}$ ounces) chopped ripe olives, drained

1 focaccia bread (about 12 ounces), halved lengthwise

4 romaine leaves

$\frac{1}{4}$ pound shaved deli ham

1 medium sweet red pepper, thinly sliced into rings

$\frac{1}{4}$ pound shaved deli turkey

1 large tomato, thinly sliced

$\frac{1}{4}$ pound thinly sliced hard salami

1 jar (7 ounces) roasted sweet red peppers, drained

4 to 6 slices provolone cheese

In a small bowl, combine mayonnaise and olives; spread over the bottom half of bread. Layer with remaining ingredients; replace bread top. Cut into wedges; secure with toothpicks.

NUTRITIONAL FACTS

1 PIECE: 113 calories, 6 g fat (2 g saturated fat), 13 mg cholesterol, 405 mg sodium, 9 g carbohydrate (1 g sugars, 1 g fiber), 5 g protein

Quick Tip

A rectangular-shaped focaccia bread, measuring about 12 inches x 8 inches, works best for this sandwich.

Party Pitas

PREP/TOTAL TIME: 15 MINUTES • **YIELD:** 16 PIECES

Whenever the ladies of our church host a shower, these pita sandwiches appear on the menu. Not only are they easy and delicious, they add color to the table.

—*Janette Root, Ellensburg, Washington*

1 package (8 ounces) cream cheese, softened
½ cup mayonnaise
½ teaspoon dill weed
¼ teaspoon garlic salt

4 whole pita breads
1½ cups fresh baby spinach
1 pound shaved fully cooked ham
½ pound thinly sliced Monterey Jack cheese

1. Combine the cream cheese, mayonnaise, dill and garlic salt. Cut each pita in half horizontally; spread 2 tablespoons cream cheese mixture on each cut surface.

2. On four pita halves, layer the spinach, ham and cheese. Top with remaining pita halves. Cut each pita into four wedges; secure with toothpicks.

NUTRITIONAL FACTS
1 PIECE: 225 calories, 15 g fat (6 g saturated fat), 45 mg cholesterol, 557 mg sodium, 10 g carbohydrate (1 g sugars, trace fiber), 12 g protein

Mini Teriyaki Turkey Sandwiches

PREP: 20 MINUTES • **COOK:** 5½ HOURS • **YIELD:** 20 SERVINGS

Preparing the pulled turkey in a delicious teriyaki sauce for these snack-size sandwiches is a breeze using a slow cooker. Serving them on lightly toasted sweet dinner rolls is a finishing touch.

—Amanda Hoop, Seaman, Ohio

2   boneless skinless turkey breast halves (2 pounds each)
⅔   cup packed brown sugar
⅔   cup reduced-sodium soy sauce
¼   cup cider vinegar
3   garlic cloves, minced

1   tablespoon minced fresh gingerroot
½   teaspoon pepper
2   tablespoons cornstarch
2   tablespoons cold water
20 Hawaiian sweet rolls
2   tablespoons butter, melted

1. Place turkey in a 5- or 6-qt. slow cooker. In a small bowl, combine brown sugar, soy sauce, vinegar, garlic, ginger and pepper; pour over turkey. Cook, covered, on low 5–6 hours or until meat is tender.

2. Remove turkey from slow cooker. In a small bowl, mix cornstarch and cold water until smooth; gradually stir into cooking liquid. When cool enough to handle, shred meat with two forks and return meat to slow cooker. Cook, covered, on high 30–35 minutes or until sauce is thickened.

3. Preheat oven to 325°. Split rolls and brush cut sides with butter; place on an ungreased baking sheet, cut side up. Bake 8–10 minutes or until toasted and golden brown. Spoon ⅓ cup turkey mixture on roll bottoms. Replace tops.

NUTRITIONAL FACTS
1 SANDWICH: 252 calories, 5 g fat (2 g saturated fat), 70 mg cholesterol, 501 mg sodium, 25 g carbohydrate (13 g sugars, 1 g fiber), 26 g protein

Sweet Potato & Bean Quesadillas

PREP/TOTAL TIME: 30 MINUTES ● **YIELD:** 4 SERVINGS

Sweet potatoes and black beans roll up together for a quesadilla that's easy, fast, fun and delicious.

—Brittany Hubbard, Gering, Nebraska

2   medium sweet potatoes

4   whole wheat tortillas (8 inches)

¾   cup canned black beans,
     rinsed and drained

½   cup shredded pepper jack cheese

¾   cup salsa

1. Scrub sweet potatoes; pierce several times with a fork. Place on a microwave-safe plate. Microwave, uncovered, on high 7–9 minutes or until very tender, turning once.

2. When cool enough to handle, cut each potato lengthwise in half. Scoop out pulp. Spread onto one half of each tortilla; top with beans and cheese. Fold other half of tortilla over filling.

3. Heat a griddle or skillet over medium heat. Cook quesadillas 2–3 minutes on each side or until golden brown and cheese is melted. Serve with salsa.

NUTRITIONAL FACTS

1 QUESADILLA WITH 3 TABLESPOONS SALSA: 306 calories, 8 g fat (3 g saturated fat), 15 mg cholesterol, 531 mg sodium, 46 g carbohydrate (9 g sugars, 6 g fiber), 11 g protein

Baked Chicken Nachos

PREP: 20 MINUTES ● **BAKE:** 15 MINUTES ● **YIELD:** 16 SERVINGS

Here's a party appetizer that's delicious and so simple. Rotisserie (or leftover) chicken keeps it quick, and the seasonings and splash of lime juice lend fantastic flavor. My husband likes this snack so much that he often requests it for dinner!

—*Gail Cawsey, Geneseo, Illinois*

2 medium sweet red peppers, diced
1 medium green pepper, diced
3 teaspoons canola oil, divided
1 can (15 ounces) black beans, rinsed and drained
1 teaspoon minced garlic
1 teaspoon dried oregano
¼ teaspoon ground cumin
2¼ cups shredded rotisserie chicken
4½ teaspoons lime juice

⅛ teaspoon salt
⅛ teaspoon pepper
7½ cups tortilla chips
8 ounces pepper jack cheese, shredded
¼ cup thinly sliced green onions
½ cup minced fresh cilantro
1 cup (8 ounces) sour cream
2 to 3 teaspoons diced pickled jalapeno peppers, optional

1. Preheat oven to 350°. In a large skillet, saute peppers in 1½ teaspoons oil for 3 minutes or until crisp-tender; transfer to a small bowl. In the same skillet, saute the beans, garlic, oregano and cumin in remaining oil for 3 minutes or until heated through.

2. Meanwhile, combine the chicken, lime juice, salt and pepper. In a greased 13x9-inch baking dish, layer half of the tortilla chips, pepper mixture, bean mixture, chicken, cheese, onions and cilantro. Repeat layers.

3. Bake, uncovered, for 15–20 minutes or until heated through. Serve with sour cream and pickled jalapenos if desired.

NUTRITIONAL FACTS
1 EACH: 221 calories, 13 g fat (5 g saturated fat), 41 mg cholesterol, 314 mg sodium, 14 g carbohydrate (2 g sugars, 2 g fiber), 12 g protein

Spicy Sweet Potato Chips & Cilantro Dip

PREP: 20 MINUTES • **BAKE:** 25 MINUTES/BATCH • **YIELD:** 12 SERVINGS (1½ CUPS DIP)

This cool, creamy dip is a great partner for the spicy sweet potato chips. They're made for each other!
—*Libby Walp, Chicago, Illinois*

2 to 3 large sweet potatoes (1¾ pounds), peeled and cut into ⅛-inch slices
2 tablespoons canola oil
1 teaspoon chili powder
½ teaspoon garlic powder
½ teaspoon taco seasoning
¼ teaspoon salt
¼ teaspoon ground cumin
¼ teaspoon pepper
⅛ teaspoon cayenne pepper

DIP:
¾ cup mayonnaise
½ cup sour cream
2 ounces cream cheese, softened
4½ teaspoons minced fresh cilantro
1½ teaspoons lemon juice
½ teaspoon celery salt
⅛ teaspoon pepper

1. Preheat oven to 400°. Place sweet potatoes in a large bowl. In a small bowl, mix oil and seasonings; drizzle over potatoes and toss to coat.

2. Arrange half of the potatoes in a single layer in two ungreased 15x10x1-inch baking pans. Bake 25–30 minutes or until golden brown, turning once. Repeat with remaining potatoes.

3. In a small bowl, beat dip ingredients until blended. Serve with chips.

NUTRITIONAL FACTS
½ CUP CHIPS WITH ABOUT 1 TABLESPOON DIP: 285 calories, 16 g fat (4 g saturated fat), 8 mg cholesterol, 217 mg sodium, 33 g carbohydrate (14 g sugars, 4 g fiber), 3 g protein

Blue Cheese Potato Chips

PREP/TOTAL TIME: 15 MINUTES • **YIELD:** 10 SERVINGS

Game day calls for something bold. I top potato chips with tomatoes, bacon and tangy blue cheese. I make two big pans, and they always disappear.

—*Bonnie Hawkins, Elkhorn, Wisconsin*

1 package (8½ ounces) kettle-cooked potato chips

2 medium tomatoes, seeded and chopped

8 bacon strips, cooked and crumbled

6 green onions, chopped

1 cup crumbled blue cheese

1. Preheat broiler. In a 15x10x1-inch baking pan, arrange potato chips in an even layer. Top with remaining ingredients.

2. Broil 4–5 inches from heat 2–3 minutes or until cheese begins to melt. Serve immediately.

NUTRITIONAL FACTS
1 SERVING: 215 calories, 14 g fat (5 g saturated fat), 17 mg cholesterol, 359 mg sodium, 16 g carbohydrate (2 g sugars, 1 g fiber), 6 g protein

Caprese Salad Kabobs

PREP/TOTAL TIME: 10 MINUTES ● **YIELD:** 12 KABOBS

Trade in the usual veggie party platter for these fun kabobs. I often make them for my family to snack on, and it's a great recipe for the kids to help with.

—*Christine Mitchell, Glendora, California*

24   grape tomatoes

12   cherry-size fresh mozzarella cheese balls

24   fresh basil leaves

2   tablespoons olive oil

2   teaspoons balsamic vinegar

On each of 12 wooden appetizer skewers, alternately thread two tomatoes, one cheese ball and two basil leaves; place on a serving plate. In a small bowl, whisk the oil and vinegar; drizzle over kabobs just before serving.

NUTRITIONAL FACTS
1 KABOB: 45 calories, 4 g fat (1 g saturated fat), 5 mg cholesterol, 12 mg sodium, 2 g carbohydrate (0 sugars, 0 fiber), 1 g protein

Pork Picadillo Lettuce Wraps

PREP: 30 MINUTES • **COOK:** 2½ HOURS • **YIELD:** 2 DOZEN

Warm pork and cool, crisp lettuce are a combination born in culinary heaven. My spin on a lettuce wrap is chock-full of scrumptious flavor and spice.
—*Janice Elder, Charlotte, North Carolina*

3 garlic cloves, minced
1 tablespoon chili powder
1 teaspoon salt
½ teaspoon pumpkin pie spice
½ teaspoon ground cumin
½ teaspoon pepper
2 pork tenderloins (1 pound each)
1 large onion, chopped

1 small Granny Smith apple, peeled and chopped
1 small sweet red pepper, chopped
1 can (10 ounces) diced tomatoes and green chilies, undrained
½ cup golden raisins
½ cup chopped pimiento-stuffed olives
24 Bibb or Boston lettuce leaves
¼ cup slivered almonds, toasted

1. In a small bowl, mix garlic and seasonings; rub over pork. Transfer to a 5-qt. slow cooker. Add onion, apple, sweet pepper and tomatoes. Cook, covered, on low 2½–3 hours or until meat is tender.

2. Remove pork; cool slightly. Shred meat into bite-size pieces; return to slow cooker. Stir in raisins and olives; heat through. Serve in lettuce leaves; sprinkle with almonds.

NUTRITIONAL FACTS
1 FILLED LETTUCE CUP: 75 calories, 3 g fat (1 g saturated fat), 21 mg cholesterol, 235 mg sodium, 5 g carbohydrate (3 g sugars, 1 g fiber), 8 g protein

Quick Tip **Keep the lid on it! Unless the recipe instructs to stir or add in ingredients, do not lift the lid while the slow cooker is operating. Every time you lift the lid, steam escapes and you add cooking time.**

Sweet & Spicy Chicken Wings

PREP: 25 MINUTES ● **COOK:** 5 HOURS ● **YIELD:** ABOUT 2½ DOZEN

The meat literally falls off the bones of these wings! Spice lovers will get a kick out of the big sprinkling of red pepper flakes.

—*Sue Bayless, Prior Lake, Minnesota*

3 pounds chicken wings	2 tablespoons Worcestershire sauce
1½ cups ketchup	1½ teaspoons crushed red pepper flakes
1 cup packed brown sugar	1 teaspoon ground mustard
1 small onion, finely chopped	1 teaspoon dried basil
¼ cup finely chopped sweet red pepper	1 teaspoon dried thyme
2 tablespoons chili powder	1 teaspoon pepper

Cut wings into three sections; discard wing tip sections. Place chicken in a 4-qt. slow cooker. In a small bowl, combine the remaining ingredients. Pour over chicken; stir until coated. Cover and cook on low for 5–6 hours or until chicken juices run clear.

NOTE: Uncooked chicken wing sections (wingettes) may be substituted for whole chicken wings.

NUTRITIONAL FACTS
1 PIECE: 95 calories, 3 g fat (1 g saturated fat), 14 mg cholesterol, 195 mg sodium, 11 g carbohydrate (11 g sugars, 0 fiber), 5 g protein

Tangy Barbecue Wings

PREP: 1 HOUR ● **COOK:** 3 HOURS ● **YIELD:** 4 DOZEN

I took these wings to work, and they vanished before I got a bite. The tangy sauce is lip-smacking good.

—*Sherry Pitzer, Troy, Missouri*

5 pounds chicken wings	1 teaspoon salt
2½ cups ketchup	1 teaspoon Worcestershire sauce
⅔ cup white vinegar	½ teaspoon onion powder
⅔ cup honey	½ teaspoon chili powder
½ cup molasses	½ to 1 teaspoon liquid smoke, optional
2 to 3 tablespoons hot pepper sauce	

1. Preheat oven to 375°. Using a sharp knife, cut through the two wing joints; discard wing tips. Arrange remaining wing pieces in two greased 15x10x1-inch baking pans. Bake 30 minutes; drain. Turn wings; bake 20–25 minutes longer or until juices run clear.

2. Meanwhile, in a large saucepan, combine remaining ingredients; bring to a boil. Reduce heat; simmer, uncovered, 30 minutes, stirring occasionally.

3. Drain wings. Place one-third of the chicken in a 5-qt. slow cooker; top with one-third of the sauce. Repeat layers twice. Cook, covered, on low 3–4 hours. Stir before serving.

NOTE: Uncooked chicken wing sections (wingettes) may be substituted for whole chicken wings.

NUTRITIONAL FACTS
1 WING (2 SECTIONS): 178 calories, 7 g fat (2 g saturated fat), 30 mg cholesterol, 458 mg sodium, 19 g carbohydrate (19 g sugars, 0 fiber), 10 g protein

Turkey-Mushroom Egg Rolls

PREP: 1¼ HOURS • **COOK:** 4 HOURS • **YIELD:** 3½ DOZEN

I slow-cook ground turkey in a hoisin, soy and sesame sauce along with fresh veggies for a finger-licking filling for egg rolls. These egg rolls are a favorite appetizer with guests—I never have leftovers!

—Sarah Herse, Brooklyn, New York

1½ pounds ground turkey
½ pound sliced fresh mushrooms
2 medium leeks (white portion only), thinly sliced
3 celery ribs, thinly sliced
½ cup hoisin sauce
2 tablespoons minced fresh gingerroot
2 tablespoons rice vinegar
2 tablespoons reduced-sodium soy sauce

1 tablespoon packed brown sugar
1 tablespoon sesame oil
2 garlic cloves, minced
½ cup sliced water chestnuts, chopped
3 green onions, thinly sliced
42 egg roll wrappers
Oil for frying
Sweet-and-sour sauce or Chinese-style mustard, optional

1. In a large skillet, cook turkey over medium heat 8–10 minutes or until no longer pink, breaking into crumbles. Transfer to a 5-qt. slow cooker.

2. Stir in mushrooms, leeks, celery, hoisin sauce, ginger, vinegar, soy sauce, brown sugar, sesame oil and garlic. Cook, covered, on low 4–5 hours or until vegetables are tender. Stir water chestnuts and green onions into turkey mixture; cool slightly.

3. With one corner of an egg roll wrapper facing you, place 2 tablespoons filling just below center of wrapper. (Cover remaining wrappers with a damp paper towel until ready to use.) Fold bottom corner over filling; moisten remaining wrapper edges with water. Fold side corners toward center over filling. Roll egg roll up tightly, pressing at tip to seal. Repeat.

4. In an electric skillet, heat ¼ inch of oil to 375°. Fry egg rolls, a few at a time, 3–4 minutes or until golden brown, turning occasionally. Drain on paper towels. If desired, serve with sweet-and-sour sauce.

NUTRITIONAL FACTS
1 EGG ROLL (CALCULATED WITHOUT SAUCE): 196 calories, 9 g fat (1 g saturated fat), 14 mg cholesterol, 284 mg sodium, 22 g carbohydrate (2 g sugars, 1 g fiber), 7 g protein

Freeze It
Cover and freeze unfried egg rolls on waxed paper-lined baking sheets until firm. Transfer to resealable plastic freezer bags; return to freezer. To use, fry egg rolls as recipe directs, increasing cooking time to 4–5 minutes.

Paddy's Reuben Dip

PREP: 5 MINUTES • **COOK:** 2 HOURS • **YIELD:** ABOUT 4 CUPS

This slow-cooked spread tastes just like the popular Reuben sandwich. Even when I double the recipe, I end up with an empty dish.

—*Mary Jane Kimmes, Hastings, Minnesota*

4 packages (2 ounces each) thinly sliced deli corned beef, finely chopped

1 package (8 ounces) cream cheese, cubed

1 can (8 ounces) sauerkraut, rinsed and drained

1 cup (8 ounces) sour cream

1 cup shredded Swiss cheese
 Rye bread or crackers

In a 1½-qt. slow cooker, combine the first five ingredients. Cover and cook on low for 2 hours or until cheese is melted; stir until blended. Serve warm with bread or crackers.

NUTRITIONAL FACTS
2 TABLESPOONS: 58 calories, 5 g fat (3 g saturated fat), 18 mg cholesterol, 126 mg sodium, 1 g carbohydrate (1 g sugars, 0 fiber), 2 g protein

Take-It Tip
Taking your church-supper contribution to the event in a slow cooker? Bring along an extension cord or two. You'll save the day as this is something the organizers may have forgotten.

Jalapeno Popper & Sausage Dip

PREP: 15 MINUTES • **COOK:** 3 HOURS • **YIELD:** 24 SERVINGS

My workplace had an appetizer contest, and I won it with my jalapeno and cheese dip. Every time I take it anywhere, folks empty the slow cooker.

—Bev Slabik, Dilworth, Minnesota

1 pound bulk spicy pork sausage

2 packages (8 ounces each) cream cheese, cubed

4 cups shredded Parmesan cheese (about 12 ounces)

1 cup (8 ounces) sour cream

1 can (4 ounces) chopped green chilies, undrained

1 can (4 ounces) diced jalapeno peppers, undrained

Assorted fresh vegetables

1. In a large skillet, cook sausage over medium heat 6–8 minutes or until no longer pink, breaking into crumbles. Using a slotted spoon, transfer sausage to a 3-qt. slow cooker.

2. Stir in cream cheese, Parmesan cheese, sour cream, chilies and peppers. Cook, covered, on low 3–3½ hours or until heated through. Stir before serving. Serve with vegetables.

NUTRITIONAL FACTS
¼ **CUP (CALCULATED WITHOUT VEGETABLES):** 180 calories, 15 g fat (8 g saturated fat), 44 mg cholesterol, 399 mg sodium, 2 g carbohydrate (1 g sugars, 0 fiber), 8 g protein

Warm Bacon Cheese Spread

PREP: 15 MINUTES • **BAKE:** 1 HOUR • **YIELD:** 4 CUPS

My friends threaten not to come by unless this dip is on the menu! The rich spread bakes right in the bread bowl and goes well with almost any dipper. Plus, cleanup is a breeze.

—*Nicole Marcotte, Smithers, British Columbia*

1 round loaf (1 pound) sourdough bread
1 package (8 ounces) cream cheese, softened
1½ cups (12 ounces) sour cream
2 cups (8 ounces) shredded cheddar cheese

1½ teaspoons Worcestershire sauce
¾ pound sliced bacon, cooked and crumbled
½ cup chopped green onions
 Assorted crackers

1. Preheat oven to 325°. Cut the top fourth off the loaf of bread; carefully hollow out the bottom, leaving a 1-inch shell. Cut the removed bread and top of loaf into cubes; set aside.

2. In a large bowl, beat cream cheese until fluffy. Add the sour cream, cheddar cheese and Worcestershire sauce until blended; stir in bacon and onions.

3. Spoon into bread shell. Wrap in a piece of heavy-duty foil (about 24 inches x 17 inches). Bake for 1 hour or until heated through. Serve with crackers and reserved bread cubes.

NUTRITIONAL FACTS
2 TABLESPOONS: 132 calories, 9 g fat (5 g saturated fat), 26 mg cholesterol, 214 mg sodium, 8 g carbohydrate (1 g sugars, 0 fiber), 5 g protein

Dijon-Bacon Dip for Pretzels

PREP/TOTAL TIME: 5 MINUTES • **YIELD:** 1¹⁄₂ CUPS

With just four ingredients that you probably already have, this quick appetizer comes together in a snap. If you like the zip of horseradish, start with one or two teaspoons and add more to your taste.

—*Isabelle Rooney, Summerville, South Carolina*

1 cup mayonnaise

¹⁄₂ cup Dijon mustard

¹⁄₄ cup real bacon bits or crumbled cooked bacon

1 to 3 teaspoons prepared horseradish

Pretzels

In a small bowl, combine the mayonnaise, mustard, bacon and horseradish. Cover and chill until serving. Serve with pretzels.

NUTRITIONAL FACTS
2 TABLESPOONS: 154 calories, 16 g fat (2 g saturated fat), 8 mg cholesterol, 428 mg sodium, 1 g carbohydrate (0 sugars, 0 fiber), 2 g protein

Take-It Tip

Taking a toddler to a potluck? They can be picky eaters, so you may want to contribute a dish you know your tykes enjoy. Or, take along some crackers, sliced veggies and a few slices of deli meat so they're sure to eat something once dinner is served.

Pepperoni Extreme Dip

PREP: 10 MINUTES • **COOK:** 3 HOURS • **YIELD:** 2¼ QUARTS

Take just 10 minutes to prep, and in a few short hours, your slow cooker will have you serving up a party-worthy appetizer to your hungry bunch, no problem!

—*Laura Magee, Houlton, Wisconsin*

 4 cups shredded cheddar cheese
 3½ cups spaghetti sauce
 2 cups mayonnaise
 1 package (8 ounces) sliced pepperoni, chopped

 1 can (6 ounces) pitted ripe olives, chopped
 1 jar (5¾ ounces) sliced green olives with pimientos, drained and chopped
 Tortilla chips

Combine the first six ingredients in a 4-qt. slow cooker coated with cooking spray. Cover and cook on low for 3 hours or until cheese is melted, stirring halfway through cooking. Serve with tortilla chips.

NUTRITIONAL FACTS
¼ CUP (CALCULATED WITHOUT TORTILLA CHIPS): 188 calories, 17 g fat (5 g saturated fat), 19 mg cholesterol, 449 mg sodium, 3 g carbohydrate (2 g sugars, 1 g fiber), 5 g protein

Hot Wing Dip

PREP: 10 MINUTES ● **COOK:** 1 HOUR ● **YIELD:** 18 SERVINGS

Since I usually have all the ingredients on hand, this is a great go-to snack for entertaining friends and family.
—*Coleen Corner, Grove City, Pennsylvania*

2 cups shredded cooked chicken
1 package (8 ounces) cream cheese, cubed
2 cups shredded cheddar cheese
1 cup ranch salad dressing

$^1\!/_2$ cup Louisiana-style hot sauce
Tortilla chips and celery sticks
Minced fresh parsley, optional

In a 3-qt. slow cooker, mix the first five ingredients. Cook, covered, on low for 1–2 hours or until cheese is melted. Serve with chips and celery. If desired, sprinkle with parsley.

NUTRITIONAL FACTS
$^1\!/_4$ **CUP (CALCULATED WITHOUT CHIPS AND CELERY):** 186 calories, 16 g fat (7 g saturated fat), 43 mg cholesterol, 235 mg sodium, 2 g carbohydrate (1 g sugars, 0 fiber), 8 g protein

Baked Onion Dip

PREP: 5 MINUTES ● **BAKE:** 40 MINUTES ● **YIELD:** 2 CUPS

Some people like this cheesy dip so much that they can't tear themselves away from the appetizer table to eat their dinner.

—*Mona Zignego, Hartford, Wisconsin*

1 cup mayonnaise
1 cup chopped sweet onion
1 tablespoon grated Parmesan cheese
¼ teaspoon garlic salt

1 cup shredded Swiss cheese
Minced fresh parsley, optional
Assorted crackers

1. Preheat oven to 325°. In a large bowl, combine mayonnaise, onion, Parmesan cheese and garlic salt; stir in Swiss cheese. Spoon into a 1-qt. baking dish.

2. Bake, uncovered, for 40 minutes or until golden brown. Sprinkle with parsley if desired. Serve with crackers.

NUTRITIONAL FACTS
2 TABLESPOONS: 131 calories, 13 g fat (3 g saturated fat), 11 mg cholesterol, 127 mg sodium, 1 g carbohydrate (1 g sugars, 0 fiber), 2 g protein

Quick Tip
To quickly chop an onion, peel and cut in half from the root to the top. Leaving root attached, place flat side down on work surface. Cut vertically through the onion, leaving the root end uncut. Cut across the onion, discarding root end. The closer the cuts, the finer the onion will be chopped.

Feta Bruschetta

PREP/TOTAL TIME: 30 MINUTES • **YIELD:** 10 APPETIZERS

You won't believe the compliments you'll receive when you greet guests with these warm appetizers. Every crispy bite offers the savory tastes of feta cheese, tomatoes, basil and garlic. They're terrific for holiday parties or most any gathering.

    —Stacey Rinehart, Eugene, Oregon

¼ cup butter, melted	2 to 3 garlic cloves, minced
¼ cup olive oil	1 tablespoon minced fresh basil or 1 teaspoon dried basil
10 slices French bread (1 inch thick)	
1 package (4 ounces) crumbled feta cheese	1 large tomato, seeded and chopped

1. Preheat oven to 350°. In a small bowl, combine butter and oil; brush onto both sides of bread. Place on a baking sheet. Bake for 8–10 minutes or until lightly browned on top.

2. In a small bowl, combine the feta cheese, garlic and basil; sprinkle over toast. Top with tomato. Bake 8–10 minutes longer or until heated through. Serve warm.

NUTRITIONAL FACTS
1 EACH: 296 calories, 14 g fat (5 g saturated fat), 18 mg cholesterol, 547 mg sodium, 35 g carbohydrate (1 g sugars, 3 g fiber), 8 g protein

Green Olive Dip

PREP: 30 MINUTES • **COOK:** 3 HOURS • **YIELD:** 8 CUPS

Olive fans will love this dip. It's cheesy and full of beef and beans. It could even be used to fill taco shells.

—Beth Dunahay, Lima, Ohio

- 1 pound ground beef
- 1 medium sweet red pepper, chopped
- 1 small onion, chopped
- 1 can (16 ounces) refried beans
- 1 jar (16 ounces) mild salsa

- 2 cups shredded part-skim mozzarella cheese
- 2 cups shredded cheddar cheese
- 1 jar (5¾ ounces) sliced green olives with pimientos, drained
  Tortilla chips

1. In a large skillet, cook the beef, pepper and onion over medium heat until meat is no longer pink; drain.

2. Transfer to a greased 3-qt. slow cooker. Add the beans, salsa, cheeses and olives. Cover and cook on low for 3–4 hours or until cheese is melted, stirring occasionally. Serve with chips.

NUTRITIONAL FACTS
¼ CUP: 96 calories, 6 g fat (3 g saturated fat), 21 mg cholesterol, 262 mg sodium, 4 g carbohydrate (1 g sugars, 1 g fiber), 7 g protein

Salmon Cheese Spread

PREP/TOTAL TIME: 5 MINUTES • **YIELD:** 1 CUP

Pickle relish livens up canned salmon in this deliciously different sandwich filling. The easy spread is good on crackers, too.

—*Mrs. Dale Cocklin, Kasilof, Alaska*

3 ounces cream cheese, softened

1 can (7$\frac{1}{2}$ ounces) salmon, drained, bones and skin removed

$\frac{1}{3}$ cup shredded cheddar cheese

$\frac{1}{4}$ cup sweet pickle relish

Crackers or bread

In a small bowl, combine the cream cheese, salmon, cheddar cheese and pickle relish. Serve with crackers or bread.

NUTRITIONAL FACTS
2 TABLESPOONS: 104 calories, 7 g fat (4 g saturated fat), 28 mg cholesterol, 265 mg sodium, 3 g carbohydrate (3 g sugars, 0 fiber), 7 g protein

Quick Tip To soften cream cheese quickly, remove the wrapper and discard it. Place the cream cheese on a microwave-safe plate and microwave on high for about 15 seconds. Add more time if necessary, but don't overheat it . . . you don't want the cream cheese to melt or cook.

Black-Eyed Pea Salsa

PREP: 10 MINUTES + CHILLING ● **YIELD:** 5 CUPS

Colorful tomatoes, green pepper and red onion contrast nicely with black-eyed peas.

—*Lynn McAllister, Mt. Ulla, North Carolina*

- 2 cans (15½ ounces each) black-eyed peas, rinsed and drained
- 2 medium tomatoes, chopped
- 1 cup chopped green pepper
- ½ cup chopped red onion
- 4 green onions, sliced

- 1 garlic clove, minced
- 1 cup Italian salad dressing
- ¼ cup sour cream
- ¼ cup minced fresh parsley
  Tortilla chips

In a medium bowl, combine the first six ingredients. In a small bowl, combine the salad dressing, sour cream and parsley. Add to the pea mixture; toss to coat. Cover and refrigerate for at least 4 hours. Serve with tortilla chips.

NUTRITIONAL FACTS
¼ CUP: 73 calories, 5 g fat (1 g saturated fat), 2 mg cholesterol, 250 mg sodium, 5 g carbohydrate (2 g sugars, 1 g fiber), 2 g protein

Slow-Cooked Salsa

PREP: 15 MINUTES ● **COOK:** 2½ HOURS + COOLING ● **YIELD:** ABOUT 2 CUPS

I love the fresh taste of homemade salsa, but as a working mother, I don't have much time to make it. So I came up with this slow-cooked version that practically makes itself!

—*Toni Menard, Lompoc, California*

10 plum tomatoes	2 jalapeno peppers
2 garlic cloves	¼ cup cilantro leaves
1 small onion, cut into wedges	½ teaspoon salt, optional

1. Core tomatoes. Cut a small slit in two tomatoes; insert a garlic clove into each slit. Place tomatoes and onion in a 3-qt. slow cooker.

2. Cut stems off jalapenos; remove seeds if a milder salsa is desired. Place jalapenos in the slow cooker.

3. Cover and cook on high for 2½–3 hours or until vegetables are softened (some may brown slightly); cool.

4. In a blender, combine the tomato mixture, cilantro and, if desired, salt; cover and process until blended. Refrigerate leftovers.

NOTE: Wear disposable gloves when cutting hot peppers; the oils can burn skin. Avoid touching your face.

NUTRITIONAL FACTS
¼ CUP: 24 calories, 0 fat (0 saturated fat), 0 cholesterol, 9 mg sodium, 5 g carbohydrate (0 sugars, 0 fiber), 1 g protein

Quick Tip

You can help out your electricity bill by turning on your slow cooker! Because of its low wattage, a slow cooker costs a lot less than a traditional oven.

Witch's Caviar

PREP: 10 MINUTES + CHILLING • **YIELD:** 4 CUPS

I like to serve triangle-shaped tortillas with this dip because they look like pointy witch hats.

—*Darlene Brenden, Salem, Oregon*

- 2 cans (4¼ ounces each) chopped ripe olives, undrained
- 2 cans (4 ounces each) chopped green chilies, undrained
- 2 medium tomatoes, seeded and chopped
- 3 green onions, chopped

- 2 garlic cloves, minced
- 1 tablespoon red wine vinegar
- 1 tablespoon olive oil
- ½ teaspoon pepper
  - Dash seasoned salt
  - Tortilla chips

In a large bowl, combine the first nine ingredients. Cover and refrigerate overnight. Serve with tortilla chips.

NUTRITIONAL FACTS
2 TABLESPOONS: 17 calories, 1 g fat (0 saturated fat), 0 cholesterol, 98 mg sodium, 1 g carbohydrate (1 g sugars, 1 g fiber), 0 protein

Lick-the-Bowl-Clean Hummus

PREP: 10 MINUTES • **COOK:** 35 MINUTES • **YIELD:** 2½ CUPS

Everyone loves hummus, but I enjoy the garlic and onion types so much that I decided to let them shine in this homemade version. I get so many compliments when I serve it!

—*Sarah Gilbert, Beaverton, Oregon*

2 large sweet onions, thinly sliced
¼ cup plus ⅓ cup olive oil, divided
1 can (15 ounces) garbanzo beans or chickpeas, rinsed and drained
¼ cup plus 2 tablespoons lemon juice
¼ cup tahini

4 garlic cloves, minced
⅛ teaspoon salt
⅛ teaspoon pepper
Baked pita chips or assorted fresh vegetables

1. In a large skillet, saute onions in ¼ cup oil until softened. Reduce heat to medium-low; cook, stirring occasionally, for 30 minutes or until deep golden brown.

2. Transfer to a food processor; add the beans, lemon juice, tahini, garlic, salt, pepper and remaining oil. Cover and process for 30 seconds or until smooth. Serve with chips.

NUTRITIONAL FACTS
¼ CUP: 218 calories, 17 g fat (2 g saturated fat), 0 cholesterol, 91 mg sodium, 14 g carbohydrate (5 g sugars, 3 g fiber), 3 g protein

Guacamole

PREP/TOTAL TIME: 10 MINUTES • **YIELD:** ABOUT 1½ CUPS

This is one of our favorite spicy snack food recipes, and it's quick and easy to prepare when friends drop by on short notice. It also makes a great side dish for a complete Southwestern-style meal. Mild or sweet peppers can be substituted for the chilies for those who like their guacamole a little less spicy.

—Anne Tipps, Duncanville, Texas

1 medium ripe avocado, halved, seeded and peeled
4½ teaspoons lemon juice
1 small tomato, seeded and finely chopped
¼ cup finely chopped onion
1 tablespoon finely chopped green chilies
1 garlic clove, minced
¼ teaspoon salt, optional
   Tortilla chips

In a large bowl, mash avocado with lemon juice. Stir in the tomato, onion, chilies, garlic and salt if desired. Cover; chill. Serve with tortilla chips.

NUTRITIONAL FACTS
2 TABLESPOONS: 29 calories, 3 g fat (0 saturated fat), 0 cholesterol, 5 mg sodium, 2 g carbohydrate (1 g sugars, 1 g fiber), 0 protein

Delightful Main Dishes to Share

Southwestern Beef Brisket

PREP: 15 MINUTES ● **BAKE:** 3 HOURS + STANDING ● **YIELD:** 12 SERVINGS

This recipe makes the beef so tender that it comes apart with a fork. When served with mashed potatoes and a vegetable, it makes a hearty meal.

—Lois McAtee, Oceanside, California

1 fresh beef brisket (3 pounds)	1 teaspoon dried oregano
1 teaspoon salt	³⁄₄ teaspoon cumin
¼ teaspoon black pepper	½ teaspoon garlic powder
2 tablespoons vegetable oil	¼ teaspoon salt
1½ cups water	⅛ to ¼ teaspoon ground red pepper
1 can (8 ounces) tomato sauce	⅛ teaspoon black pepper
1 small onion, chopped	3 medium sweet red peppers, cut into strips
2 tablespoons red wine vinegar	1½ cups sliced carrots (1-inch chunks)
1 tablespoon chili powder	

Preheat oven to 325°. Season beef with salt and pepper. In a Dutch oven, heat oil; brown beef on both sides. Meanwhile, in a bowl, combine the next 11 ingredients. Pour over meat. Cover and bake for 2 hours. Add red peppers and carrots; bake 1 hour longer or until meat is tender. Remove meat from the pan; allow to stand 15 minutes before cutting. To thicken juices, bring to a boil. Cook, uncovered, 13–15 minutes or until thickened, stirring occasionally.

NUTRITIONAL FACTS
1 SLICE: 188 calories, 7 g fat (2 g saturated fat), 48 mg cholesterol, 389 mg sodium, 6 g carbohydrate (3 g sugars, 2 g fiber), 24 g protein

Quick Tip

We create one of our favorite sandwiches using leftover beef brisket. I layer the meat, sauteed onion and green pepper on a toasted sandwich roll and top with Swiss cheese. Then I pop it under the broiler to melt the cheese for a tasty Philly-style sandwich.—Donna H., Willard, MO

Java Roast Beef

PREP: 10 MINUTES ● **COOK:** 8 HOURS ● **YIELD:** 12 SERVINGS

Coffee adds richness to the gravy, which is perfect for sopping up with crusty bread or draping over mashed potatoes.

—*Charla Sackmann, Orange City, Iowa*

5 garlic cloves, minced	1½ cups strong brewed coffee
1½ teaspoons salt	2 tablespoons cornstarch
¾ teaspoon pepper	¼ cup cold water
1 boneless beef chuck roast (3 to 3½ pounds)	

1. Mix garlic, salt and pepper; rub over beef. Transfer to a 4-qt. slow cooker. Pour coffee around meat. Cook, covered, on low 8–10 hours or until meat is tender.

2. Remove roast to a serving plate; keep warm. Transfer cooking juices to a small saucepan; skim off fat. Bring to a boil. In a small bowl, mix cornstarch and water until smooth; gradually stir into cooking juices. Bring to a boil; cook and stir 1–2 minutes or until thickened. Serve with roast.

NUTRITIONAL FACTS
3 OUNCES COOKED BEEF WITH ABOUT 2 TABLESPOONS GRAVY: 199 calories, 11 g fat (4 g saturated fat), 74 mg cholesterol, 342 mg sodium, 2 g carbohydrate (0 sugars, 0 fiber), 22 g protein

Thai Coconut Beef

PREP: 30 MINUTES • **COOK:** 8¾ HOURS • **YIELD:** 10 SERVINGS

My husband and I love Thai food, but going out on weeknights can be challenging with busy schedules. I wanted to create a Thai-inspired dinner that could double as an easy lunch the following day. The beef is fantastic in this dish, but chicken or pork would be equally delicious!

—Ashley Lecker, Green Bay, Wisconsin

1 boneless beef chuck roast (3 pounds), halved
1 teaspoon salt
1 teaspoon pepper
1 large sweet red pepper, sliced
1 can (13.66 ounces) coconut milk
¾ cup beef stock
½ cup creamy peanut butter
¼ cup red curry paste
2 tablespoons soy sauce
2 tablespoons honey
2 teaspoons minced fresh gingerroot
½ pound fresh sugar snap peas, trimmed
¼ cup minced fresh cilantro
Hot cooked brown or white rice
Optional toppings: thinly sliced green onions, chopped peanuts, hot sauce and lime wedges

1. Sprinkle beef with salt and pepper. Place beef and pepper slices in a 5-qt. slow cooker. In a bowl, whisk coconut milk, beef stock, peanut butter, curry paste, soy sauce, honey and ginger; pour over meat. Cook, covered, on low 7–8 hours or until meat is tender.

2. Remove beef; cool slightly. Skim fat from reserved juices. Shred beef with two forks. Return beef to slow cooker; stir in snap peas. Cook, covered, on low 45–60 minutes longer or until peas are crisp-tender. Stir in cilantro. Serve with rice and, if desired, toppings of your choice.

NUTRITIONAL FACTS
1 CUP (CALCULATED WITHOUT RICE AND TOPPINGS): 421 calories, 28 g fat (14 g saturated fat), 88 mg cholesterol, 731 mg sodium, 12 g carbohydrate (7 g sugars, 2 g fiber), 32 g protein

Freeze It **Place cooled meat mixture in freezer containers. To use, partially thaw in refrigerator overnight. Microwave, covered, on high in a microwave-safe dish until heated through, gently stirring and adding a little broth or water if necessary.**

Bavarian Pot Roast

PREP: 15 MINUTES • **COOK:** 2¾ HOURS • **YIELD:** 10 SERVINGS

Since all of my grandparents were German, it's no wonder that so many Bavarian recipes have been handed down to me. Because the Midwest has such a large German population, I feel this recipe represents the area well.
—*Susan Robertson, Hamilton, Ohio*

1 boneless beef chuck pot roast (about 3 pounds)
2 tablespoons canola oil
1¼ cups water
¾ cup beer or beef broth
1 can (8 ounces) tomato sauce
½ cup chopped onion
2 tablespoons sugar

1 tablespoon vinegar
2 teaspoons salt
1 teaspoon ground cinnamon
1 bay leaf
½ teaspoon pepper
½ teaspoon ground ginger
Cornstarch and water, optional

1. In a Dutch oven, brown roast in hot oil. In a bowl, combine water, beer, tomato sauce, onion, sugar, vinegar, salt, cinnamon, bay leaf, pepper and ginger. Pour over meat and bring to a boil. Reduce heat; cover and simmer until meat is tender, about 2½–3 hours.

2. Remove meat. Discard bay leaf. If desired, thicken juices with cornstarch and water.

NUTRITIONAL FACTS
1 EACH: 281 calories, 16 g fat (5 g saturated fat), 88 mg cholesterol, 633 mg sodium, 5 g carbohydrate (4 g sugars, 0 fiber), 27 g protein

Freeze It
Place sliced pot roast in freezer containers; top with cooking juices. Cool and freeze. To use, partially thaw in refrigerator overnight. Microwave, covered, on high in a microwave-safe dish until heated through, gently stirring and adding a little broth to pot roast if necessary.

Marinated Pot Roast

PREP: 10 MINUTES + MARINATING ● **COOK:** 8 HOURS ● **YIELD:** 12 SERVINGS

I've long used whole or ground cloves as my secret ingredient in cooking and baking. Added to an overnight marinade, they provide the gravy in this meaty main dish with great flavor.

—*Marijane Rea, Milwaukie, Oregon*

1 cup dry white wine or beef broth	¼ teaspoon pepper
⅓ cup reduced-sodium soy sauce	4 whole cloves
1 tablespoon olive oil	1 beef top round roast (4 pounds)
4 garlic cloves, minced	5 teaspoons cornstarch
2 green onions, thinly sliced	5 teaspoons cold water
1½ teaspoons ground ginger	

1. In a gallon-size resealable plastic bag, combine the first eight ingredients. Cut roast in half; add to marinade. Seal bag and turn to coat; refrigerate overnight.

2. Place roast and marinade in a 5-qt. slow cooker. Cover and cook on low for 8–10 hours or until meat is tender. Remove roast to a serving platter and keep warm. Pour cooking juices into a 2-cup measuring cup; discard whole cloves.

3. In a saucepan, combine cornstarch and cold water until smooth; stir in 1½ cups cooking juices. Bring to a boil; cook and stir for 2 minutes or until thickened. Serve with the roast.

NUTRITIONAL FACTS
3 OUNCES COOKED BEEF: 174 calories, 6 g fat (2 g saturated fat), 59 mg cholesterol, 255 mg sodium, 3 g carbohydrate (0 sugars, 1 g fiber), 25 g protein

Saucy Italian Roast

PREP: 10 MINUTES ● **COOK:** 8 HOURS ● **YIELD:** 10 SERVINGS

This tender roast is one of my favorite slow cooker meals. I thicken the juices with a little flour and add ketchup, then serve the sauce and beef slices over pasta.

—*Jan Roat, Red Lodge, Montana*

$\frac{1}{2}$ to 1 teaspoon salt
  $\frac{1}{2}$ teaspoon garlic powder
  $\frac{1}{4}$ teaspoon pepper
  1 beef rump roast or bottom round roast (3 to 3$\frac{1}{2}$ pounds)
  1 jar (4$\frac{1}{2}$ ounces) sliced mushrooms, drained

  1 medium onion, diced
  1 jar (14 ounces) spaghetti sauce
$\frac{1}{4}$ to $\frac{1}{2}$ cup red wine or beef broth
     Hot cooked pasta

1. In a small bowl, combine the salt, garlic powder and pepper; rub over roast. Place in a 5-qt. slow cooker. Top with mushrooms and onion. In a medium bowl, combine the spaghetti sauce and wine; pour over meat and vegetables.

2. Cover and cook on low for 8–10 hours or until meat is tender. Slice roast; serve with pasta and pan juices.

NUTRITIONAL FACTS
4 OUNCES COOKED BEEF (CALCULATED WITHOUT PASTA): 218 calories, 8 g fat (3 g saturated fat), 82 mg cholesterol, 415 mg sodium, 6 g carbohydrate (3 g sugars, 1 g fiber), 28 g protein

Quick Tip **Don't flip your lid! To keep your dish's cover on while driving to the church supper, simply set a rubber band around the lid's knob and over one of the dish's handles. Pull another rubber band around the knob and over the other handle.**

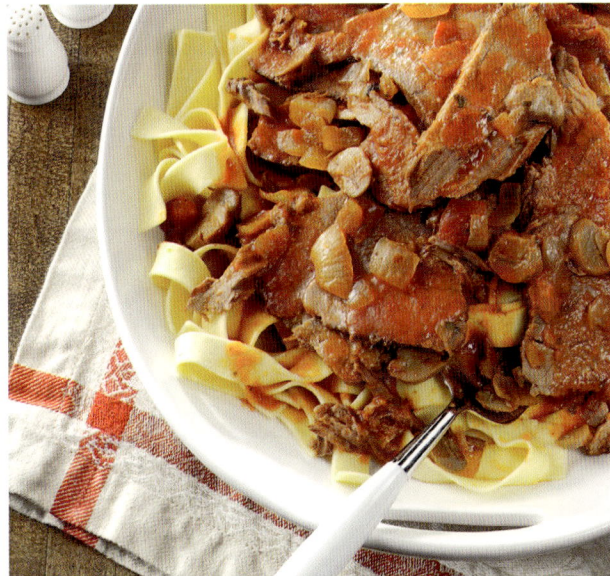

Louisiana Round Steak

PREP: 20 MINUTES ● **COOK:** 7 HOURS ● **YIELD:** 6 SERVINGS

This beefy main dish is always a big hit with the men in our family. After simmering in a slow cooker, the steak takes on a robust taste, and the filling portions are just what we love.

—*Megan Rohlck, Vermillion, South Dakota*

2 pounds sweet potatoes, peeled and cut into 1-inch pieces
1 large onion, chopped
1 medium green pepper, sliced
2 beef top round steaks ($\frac{3}{4}$ inch thick and 1 pound each)
1 teaspoon salt, divided
2 tablespoons olive oil
1 garlic clove, minced

3 tablespoons all-purpose flour
1 can (28 ounces) diced tomatoes, undrained
$\frac{1}{2}$ cup beef broth
1 teaspoon sugar
$\frac{1}{2}$ teaspoon dried thyme
$\frac{1}{2}$ teaspoon pepper
$\frac{1}{4}$ teaspoon hot pepper sauce

1. Place the sweet potatoes, onion and green pepper in a 6-qt. slow cooker. Cut each steak into three serving-size pieces; sprinkle with $\frac{1}{2}$ teaspoon salt. In a large skillet over medium heat, brown steaks in oil in batches on both sides. Place steaks over vegetables, reserving drippings in pan.

2. Add garlic to drippings; cook and stir for 1 minute. Stir in flour until blended. Stir in the remaining ingredients and remaining salt. Bring to a boil, stirring constantly. Cook and stir for 4–5 minutes or until thickened. Pour over meat. Cover and cook on low for 7–9 hours or until beef is tender.

NUTRITIONAL FACTS
1 STEAK WITH 1$\frac{1}{4}$ CUPS TOMATO MIXTURE: 576 calories, 14 g fat (4 g saturated fat), 170 mg cholesterol, 1031 mg sodium, 37 g carbohydrate (16 g sugars, 5 g fiber), 71 g protein

Quick Tip
Some newer slow cookers seem to heat up more quickly than older ones. If you have an older model and your recipe directs to cook on low, you may want to set it on the highest setting for the first hour of cooking to ensure food safety.

Asian-Style Round Steak

PREP: 20 MINUTES • **COOK:** 7 HOURS • **YIELD:** 8 SERVINGS

I've long relied on this hearty dish loaded with veggies to satisfy my family. My friend gave me the recipe two decades ago, and all I added was a little more meat, plus celery and mushrooms.

—*Marilyn Wolfe, Des Moines, Iowa*

2 pounds beef top round steak, cut into 3-inch strips
2 tablespoons canola oil
3 celery ribs, chopped
1 cup chopped onion
¼ cup reduced-sodium soy sauce
1 teaspoon sugar
½ teaspoon salt
½ teaspoon minced garlic
¼ teaspoon ground ginger
¼ teaspoon pepper

2 medium green peppers, julienned
1 can (15 ounces) tomato sauce
1 can (14 ounces) bean sprouts, rinsed and drained
1 can (8 ounces) sliced water chestnuts, drained
1 jar (4½ ounces) sliced mushrooms, drained
1 tablespoon cornstarch
½ cup cold water
Hot cooked rice

1. In a large skillet, brown meat in oil on all sides. Transfer meat and drippings to a 5-qt. slow cooker. In a bowl, combine the celery, onion, soy sauce, sugar, salt, garlic, ginger and pepper; pour over meat. Cover and cook on low for 5½– to 6 hours or until meat is tender.

2. Add the green peppers, tomato sauce, bean sprouts, water chestnuts and mushrooms; cover and cook on low 1 hour longer.

3. In a small bowl or measuring cup, combine cornstarch and water until smooth; stir into beef mixture. Cover and cook on high for 30 minutes or until sauce is thickened. Serve with rice.

NUTRITIONAL FACTS
1 CUP: 239 calories, 7 g fat (2 g saturated fat), 64 mg cholesterol, 980 mg sodium, 14 g carbohydrate (4 g sugars, 3 g fiber), 29 g protein

Quick Tip   **It is not always necessary to brown meats before placing them in a slow cooker. However, browning can improve the visual appeal of the meat and produce a richer flavor.**

Slow-Cooked Hungarian Goulash

PREP: 15 MINUTES ● **COOK:** 8 HOURS ● **YIELD:** 8 SERVINGS

I enjoy sharing recipes with friends and family. This one's great for potluck suppers, too.

—*Jackie Kohn, Duluth, Minnesota*

2 pounds beef top round steak, cut into 1-inch cubes
1 cup chopped onion
2 tablespoons all-purpose flour
1½ teaspoons paprika
1 teaspoon garlic salt

½ teaspoon pepper
1 can (14½ ounces) diced tomatoes, undrained
1 bay leaf
1 cup (8 ounces) sour cream
Hot cooked egg noodles

1. Place beef and onion in a 3-qt. slow cooker. In a small bowl, combine the flour, paprika, garlic salt and pepper; sprinkle over beef and stir to coat. Stir in tomatoes; add bay leaf. Cover and cook on low for 8–10 hours or until meat is tender.

2. Discard bay leaf. Just before serving, stir in sour cream; heat through. Serve with noodles.

NUTRITIONAL FACTS
1 CUP: 224 calories, 8 g fat (5 g saturated fat), 83 mg cholesterol, 339 mg sodium, 7 g carbohydrate (4 g sugars, 1 g fiber), 27 g protein

Make It Ahead Before adding sour cream, cool stew. Freeze stew in freezer containers. To use, partially thaw in refrigerator overnight. Heat through in a saucepan, stirring occasionally and adding a little broth if necessary. Remove from heat; stir in sour cream.

Beef and Beans

PREP: 10 MINUTES • **COOK:** 6½ HOURS • **YIELD:** 8 SERVINGS

My deliciously spicy steak and beans will have family and friends asking for more. It's a favorite in my recipe collection.

—*Marie Leadmon, Bethesda, Maryland*

1½ pounds boneless round steak
1 tablespoon prepared mustard
1 tablespoon chili powder
½ teaspoon salt
¼ teaspoon pepper
1 garlic clove, minced

2 cans (14½ ounces each) diced tomatoes, undrained
1 medium onion, chopped
1 beef bouillon cube, crushed
1 can (16 ounces) kidney beans, rinsed and drained
Hot cooked rice

Cut steak into thin strips. Combine mustard, chili powder, salt, pepper and garlic in a bowl; add steak and toss to coat. Transfer to a 3-qt. slow cooker; add tomatoes, onion and bouillon. Cover and cook on low for 6–8 hours. Stir in beans; cook 30 minutes longer. Serve over rice.

NUTRITIONAL FACTS
1 CUP (CALCULATED WITHOUT RICE): 185 calories, 3 g fat (1 g saturated fat), 47 mg cholesterol, 584 mg sodium, 16 g carbohydrate (5 g sugars, 5 g fiber), 24 g protein

Beef Burgundy with Noodles

PREP: 10 MINUTES • **COOK:** 5 HOURS • **YIELD:** 6 SERVINGS

To save time, the night before serving this tasty dish, I cut up the vegetables and store them in the fridge in separate containers. Prep takes only minutes the next morning. At dinnertime, I simply cook the noodles and bake some cheesy garlic toast for a warm, hearty, fuss-free meal!

—*Mary Jo Nikolaus, Mansfield, Ohio*

1½ pounds beef stew meat, cut into 1-inch cubes
½ pound whole fresh mushrooms, halved
4 medium carrots, chopped
1 can (10¾ ounces) condensed golden mushroom soup, undiluted
1 large onion, cut into thin wedges

½ cup Burgundy wine or beef broth
¼ cup quick-cooking tapioca
½ teaspoon salt
¼ teaspoon dried thyme
¼ teaspoon pepper
  Hot cooked egg noodles

1. In a 5-qt. slow cooker, combine the first 10 ingredients.

2. Cover and cook on low for 5–6 hours or until meat is tender. Serve with noodles.

NUTRITIONAL FACTS
1 CUP (CALCULATED WITHOUT NOODLES): 273 calories, 9 g fat (3 g saturated fat), 73 mg cholesterol, 642 mg sodium, 19 g carbohydrate (5 g sugars, 3 g fiber), 24 g protein

Quick Tip **Avoid adding dry pasta to a slow cooker; it will become sticky. It is better to cook it according to package directions and stir it into the slow cooker just before serving.**

Garlic Lover's Beef Stew

PREP: 30 MINUTES • **COOK:** 8 HOURS • **YIELD:** 10 SERVINGS

The wine gives a mellow flavor to this stew that has tender pieces of beef and carrots. We like to serve it over mashed potatoes, but you could also use noodles.

—*Alissa Brown, Ft. Washington, Pennsylvania*

1 boneless beef chuck roast (3 pounds), cut into 2-inch pieces

1¼ teaspoons salt

¾ teaspoon coarsely ground pepper

½ cup all-purpose flour

2 tablespoons olive oil

12 garlic cloves, minced

1 cup dry red wine or reduced-sodium beef broth

2 cans (14½ ounces each) diced tomatoes, undrained

1 can (14½ ounces) reduced-sodium beef broth

6 medium carrots, thinly sliced

2 medium onions, chopped

2 tablespoons tomato paste

2 teaspoons minced fresh rosemary or ½ teaspoon dried rosemary, crushed

2 teaspoons minced fresh thyme or ½ teaspoon dried thyme

2 bay leaves
  Dash ground cloves
  Hot mashed potatoes

1. Sprinkle beef with salt, pepper and flour; toss to coat.

2. In a large skillet, heat oil over medium-high heat. Brown beef in batches. Remove with a slotted spoon. Reduce heat to medium. Add garlic; cook and stir 1 minute.

3. Add wine to skillet, stirring to loosen browned bits from pan. Transfer to a 5- or 6-qt. slow cooker. Stir in tomatoes, broth, carrots, onions, tomato paste, rosemary, thyme, bay leaves, cloves and beef.

4. Cook, covered, on low 8–10 hours or until beef is tender. Remove bay leaves. Serve with mashed potatoes.

NUTRITIONAL FACTS
1 CUP (CALCULATED WITHOUT POTATOES): 330 calories, 16 g fat (5 g saturated fat), 89 mg cholesterol, 586 mg sodium, 17 g carbohydrate (6 g sugars, 3 g fiber), 29 g protein

Easy Ropa Vieja Stew

PREP: 25 MINUTES ● **COOK:** 6 HOURS ● **YIELD:** 8 SERVINGS

Use your slow cooker for this meaty Cuban classic, which offers bold flavors without a lot of hands-on time.

—Denise Nyland, Panama City, Florida

1 boneless beef chuck roast (2 pounds), cut in half
2 tablespoons olive oil
2 large onions, coarsely chopped
2 large green peppers, coarsely chopped
4 jalapeno peppers, seeded and minced
1 habanero pepper, seeded and minced
3 cans (14½ ounces each) diced tomatoes, undrained
½ cup water

6 garlic cloves, minced
2 tablespoons minced fresh cilantro
4 teaspoons beef bouillon granules
2 teaspoons pepper
1½ teaspoons ground cumin
1 teaspoon dried oregano
½ cup pimiento-stuffed olives, coarsely chopped
Hot cooked rice, optional

1. In a large skillet, brown beef in oil on all sides. Transfer meat to a 5-qt. slow cooker. Add onions and peppers. In a bowl, combine tomatoes, water, garlic, cilantro, beef bouillon, pepper, cumin and oregano; pour over vegetables.

2. Cover and cook on low for 6–8 hours or until meat is tender. Remove beef; cool slightly. Skim fat from cooking juices; stir in olives. Shred beef with two forks and return to slow cooker; heat through. Serve with rice if desired.

NOTE: Wear disposable gloves when cutting hot peppers; the oils can burn skin. Avoid touching your face.

NUTRITIONAL FACTS
1⅓ CUPS (CALCULATED WITHOUT RICE): 306 calories, 16 g fat (5 g saturated fat), 74 mg cholesterol, 821 mg sodium, 16 g carbohydrate (8 g sugars, 4 g fiber), 25 g protein

Freeze It **Transfer individual portions of stew to freezer containers and freeze. To use, partially thaw in refrigerator overnight. Heat through in a saucepan, stirring occasionally and adding a little water if necessary.**

Spinach & Feta Stuffed Flank Steak

PREP: 30 MINUTES ● **COOK:** 6 HOURS ● **YIELD:** 6 SERVINGS

If you need a main dish recipe from a slow cooker that offers an upscale feel, this one is a great choice. Elegant enough for company, the rolled flank steak looks pretty on a plate.

—*Steven Schend, Grand Rapids, Michigan*

- 1 beef flank steak (1½ pounds)
- 2 cups crumbled feta cheese
- 3 cups fresh baby spinach
- ½ cup oil-packed sun-dried tomatoes, drained and chopped
- ½ cup finely chopped onion
- 5 tablespoons all-purpose flour, divided
- ½ teaspoon salt
- ½ teaspoon pepper
- 2 tablespoons canola oil
- 1 cup beef broth
- 1 tablespoon Worcestershire sauce
- 2 teaspoons tomato paste
- ⅓ cup dry red wine or additional beef broth
  Hot cooked egg noodles, optional

1. Starting at one long side, cut steak horizontally in half to within ½ inch of opposite side. Open steak flat; cover with plastic wrap. Pound with a meat mallet to ½-inch thickness. Remove plastic.

2. Sprinkle 1 cup cheese over steak to within 1 inch of edges. Layer with spinach, tomatoes, onion and remaining cheese. Roll up jelly-roll style, starting with a long side; tie at 1½-inch intervals with kitchen string. Sprinkle with 2 tablespoons flour, salt and pepper.

3. In a large skillet, heat oil over medium heat. Brown beef on all sides; drain. Transfer to a 6-qt. oval slow cooker. In a small bowl, mix broth, Worcestershire sauce and tomato paste; pour over top. Cook, covered, on low 6–8 hours or until meat is tender.

4. Remove beef to a platter; keep warm. Transfer cooking juices to a small saucepan; skim fat. Bring juices to a boil. Mix remaining flour and wine until smooth; gradually stir into pan. Return to a boil; cook and stir 1–2 minutes or until thickened. Serve beef with gravy and, if desired, noodles.

NUTRITIONAL FACTS
1 SLICE WITH 3 TABLESPOONS GRAVY (CALCULATED WITHOUT NOODLES): 367 calories, 20 g fat (8 g saturated fat), 74 mg cholesterol, 838 mg sodium, 11 g carbohydrate (1 g sugars, 3 g fiber), 31 g protein

Li'l Cheddar Meat Loaves

PREP: 15 MINUTES ● **BAKE:** 25 MINUTES ● **YIELD:** 8 SERVINGS

I got this recipe from my aunt when I was a teen and have made these miniature loaves many times since. My husband and three children count this main dish among their favorites.

—*Kathy Bowron, Cocolalla, Idaho*

1 large egg	$\frac{1}{2}$ teaspoon salt
$\frac{3}{4}$ cup whole milk	1 pound ground beef
1 cup shredded cheddar cheese	$\frac{2}{3}$ cup ketchup
$\frac{1}{2}$ cup quick-cooking oats	$\frac{1}{2}$ cup packed brown sugar
$\frac{1}{2}$ cup chopped onion	$1\frac{1}{2}$ teaspoons prepared mustard

1. Preheat oven to 350°. In a large bowl, whisk egg and milk. Stir in the cheese, oats, onion and salt. Crumble beef over mixture and mix well. Shape into eight loaves; place in a greased 13x9-inch baking dish. In a small bowl, combine the ketchup, brown sugar and mustard; spoon over loaves.

2. Bake, uncovered, for 25–30 minutes or until no pink remains and a meat thermometer reads 160°.

NUTRITIONAL FACTS
1 EACH: 279 calories, 13 g fat (6 g saturated fat), 81 mg cholesterol, 547 mg sodium, 25 g carbohydrate (20 g sugars, 1 g fiber), 17 g protein

Quick Tip

When setting up a reunion, block party or potluck, mark the table with sticky notes labeled for main dishes, sides, salads, drinks and desserts. Attendees will know where to place items and not have to ask.

Sweet 'n' Tender Cabbage Rolls

PREP: 40 MINUTES • **COOK:** 7 HOURS • **YIELD:** 7 SERVINGS

I've used this recipe for more than 30 years, and the extra time it takes to assemble the rolls is well worth the effort. I always make two batches because they go so fast. You can assemble the night before and cook the next day.

—*Sonja Benz, Carmel, Indiana*

1 large head cabbage
2 large eggs, lightly beaten
½ cup 2% milk
2 cups cooked long-grain rice
2 jars (4½ ounces each) sliced mushrooms, well drained
1 small onion, chopped
2 teaspoons salt
1 teaspoon dried parsley flakes
1 teaspoon dried oregano

1 teaspoon dried basil
½ teaspoon pepper
2 pounds lean ground beef (90% lean)

SAUCE:
2 cans (8 ounces each) tomato sauce
½ cup packed brown sugar
2 tablespoons lemon juice
2 teaspoons Worcestershire sauce

1. Cook cabbage in boiling water just until leaves fall off head. Set aside 14 large leaves for rolls. (Refrigerate remaining cabbage for another use.) Cut out the thick vein from the bottom of each reserved leaf, making a V-shaped cut.

2. In a large bowl, combine the eggs, milk, rice, mushrooms, onion and seasonings. Crumble beef over mixture and mix well. Place about ½ cup on each cabbage leaf; overlap cut ends and fold in sides, beginning from the cut end. Roll up completely to enclose filling.

3. Place seven rolls, seam side down, in a 5-qt. slow cooker. Combine sauce ingredients; pour half over cabbage rolls. Top with remaining rolls and sauce. Cover and cook on low for 7–8 hours or until a thermometer reads 160°.

NUTRITIONAL FACTS
2 EACH: 389 calories, 12 g fat (5 g saturated fat), 141 mg cholesterol, 1243 mg sodium, 39 g carbohydrate (20 g sugars, 3 g fiber), 31 g protein

Zucchini Pizza Casserole

PREP: 20 MINUTES ● **BAKE:** 40 MINUTES ● **YIELD:** 8 SERVINGS

I grow zucchini by the bushel, so this pizza casserole is one of my dinnertime go-to's. My hungry husband and kids gobble it right up.

—Lynn Bernstetter, White Bear Lake, Minnesota

4 cups shredded unpeeled zucchini
½ teaspoon salt
2 large eggs
½ cup grated Parmesan cheese
2 cups shredded part-skim mozzarella cheese, divided

1 cup shredded cheddar cheese, divided
1 pound ground beef
½ cup chopped onion
1 can (15 ounces) Italian tomato sauce
1 medium green pepper, chopped

1. Preheat oven to 400°. Place zucchini in colander; sprinkle with salt. Let stand 10 minutes, then squeeze out moisture.

2. In a large bowl, combine zucchini with eggs, Parmesan and half of mozzarella and cheddar cheeses. Press into a greased 13x9-inch or 3-qt. baking dish. Bake 20 minutes.

3. Meanwhile, in a large saucepan, cook beef and onion over medium heat, crumbling beef, until meat is no longer pink; drain. Add tomato sauce; spoon over zucchini mixture. Sprinkle with remaining cheeses; add green pepper. Bake until heated through, about 20 minutes longer.

NUTRITIONAL FACTS
1 CUP: 315 calories, 20 g fat (10 g saturated fat), 119 mg cholesterol, 855 mg sodium, 10 g carbohydrate (4 g sugars, 2 g fiber), 25 g protein

Freeze It **Cool baked casserole; cover and freeze. To use, partially thaw in refrigerator overnight. Remove from refrigerator 30 minutes before baking. Preheat oven to 350°. Unwrap casserole; reheat on a lower oven rack until heated through and a thermometer inserted in center reads 165°.**

Church Supper Spaghetti

PREP: 50 MINUTES • **BAKE:** 20 MINUTES • **YIELD:** 12 SERVINGS

Because this recipe feeds so many, I often take it to church dinners and potlucks. This colorful dish also comes in handy when we have lots of help to feed on our farm.

—*Verlyn Wilson, Wilkinson, Indiana*

1 pound ground beef	1 package (10 ounces) frozen corn, thawed
1 large onion, chopped	1 package (10 ounces) frozen peas, thawed
1 medium green pepper, chopped	1 can (4 ounces) mushroom stems and pieces, drained
1 can (14½ ounces) diced tomatoes, undrained	Salt and pepper to taste
1 cup water	12 ounces spaghetti, cooked and drained
2 tablespoons chili powder	2 cups shredded cheddar cheese, divided

1. In a large skillet, cook beef, onion and green pepper over medium heat until meat is no longer pink. Add tomatoes, water and chili powder. Cover and simmer for 30 minutes. Add the corn, peas, mushrooms, salt and pepper. Stir in spaghetti.

2. Preheat oven to 350°. Layer half of the mixture in a greased 4-qt. baking dish. Sprinkle with 1 cup cheese; repeat layers.

3. Bake, uncovered, for 20 minutes or until heated through.

NOTE: To give Church Supper Spaghetti a new flavor twist, use Italian, Mexican or Cajun diced tomatoes in place of the plain diced tomatoes.

NUTRITIONAL FACTS
1 EACH: 290 calories, 10 g fat (6 g saturated fat), 39 mg cholesterol, 259 mg sodium, 34 g carbohydrate (5 g sugars, 4 g fiber), 17 g protein

Take-It Tip

Don't forget about the utensils! Whether your casserole needs to be dished out with a slotted spoon, pasta fork or another serving tool, remember to pack it up before heading out the door.

Beef Bolognese with Linguine

PREP: 30 MINUTES • **COOK:** 3½ HOURS • **YIELD:** 18 SERVINGS

After much research, tasting and tweaking, I finally came up with this recipe, based on a dish from an Italian restaurant where I worked. It's perfect for feeding a house full of holiday guests the Sunday before or after Christmas.

—*Christine Wendland, Browns Mills, New Jersey*

3 pounds lean ground beef (90% lean)	1½ teaspoons coarsely ground pepper
⅓ cup olive oil	¼ teaspoon crushed red pepper flakes
3 medium onions, chopped	1½ cups dry red wine
3 large carrots, chopped	3 cans (28 ounces each) diced tomatoes, undrained
6 celery ribs, chopped	
1 can (12 ounces) tomato paste, divided	1½ cups beef stock
9 garlic cloves, sliced	6 bay leaves
3 tablespoons dried parsley flakes	3 cups 2% milk
5 teaspoons kosher salt	¾ cup grated Parmesan cheese
3 teaspoons dried basil	Hot cooked linguine
3 teaspoons dried marjoram	Additional grated Parmesan cheese, optional

1. In a stockpot, cook half of the beef over medium heat for 8–10 minutes or until no longer pink, breaking into crumbles. Remove beef with a slotted spoon; set aside. Pour off drippings. Repeat with remaining beef.

2. In the same stockpot, heat oil over medium heat. Add the onions, carrots and celery; cook and stir until tender. Stir in 1 cup tomato paste; cook and stir 3 minutes longer. Add the garlic, seasonings and beef.

3. Stir in wine. Bring to a boil; cook until almost evaporated. Add tomatoes, stock and bay leaves; return to a boil. Reduce heat; simmer, uncovered, for 3 hours or until desired consistency, stirring in milk halfway through cooking.

4. Remove bay leaves. Stir in cheese and remaining tomato paste; heat through. Serve with linguine and, if desired, additional cheese.

NUTRITIONAL FACTS
1 CUP (CALCULATED WITHOUT PASTA AND ADDITIONAL CHEESE): 270 calories, 12 g fat (4 g saturated fat), 53 mg cholesterol, 929 mg sodium, 17 g carbohydrate (10 g sugars, 4 g fiber), 20 g protein

Mexican Lasagna

PREP: 20 MINUTES ● **BAKE:** 65 MINUTES + STANDING ● **YIELD:** 12 SERVINGS

I collect cookbooks and recipes (this one is from my son's mother-in-law). My husband teases me that I won't live long enough to try half of the recipes in my files!

—*Rose Ann Buhle, Minooka, Illinois*

- 2 pounds ground beef
- 1 can (16 ounces) refried beans
- 1 can (4 ounces) chopped green chilies
- 1 envelope taco seasoning
- 2 tablespoons hot salsa
- 12 ounces uncooked lasagna noodles
- 4 cups shredded Colby–Monterey Jack cheese, divided

- 1 jar (16 ounces) mild salsa
- 2 cups water
- 2 cups (16 ounces) sour cream
- 1 can (2¼ ounces) sliced ripe olives, drained
- 3 green onions, chopped
- 1 medium tomato, chopped, optional

1. Preheat oven to 350°. In a large skillet, cook beef over medium heat until no longer pink; drain. Stir in beans, chilies, taco seasoning and hot salsa.

2. In a greased 13x9-inch baking dish, layer a third of the noodles and meat mixture. Sprinkle with 1 cup of cheese. Repeat layers twice.

3. Combine mild salsa and water; pour over top. Cover and bake 1 hour or until heated through.

4. Top with sour cream, olives, onions, tomatoes, if desired, and remaining cheese. Bake, uncovered, 5 minutes. Let stand 10–15 minutes before cutting.

NUTRITIONAL FACTS
1 SERVING: 521 calories, 28 g fat (16 g saturated fat), 110 mg cholesterol, 909 mg sodium, 36 g carbohydrate (4 g sugars, 3 g fiber), 29 g protein

Tomato–French Bread Lasagna

PREP: 30 MINUTES • **BAKE:** 40 MINUTES • **YIELD:** 10 SERVINGS

For a big, hearty meal, I make this recipe as a side dish to go with veal cutlets or a roast. But you could also serve the beefy lasagna as a main dish. Just pair it with a tossed green salad and loaf of garlic bread.

—*Patricia Collins, Imbler, Oregon*

  1 pound ground beef
  $\frac{1}{3}$ cup chopped onion
  $\frac{1}{3}$ cup chopped celery
  2 garlic cloves, minced
  14 slices French bread ($\frac{1}{2}$ inch thick)
  4 large tomatoes, sliced $\frac{1}{2}$ inch thick
  1 teaspoon dried basil
  1 teaspoon dried parsley flakes
  1 teaspoon dried oregano
  1 teaspoon dried rosemary, crushed
  1 teaspoon garlic powder
  $\frac{3}{4}$ teaspoon salt
  $\frac{1}{2}$ teaspoon pepper
  2 teaspoons olive oil, divided
  3 tablespoons butter
  3 tablespoons all-purpose flour
  $1\frac{1}{2}$ cups whole milk
  $\frac{1}{3}$ cup grated Parmesan cheese
  2 cups shredded mozzarella cheese

1. Preheat oven to 350°. In a skillet, cook beef, onion, celery and garlic over medium heat until beef is no longer pink; drain and set aside. Toast bread; line the bottom of an ungreased 13x9-inch baking dish with 10 slices. Top with half of the meat mixture and half of the tomatoes.

2. In a small bowl, combine seasonings; sprinkle half over tomatoes. Drizzle with 1 teaspoon oil. Crumble remaining bread over top. Repeat layers of meat, tomatoes, seasonings and oil.

3. In a saucepan over medium heat, melt the butter; stir in flour until smooth. Gradually stir in milk; bring to a boil. Cook and stir until thickened and bubbly, about 2 minutes. Remove from the heat; stir in Parmesan. Pour over casserole. Top with mozzarella. Bake, uncovered, for 40–45 minutes or until bubbly and cheese is golden brown.

NUTRITIONAL FACTS
1 EACH: 280 calories, 16 g fat (8 g saturated fat), 56 mg cholesterol, 500 mg sodium, 17 g carbohydrate (4 g sugars, 2 g fiber), 17 g protein

Ground Beef Spiral Bake

PREP: 40 MINUTES • **BAKE:** 25 MINUTES • **YIELD:** 2 CASSEROLES (8 SERVINGS EACH)

We got this recipe from a restaurant cook who lived in the duplex beside my mother-in-law. It was one of his favorites. It is easy to make, tastes great and freezes well. Both my mother-in-law and her neighbor are gone now, but this recipe always brings back happy memories!

—*Monika Rahn, Dillsburg, Pennsylvania*

1 package (16 ounces) spiral pasta
2 pounds ground beef
2/3 cup chopped onion
1 teaspoon minced garlic
2 jars (26 ounces each) spaghetti sauce

2 tablespoons tomato paste
1 teaspoon dried basil
1 teaspoon dried oregano
4 cups shredded part-skim mozzarella cheese

1. Preheat oven to 350°. Cook pasta according to package directions; drain. Meanwhile, in a Dutch oven, cook beef and onion over medium heat until meat is no longer pink. Add garlic; cook 1 minute longer. Drain. Stir in the spaghetti sauce, tomato paste, basil and oregano. Bring to a boil. Reduce heat; simmer, uncovered, for 5–10 minutes.

2. Stir pasta into meat mixture. Transfer to two greased 13x9-inch baking dishes. Sprinkle each with 2 cups cheese. Cover and freeze one casserole for up to 3 months.

3. Bake the remaining casserole, uncovered, for 25–30 minutes or until heated through.

NUTRITIONAL FACTS
3/4 CUP: 359 calories, 15 g fat (6 g saturated fat), 54 mg cholesterol, 627 mg sodium, 32 g carbohydrate (8 g sugars, 3 g fiber), 23 g protein

Freeze It
Thaw in the refrigerator overnight. Bake, uncovered, at 350° for 35–40 minutes or until heated through.

Mozzarella Baked Spaghetti

PREP: 20 MINUTES • **BAKE:** 30 MINUTES + STANDING • **YIELD:** 8 SERVINGS

This satisfying pasta bake is quick to make and will please young and old alike. Add a salad and breadsticks, and you're ready for company.

—*Betty Rabe, Mahtomedi, Minnesota*

8 ounces uncooked spaghetti, broken into thirds
1 large egg
½ cup whole milk
½ teaspoon salt
½ pound ground beef
½ pound bulk Italian sausage

1 small onion, chopped
¼ cup chopped green pepper
1 jar (14 ounces) meatless spaghetti sauce
1 can (8 ounces) tomato sauce
1 to 2 cups shredded part-skim mozzarella cheese

1. Preheat oven to 350°. Cook spaghetti according to package directions.

2. Meanwhile, in a large bowl, beat egg, milk and salt. Drain spaghetti; add to egg mixture and toss to coat. Transfer to a greased 13x9-inch baking dish.

3. In a large skillet, cook beef, sausage, onion and green pepper over medium heat until meat is no longer pink; drain. Stir in spaghetti sauce and tomato sauce. Spoon over the spaghetti mixture.

4. Bake, uncovered, 20 minutes. Sprinkle with the cheese. Bake 10 minutes longer or until cheese is melted. Let stand 10 minutes before cutting.

NUTRITIONAL FACTS
1 EACH: 286 calories, 11 g fat (5 g saturated fat), 65 mg cholesterol, 718 mg sodium, 29 g carbohydrate (6 g sugars, 2 g fiber), 17 g protein

Freeze It **Cool spaghetti completely before tossing with egg mixture. Transfer to baking dish; cover and refrigerate. Meanwhile, prepare meat sauce and cool completely before spooning over spaghetti mixture. Cover and freeze unbaked casserole. To use, partially thaw in refrigerator overnight. Remove from refrigerator 30 minutes before baking. Preheat oven to 350°. Bake as directed, increasing time as necessary to heat through and for a thermometer inserted in center to read 165°.**

Italian Meatball Tortes

PREP: 1¼ HOURS + RISING ● **BAKE:** 30 MINUTES ● **YIELD:** 2 TORTES (6 SERVINGS EACH)

With classic Italian flavor, this hearty pie—filled with tomatoes, mozzarella and moist homemade meatballs—will be a hit with your family. Preparation takes some time, but it's well worth it.
—*Sandy Blessing, Ocean Shores, Washington*

1 package (¼ ounce) active dry yeast
¼ cup warm water (110° to 115°)
¾ cup warm whole milk (110° to 115°)
¼ cup sugar
¼ cup shortening
1 large egg
1 teaspoon salt
3½ to 3¾ cups all-purpose flour

MEATBALLS:
1 can (5 ounces) evaporated milk
2 large eggs, lightly beaten
1 cup quick-cooking oats
1 cup crushed saltines
½ cup chopped onion
½ cup chopped celery
2 teaspoons salt
2 teaspoons chili powder
½ teaspoon garlic powder
½ teaspoon pepper
3 pounds ground beef

FILLING:
1 can (15 ounces) crushed tomatoes
½ cup chopped onion
⅓ cup grated Parmesan cheese
1½ teaspoons dried basil
1½ teaspoons dried oregano
1 teaspoon minced fresh parsley
1 teaspoon salt
1½ cups shredded part-skim mozzarella cheese

1. In a large bowl, dissolve yeast in warm water. Add the milk, sugar, shortening, egg, salt and 2 cups flour. Beat until smooth. Stir in enough remaining flour to form a soft dough.

2. Turn onto a floured surface; knead until smooth and elastic, about 6–8 minutes. Place in a greased bowl, turning once to grease the top. Cover and let rise in a warm place until doubled, 1–1½ hours.

3. In a large bowl, combine the milk, eggs, oats, saltines, onion, celery and seasonings. Crumble beef over mixture and mix well. Shape into 1½-inch balls. In a large skillet over medium heat, cook meatballs in batches until no longer pink.

4. Meanwhile, place tomatoes and onion in a small saucepan. Bring to a boil. Reduce heat; simmer, uncovered, for 10 minutes or until slightly thickened. Stir in the Parmesan cheese, herbs and salt.

5. Punch dough down. Divide into three portions. Roll two portions into 11-inch circles; line the bottoms and press partially up the sides of two greased 9-inch springform pans. Roll third portion into a 12x10-inch rectangle; cut into twelve 10x1-inch strips.

6. Place meatballs in prepared crusts; top with tomato mixture and mozzarella cheese. Make lattice crusts with strips of dough; trim and seal edges. Cover and let rise for 30 minutes.

7. Preheat oven to 350°. Bake 30–35 minutes or until golden brown. Cut into wedges.

NUTRITIONAL FACTS
1 PIECE: 560 calories, 26 g fat (10 g saturated fat), 154 mg cholesterol, 1119 mg sodium, 43 g carbohydrate (8 g sugars, 3 g fiber), 37 g protein

Quick Tip   For meatballs to cook evenly, it's important for them to be the same size. One way to do this is to lightly pat the meat mixture into a 1-inch-thick rectangle. Cut the rectangle into the same number of squares as meatballs in the recipe. Gently roll each square into a ball. Or, using a $1\frac{1}{2}$- or $1\frac{3}{4}$-inch-diameter scoop, scoop the mixture into portions of equal size. Gently roll each into a ball.

Sesame Pork Roast

PREP: 10 MINUTES + MARINATING • **COOK:** 9 HOURS • **YIELD:** 8 SERVINGS

I marinate a boneless cut of pork in a tangy sauce overnight before cooking it slowly the next day. The result is a tasty roast that's pull-apart tender.

—*Sue Brown, San Miguel, California*

1 boneless pork shoulder butt roast
  (4 pounds)
2 cups water
½ cup soy sauce
¼ cup sesame seeds, toasted
¼ cup molasses

¼ cup cider or white wine vinegar
4 green onions, sliced
2 teaspoons garlic powder
¼ teaspoon cayenne pepper
3 tablespoons cornstarch
¼ cup cold water

1. Cut roast in half; place in a large resealable plastic bag. In a small bowl, combine the water, soy sauce, sesame seeds, molasses, vinegar, onions, garlic powder and cayenne. Pour half over the roast. Seal bag and turn to coat; refrigerate overnight. Cover and refrigerate remaining marinade.

2. Drain and discard marinade. Place roast in a 5-qt. slow cooker; add the reserved marinade. Cover and cook on high for 1 hour. Reduce temperature to low; cook 8–9 hours longer or until meat is tender.

3. Remove meat to a serving platter; keep warm. Skim fat from cooking juices; transfer to a small saucepan. Bring liquid to a boil. In a small bowl or measuring cup, combine cornstarch and cold water until smooth. Gradually stir into the pan. Bring to a boil; cook and stir for 2 minutes or until thickened. Serve with meat.

NUTRITIONAL FACTS
6 OUNCES COOKED PORK: 433 calories, 24 g fat (8 g saturated fat), 135 mg cholesterol, 835 mg sodium, 10 g carbohydrate (6 g sugars, 1 g fiber), 41 g protein

Italian Shredded Pork Stew

PREP: 20 MINUTES ● **COOK:** 8 HOURS ● **YIELD:** 9 SERVINGS (3½ QUARTS)

Need a warm meal for a blustery night? Throw together this slow-cooked stew that's brightened with fresh sweet potatoes, kale and Italian seasoning. The shredded pork is so tender, you're going to want to make this again and again.

—*Robin Jungers, Campbellsport, Wisconsin*

2 medium sweet potatoes, peeled and cubed
2 cups chopped fresh kale
1 large onion, chopped
3 garlic cloves, minced
1 boneless pork shoulder butt roast
    (2½ to 3½ pounds)
1 can (14 ounces) white kidney or cannellini
    beans, rinsed and drained
1½ teaspoons Italian seasoning
½ teaspoon salt
½ teaspoon pepper
3 cans (14½ ounces each) chicken broth
    Sour cream, optional

1. Place the sweet potatoes, kale, onion and garlic in a 5-qt. slow cooker. Place roast on vegetables. Add the beans and seasonings. Pour broth over top. Cover and cook on low for 8–10 hours or until meat is tender.

2. Remove meat; cool slightly. Skim fat from cooking juices. Shred pork with two forks and return to slow cooker; heat through. Garnish servings with sour cream if desired.

NUTRITIONAL FACTS
1½ CUPS (CALCULATED WITHOUT SOUR CREAM): 283 calories, 13 g fat (5 g saturated fat), 78 mg cholesterol, 860 mg sodium, 15 g carbohydrate (4 g sugars, 3 g fiber), 24 g protein

Quick Tip
Vegetables, especially potatoes and root vegetables (such as carrots), tend to cook slower than meat. Place these vegetables on the bottom and around the sides of the slow cooker and put meat on top of the vegetables. Add tender vegetables, like peas and zucchini, or those you'd prefer to be crisp-tender, during the last 15 to 60 minutes.

Low & Slow Pork Verde

PREP: 15 MINUTES ● **COOK:** 5 HOURS ● **YIELD:** 8 SERVINGS

My family loves this versatile pork dish. We like to have it over a serving of cheesy grits, but it also goes well with rice or potatoes. Leftovers make an excellent starter for white chili.

—Val Ruble, Ava, Missouri

1 boneless pork shoulder butt roast (3½ to 4 pounds)
1 large onion, chopped
1 jar (16 ounces) salsa verde
2 cans (4 ounces each) chopped green chilies
2 teaspoons ground cumin
1 teaspoon dried oregano

1 teaspoon salt
1 teaspoon pepper
¼ teaspoon crushed red pepper flakes
⅛ teaspoon ground cinnamon
¼ cup minced fresh cilantro
Hot cooked grits
Sour cream, optional

1. Place pork and onion in a 4-qt. slow cooker. In a small bowl, combine salsa, chilies, cumin, oregano, salt, pepper, pepper flakes and cinnamon; pour over meat. Cook, covered, on low 5–6 hours or until meat is tender.

2. Remove roast; cool slightly. Skim fat from cooking juices. Shred pork with two forks. Return pork to slow cooker; heat through. Stir in cilantro. Serve with grits and, if desired, sour cream.

NUTRITIONAL FACTS
1 CUP (CALCULATED WITHOUT GRITS AND SOUR CREAM): 349 calories, 20 g fat (7 g saturated fat), 118 mg cholesterol, 872 mg sodium, 8 g carbohydrate (3 g sugars, 1 g fiber), 34 g protein

Freeze It **Freeze cooled meat mixture in freezer containers. To use, partially thaw in refrigerator overnight. Microwave, covered, on high in a microwave-safe dish until heated through, gently stirring and adding a little broth if necessary.**

Dijon-Rubbed Pork with Rhubarb Sauce

PREP: 15 MINUTES ● **BAKE:** 1 HOUR + STANDING ● **YIELD:** 12 SERVINGS (1½ CUPS SAUCE)

This moist and tender pork loin roast is served with a rhubarb sauce that's just delicious! It is great for company and makes an extra-special weeknight meal.

—Marilyn Rodriguez, Fairbanks, Alaska

1   boneless pork loin roast (3 pounds)
¼   cup Dijon mustard
6   garlic cloves, minced
1   tablespoon minced fresh rosemary or
    1 teaspoon dried rosemary, crushed
¾   teaspoon salt
½   teaspoon pepper

SAUCE:

3   cups sliced fresh or frozen rhubarb
⅓   cup orange juice
⅓   cup sugar
1   tablespoon cider vinegar

1. Preheat oven to 350°. Score the surface of the pork, making diamond shapes ¼ inch deep. In a small bowl, combine the mustard, garlic, rosemary, salt and pepper; rub over pork.

2. Coat a roasting pan and rack with cooking spray; place pork on rack in pan. Bake, uncovered, for 1 hour or until a thermometer reads 145°. Let stand for 10 minutes before slicing.

3. In a small saucepan, bring the sauce ingredients to a boil. Reduce heat; cover and simmer for 8–12 minutes or until rhubarb is tender. Serve warm with pork.

NOTE: If using frozen rhubarb, measure rhubarb while still frozen, then thaw completely. Drain in a colander, but do not press liquid out.

NUTRITIONAL FACTS
3 OUNCES COOKED PORK: 181 calories, 6 g fat (2 g saturated fat), 56 mg cholesterol, 308 mg sodium, 9 g carbohydrate (7 g sugars, 1 g fiber), 23 g protein

Glazed Rosemary Pork Roast

PREP: 20 MINUTES ● **COOK:** 4 HOURS ● **YIELD:** 8 SERVINGS

For a change of pace, I'll serve this special pork roast at holiday gatherings. It's a welcome break from traditional turkey or ham, and when dressed with an herb-infused glaze featuring rosemary, thyme and sage, its flavor is unbeatable.

—*Joyce Manier, Beech Grove, Indiana*

1 boneless pork loin roast (3 pounds)	1 teaspoon rubbed sage
1 tablespoon butter	1 teaspoon grated orange peel
1 teaspoon olive oil	½ teaspoon pepper
1 large onion, sliced	¼ teaspoon salt
1 tablespoon brown sugar	⅔ cup apricot jam
1 tablespoon minced fresh rosemary	½ cup orange juice
1 teaspoon dried thyme	1 bay leaf

1. Cut roast in half. In a large skillet, brown roast in butter and oil on all sides. Transfer to a 4- or 5-qt. slow cooker.

2. Add onion to the same skillet; cook and stir until tender. Stir in the brown sugar, herbs, orange peel, pepper and salt. Spread over pork. Combine jam and orange juice; pour over top. Add bay leaf.

3. Cover and cook on low for 4 hours or until a meat thermometer reads 160°. Discard bay leaf.

NUTRITIONAL FACTS
5 OUNCES COOKED PORK: 314 calories, 10 g fat (4 g saturated fat), 88 mg cholesterol, 145 mg sodium, 22 g carbohydrate (13 g sugars, 1 g fiber), 33 g protein

Quick Tip **When cooking a roast over 3 pounds in a slow cooker, be sure to cut it in half before placing it in the slow cooker. This ensures thorough cooking.**

Apple-Cinnamon Pork Loin

PREP: 20 MINUTES • **COOK:** 6 HOURS • **YIELD:** 6 SERVINGS

I love making this slow-cooked dish for chilly fall dinners with my family—the comforting apple-cinnamon aroma fills our whole house. The pork roast tastes even better served with homemade mashed potatoes.

—*Rachel Schultz, Lansing, Michigan*

1 boneless pork loin roast (2 to 3 pounds)	¼ cup honey
½ teaspoon salt	1 small red onion, halved and sliced
¼ teaspoon pepper	1 tablespoon ground cinnamon
1 tablespoon canola oil	Minced fresh parsley, optional
3 medium apples, peeled and sliced, divided	

1. Sprinkle roast with salt and pepper. In a large skillet, brown roast in oil on all sides; cool slightly. With a paring knife, cut about sixteen 3-inch-deep slits in sides of roast; insert one apple slice into each slit.

2. Place half of the remaining apples in a 4-qt. slow cooker. Place roast over apples. Drizzle with honey; top with onion and remaining apples. Sprinkle with cinnamon.

3. Cover and cook on low for 6–8 hours or until meat is tender. Remove pork and apple mixture; keep warm.

4. Transfer cooking juices to a small saucepan. Bring to a boil; cook until liquid is reduced by half. Serve with pork and apple mixture. Sprinkle with parsley if desired.

NUTRITIONAL FACTS
1 SERVING: 290 calories, 10 g fat (3 g saturated fat), 75 mg cholesterol, 241 mg sodium, 22 g carbohydrate (19 g sugars, 2 g fiber), 29 g protein

Honey-Orange Glazed Pork Loin

PREP: 10 MINUTES • **BAKE:** 1¼ HOURS + STANDING • **YIELD:** 12 SERVINGS

After finding this idea in a magazine, I changed it up to make it my own. I like to keep a pork loin in the freezer so we can have this special dish anytime.

—*Marlys Peterson, Centerville, South Dakota*

1	cup orange juice		1	tablespoon ground cumin
½	cup cider vinegar		1½	teaspoons ground cinnamon
½	cup packed brown sugar		1	boneless whole pork loin roast (4 pounds)
¼	cup honey		1	teaspoon salt
2	tablespoons chili powder		¼	teaspoon pepper
1	tablespoon ground coriander			Orange slices, optional

1. In a small saucepan, combine the first eight ingredients. Bring to a boil. Reduce heat; simmer, uncovered, for 45 minutes or until glaze is reduced to 1 cup.

2. Preheat oven to 350°. Sprinkle pork with salt and pepper. Place on a rack in a shallow roasting pan lined with heavy-duty foil. Bake for 1¼ to 1¾ hours or until a meat thermometer reads 160°, brushing occasionally with glaze. Let stand for 10 minutes before slicing. If desired, serve with orange slices.

NUTRITIONAL FACTS
4 OUNCES COOKED PORK: 263 calories, 7 g fat (3 g saturated fat), 75 mg cholesterol, 258 mg sodium, 19 g carbohydrate (17 g sugars, 1 g fiber), 30 g protein

Take-It Tip **If you know you'll be preparing large cuts of meat for a church social, potluck or other fundraiser, watch for sales at grocery stores and stock up in advance. Freeze the meat until needed. Prepare the entree a day before the event, slicing it early on so it can be served easily at the function.**

Pork Tenderloin Medallions with Strawberry Sauce

PREP: 15 MINUTES • **COOK:** 20 MINUTES • **YIELD:** 8 SERVINGS

Pork tenderloin paired with strawberries is a heavenly match, made even more special with a tangy feta garnish. Serve with roasted spring vegetables.

—Katie Wollgast, Florissant, Missouri

1½ cups reduced-sodium beef broth	1 teaspoon garlic powder
2 cups chopped fresh strawberries, divided	½ teaspoon salt
½ cup white wine vinegar	½ teaspoon pepper
¼ cup packed brown sugar	2 tablespoons canola oil
¼ cup reduced-sodium soy sauce	2 tablespoons cornstarch
3 garlic cloves, minced	2 tablespoons cold water
2 pounds pork tenderloin, cut into ½-inch slices	½ cup crumbled feta cheese
	½ cup chopped green onions

1. In a large saucepan, combine broth, 1 cup strawberries, vinegar, brown sugar, soy sauce and garlic; bring to a boil. Reduce heat; simmer, uncovered, 15 minutes or until slightly thickened. Strain mixture and set aside liquid, discarding solids.

2. Sprinkle pork with garlic powder, salt and pepper. In a large skillet, heat oil over medium heat. Brown pork in batches on both sides. Remove and keep warm.

3. Add broth mixture to the pan; bring to a boil. In a small bowl, combine cornstarch and water until smooth and gradually stir into skillet.

4. Return pork to the pan. Bring to a boil. Reduce heat; cook and stir 2 minutes or until sauce is thickened and pork is tender. Top each serving with cheese, onions and remaining strawberries.

NUTRITIONAL FACTS
1 SERVING: 244 calories, 9 g fat (2 g saturated fat), 68 mg cholesterol, 649 mg sodium, 15 g carbohydrate (9 g sugars, 1 g fiber), 25 g protein

Chili-Spiced Pork Chops

PREP/TOTAL TIME: 30 MINUTES ● **YIELD:** 6 SERVINGS

I like my food spicy, and my husband likes his mild. This pleasantly spiced dish makes us both happy—and our son enjoys it, too. It's easy to make, and I always have all the ingredients on hand.

—*Andrea Keith, Kentwood, Michigan*

$\frac{3}{4}$ cup seasoned bread crumbs

3 tablespoons chili powder

$\frac{1}{2}$ teaspoon seasoned salt

1 large egg

$\frac{1}{4}$ cup fat-free milk

6 bone-in pork rib chops
(7 ounces each, $\frac{3}{4}$ inch thick)

1. Preheat oven to 350°. In a shallow bowl, combine the bread crumbs, chili powder and seasoned salt. In another shallow bowl, combine the egg and milk. Dip chops in egg mixture, then coat with crumb mixture.

2. Transfer to a 15x10x1-inch baking pan coated with cooking spray. Bake 20–25 minutes or until meat reaches desired doneness (for medium-rare, a thermometer should read 145°; medium, 160°). Let stand 5 minutes before serving.

NUTRITIONAL FACTS
1 PORK CHOP: 299 calories, 12 g fat (4 g saturated fat), 120 mg cholesterol, 448 mg sodium, 12 g carbohydrate (0 sugars, 1 g fiber), 34 g protein

Quick Tip **A pinch of ground cloves is a terrific addition to pork chops, pork roast and traditional bread dressing.—Lenore G., Woodbury, MN**

Pork Chops & Acorn Squash

PREP: 15 MINUTES ● **COOK:** 4 HOURS ● **YIELD:** 6 SERVINGS

My husband and I can never get enough fresh buttery squash from our garden. These chops cook up sweet and tender in the slow cooker, and the classic, comfort-food flavor doesn't take up my whole day to prepare.

—*Mary Johnson, Coloma, Wisconsin*

6 boneless pork loin chops (4 ounces each)
2 medium acorn squash, halved lengthwise, seeded and sliced
½ cup packed brown sugar
2 tablespoons butter, melted

1 tablespoon orange juice
¾ teaspoon salt
¾ teaspoon browning sauce, optional
½ teaspoon grated orange peel

Place pork chops in a 5-qt. slow cooker; add squash. In a small bowl, mix remaining ingredients; pour over squash. Cook, covered, on low 4–6 hours or until pork is tender.

NUTRITIONAL FACTS
1 PORK CHOP WITH ⅔ CUP SQUASH (CALCULATED WITHOUT BROWNING SAUCE): 317 calories, 10 g fat (5 g saturated fat), 65 mg cholesterol, 365 mg sodium, 34 g carbohydrate (22 g sugars, 2 g fiber), 23 g protein

Make It Ahead

Many slow cooker recipes cook all day. It may be easier to place all ingredients in the crock the night before, then cover and refrigerate overnight. In the morning, place the crock in the slow cooker and select the temperature. *Do not preheat your slow cooker.*

Pork Chops with Scalloped Potatoes

PREP: 25 MINUTES ● **BAKE:** 1½ HOURS ● **YIELD:** 6 SERVINGS

Mom always managed to put a delicious, hearty meal on the table for us and for our farmhands. This all-in-one comforting main dish reminds me of home.

—*Bernice Morris, Marshfield, Missouri*

3 tablespoons butter	2 tablespoons canola oil
3 tablespoons all-purpose flour	Additional salt and pepper, optional
1½ teaspoons salt	6 cups thinly sliced peeled potatoes
¼ teaspoon pepper	1 medium onion, sliced
1 can (14½ ounces) chicken broth	Paprika and minced fresh parsley, optional
6 pork rib or loin chops (¾ inch thick)	

1. Preheat oven to 350°. In a small saucepan, melt butter; stir in the flour, salt and pepper until smooth. Add broth. Bring to a boil; cook and stir for 1 minute or until thickened. Remove from the heat and set aside.

2. In a large skillet, brown the pork chops on both sides in oil; sprinkle with additional salt and pepper if desired.

3. In a greased 13x9-inch baking dish, layer potatoes and onion. Pour broth mixture over layers. Place pork chops on top.

4. Cover and bake for 1 hour; uncover and bake 30 minutes longer or until meat and potatoes are tender. If desired, sprinkle with paprika and parsley.

NUTRITIONAL FACTS
1 SERVING: 574 calories, 29 g fat (11 g saturated fat), 128 mg cholesterol, 1015 mg sodium, 36 g carbohydrate (3 g sugars, 3 g fiber), 40 g protein

Lazy Man's Ribs

PREP: 20 MINUTES ● **COOK:** 5 HOURS ● **YIELD:** 4 SERVINGS

I'll have to admit these ribs are finger-lickin' good and fall-off-the-bone tender! I've made them for a lot of my buddies—including my preacher—and some have even suggested that I try bottling my sauce and selling it to the public!

—Allan Stackhouse Jr., Jennings, Louisiana

2½ pounds pork baby back ribs, cut into eight pieces
2 teaspoons Cajun seasoning
1 medium onion, sliced
1 cup ketchup
½ cup packed brown sugar
⅓ cup orange juice
⅓ cup cider vinegar
¼ cup molasses

2 tablespoons Worcestershire sauce
1 tablespoon barbecue sauce
1 teaspoon stone-ground mustard
1 teaspoon paprika
½ teaspoon garlic powder
½ teaspoon liquid smoke, optional
Dash salt
5 teaspoons cornstarch
1 tablespoon cold water

1. Rub ribs with Cajun seasoning. Layer ribs and onion in a 5-qt. slow cooker. In a small bowl, combine the ketchup, brown sugar, orange juice, vinegar, molasses, Worcestershire sauce, barbecue sauce, mustard, paprika, garlic powder, liquid smoke, if desired, and salt. Pour over ribs. Cover and cook on low for 5–6 hours or until meat is tender.

2. Remove ribs and keep warm. Strain cooking juices and skim fat; transfer to a small saucepan. In a small bowl, combine cornstarch and water until smooth; stir into juices. Bring to a boil; cook and stir for 2 minutes or until thickened. Serve with ribs.

NUTRITIONAL FACTS
2 EACH: 753 calories, 39 g fat (14 g saturated fat), 153 mg cholesterol, 1335 mg sodium, 70 g carbohydrate (52 g sugars, 2 g fiber), 33 g protein

Tender Spareribs

PREP: 10 MINUTES • **COOK:** 5½ HOURS • **YIELD:** 8 SERVINGS

Even my three little ones love this easy-to-make and delicious-to-eat meal. The succulent meat falls right off the bone!

—*Julie Czmer, West Bloomfield, Michigan*

4	pounds pork spareribs, cut into serving-size pieces	¼	cup molasses
¼	cup soy sauce	3	tablespoons cider vinegar
¼	cup prepared mustard	2	tablespoons Worcestershire sauce
		1 to 2	teaspoons hot pepper sauce

Place ribs in a 5-qt. slow cooker. Combine the remaining ingredients; pour over ribs. Cover and cook on low for 5–6 hours or until meat is tender.

NUTRITIONAL FACTS
1 SERVING: 460 calories, 32 g fat (12 g saturated fat), 128 mg cholesterol, 691 mg sodium, 9 g carbohydrate (6 g sugars, 0 fiber), 32 g protein

Take-It Tip **Transporting more than one slow cooker to the church supper and can't find a cardboard box to carry them in? Try setting them in a sturdy laundry basket.**

Farmhouse Pork and Apple Pie

PREP: 70 MINUTES ● **BAKE:** 2 HOURS ● **YIELD:** 10 SERVINGS

I've always loved pork and apples together, and this recipe combines them nicely to create a comforting main dish. It calls for a bit of preparation, but my family and I agree that its wonderful flavor makes it well worth the extra effort.

—*Suzanne Strocsher, Bothell, Washington*

1 pound sliced bacon, cut into 2-inch pieces
3 medium onions, chopped
3 pounds boneless pork, cut into 1-inch cubes
¾ cup all-purpose flour
 Canola oil, optional
3 medium tart apples, peeled and chopped
1 teaspoon rubbed sage
½ teaspoon ground nutmeg

1 teaspoon salt
¼ teaspoon pepper
1 cup apple cider
½ cup water
4 medium potatoes, peeled and cubed
½ cup whole milk
5 tablespoons butter, divided
 Additional salt and pepper
 Minced fresh parsley, optional

1. Preheat oven to 325°. Cook bacon in an ovenproof 12-inch skillet until crisp. Remove with a slotted spoon to paper towels to drain. In drippings, saute onions until tender; remove with slotted spoon and set aside. Dust pork lightly with flour. Brown a third at a time in drippings, adding oil if needed. Remove from the heat and drain.

2. To the pork, add the bacon, onions, apples, sage, nutmeg, salt and pepper. Stir in cider and water. Cover and bake for 2 hours or until pork is tender.

3. Place potatoes in a large saucepan and cover with water. Bring to a boil. Reduce heat; cover and cook for 10–15 minutes or until tender.

4. Drain and mash with milk and 3 tablespoons butter. Add salt and pepper to taste. Remove skillet from the oven and spread potatoes over pork mixture.

5. Melt remaining butter; brush over potatoes. Broil 6 inches from the heat for 5 minutes or until topping is browned. Sprinkle with parsley if desired.

NUTRITIONAL FACTS
1 EACH: 467 calories, 22 g fat (9 g saturated fat), 110 mg cholesterol, 603 mg sodium, 32 g carbohydrate (11 g sugars, 3 g fiber), 36 g protein

Sausage Ratatouille

PREP: 20 MINUTES • **COOK:** 25 MINUTES • **YIELD:** 24 SERVINGS

You'll feel like *Ratatouille*'s great chef, Remy, when you serve this veggie-packed dish party guests will rave about. Don't let the ingredient list fool you: Pantry staples and an easy-cook method make this one a cinch.
—*Janine Freeman, Blaine, Washington*

2 pounds sweet Italian sausage links, cut into ½-inch slices
½ pound fresh green beans, trimmed and cut into 2-inch pieces
2 medium green peppers, julienned
1 large onion, chopped
5 shallots, chopped
2 garlic cloves, minced
2 tablespoons butter
2 tablespoons olive oil
4 medium zucchini, quartered and sliced
5 plum tomatoes, chopped
½ teaspoon sugar
½ teaspoon salt
¼ teaspoon pepper
¼ teaspoon crushed red pepper flakes
⅛ teaspoon ground allspice
¼ cup minced fresh parsley
⅓ cup grated Parmesan cheese
Hot cooked rice

1. In a large skillet, cook sausage over medium heat until no longer pink; drain. Remove and keep warm.

2. In the same skillet, cook the beans, green peppers, onion, shallots and garlic in butter and oil over medium heat until tender. Stir in the zucchini, tomatoes, sugar, salt, pepper, pepper flakes and allspice. Cook and stir for 6–8 minutes or until vegetables are tender.

3. Stir in sausage and parsley; heat through. Sprinkle with cheese. Serve with rice.

NUTRITIONAL FACTS
½ CUP (CALCULATED WITHOUT RICE): 168 calories, 12 g fat (5 g saturated fat), 30 mg cholesterol, 396 mg sodium, 7 g carbohydrate (3 g sugars, 1 g fiber), 8 g protein

Eggplant Sausage Casserole

PREP: 45 MINUTES ● **BAKE:** 45 MINUTES + STANDING ● **YIELD:** 12 SERVINGS

If you want your kids to happily eat their eggplant, serve it in this lovely layered casserole. Our whole family enjoys it. Always a popular potluck item, it's a great company dish, as well.

—*Carol Mieske, Red Bluff, California*

- 1 package (16 ounces) penne pasta
- 2 pounds bulk Italian sausage
- 1 medium eggplant, peeled and cubed
- 1 large onion, chopped
- 2 tablespoons olive oil
- 2 garlic cloves, minced
- 1 can (28 ounces) diced tomatoes, undrained
- 1 can (6 ounces) tomato paste
- 1 teaspoon salt
- 1 teaspoon dried basil
- 1 teaspoon paprika
- 1 carton (15 ounces) ricotta cheese
- 4 cups shredded part-skim mozzarella cheese, divided

1. Preheat oven to 350°. Cook pasta according to package directions. Meanwhile, in a large skillet, cook sausage over medium heat until no longer pink; drain. Set sausage aside.

2. In the same skillet, saute eggplant and onion in oil. Add garlic; cook 1 minute longer. Stir in the tomatoes, tomato paste, salt, basil and paprika; simmer, partially covered, for 15 minutes. Remove from the heat. Drain pasta; stir into eggplant mixture. Add sausage.

3. Spread half of the sausage mixture in a greased 13x9-inch baking dish. Spread with ricotta cheese. Top with half of the cheese and remaining sausage mixture.

4. Cover and bake for 40 minutes. Uncover; sprinkle with remaining cheese. Bake 5 minutes longer or until cheese is melted. Let stand for 10 minutes before serving.

NUTRITIONAL FACTS
1 EACH: 606 calories, 36 g fat (15 g saturated fat), 94 mg cholesterol, 1066 mg sodium, 41 g carbohydrate (11 g sugars, 4 g fiber), 31 g protein

Sausage Lasagna Rolls

PREP: 45 MINUTES ● **BAKE:** 45 MINUTES ● **YIELD:** 2 CASSEROLES (6 SERVINGS EACH)

Who said lasagna noodles have to lie flat? This artful interpretation of layered comfort food—with a twist—is what we like to call "casser-roll."

—*Kali Wraspir, Olympia, Washington*

12 lasagna noodles
1 pound bulk Italian sausage
2 jars (26 ounces each) spaghetti sauce
1 carton (15 ounces) ricotta cheese
2 cups shredded part-skim mozzarella cheese, divided
¾ cup shredded Parmesan cheese, divided
1 large egg
2 tablespoons minced fresh parsley or 2 teaspoons dried parsley flakes

2½ teaspoons minced fresh rosemary or ¾ teaspoon dried rosemary, crushed
2 teaspoons lemon juice
1½ teaspoons minced fresh thyme or ½ teaspoon dried thyme
1 teaspoon grated lemon peel
1 teaspoon coarsely ground pepper
½ teaspoon salt

1. Preheat oven to 350°. Cook noodles according to package directions.

2. Meanwhile, in a large skillet, cook sausage over medium heat until no longer pink; drain. Stir in spaghetti sauce.

3. In a large bowl, combine ricotta, 1 cup mozzarella, ¼ cup Parmesan, egg, parsley, rosemary, lemon juice, thyme, lemon peel, pepper and salt. Drain noodles. Spread 2 tablespoons cheese mixture on each noodle; carefully roll up.

4. Spread ⅔ cup meat sauce into each of two greased 11x7-inch baking dishes. Place roll-ups seam side down over sauce. Top with remaining meat sauce. Sprinkle with remaining mozzarella and Parmesan cheeses.

5. Cover and bake 45–50 minutes or until bubbly.

NUTRITIONAL FACTS
1 EACH: 380 calories, 18 g fat (8 g saturated fat), 64 mg cholesterol, 1113 mg sodium, 34 g carbohydrate (12 g sugars, 3 g fiber), 21 g protein

Freeze It **Cover and freeze unbaked casseroles up to 3 months. To use, thaw in the refrigerator overnight. Remove from refrigerator 30 minutes before baking. Preheat oven to 350°. Cover and bake 50–60 minutes or until bubbly.**

Florentine Spaghetti Bake

PREP: 30 MINUTES • **BAKE:** 1 HOUR + STANDING • **YIELD:** 9 SERVINGS

This plate-filling sausage dish appeals to most every appetite, from basic meat-and-potatoes fans to gourmets. My daughter, a Montana wheat rancher's wife, says she serves it often to satisfy her hardworking family.

—Lorraine Martin, Lincoln, California

- 8 ounces uncooked spaghetti
- 1 pound bulk Italian sausage
- 1 large onion, chopped
- 1 garlic clove, minced
- 1 jar (24 ounces) pasta sauce
- 1 can (4 ounces) mushroom stems and pieces, drained
- 1 large egg, lightly beaten

- 2 cups (16 ounces) 4% cottage cheese
- 1 package (10 ounces) frozen chopped spinach, thawed and squeezed dry
- $\frac{1}{4}$ cup grated Parmesan cheese
- $\frac{1}{2}$ teaspoon seasoned salt
- $\frac{1}{4}$ teaspoon pepper
- 2 cups shredded part-skim mozzarella cheese

1. Preheat oven to 375°. Cook pasta according to package directions. Meanwhile, in a large skillet over medium heat, cook sausage and onion, crumbling meat, until sausage is no longer pink. Add garlic; cook 1 minute longer. Drain. Stir in pasta sauce and mushrooms. Bring to a boil. Reduce heat; cover and cook until heated through, about 15 minutes.

2. Drain pasta. Combine the egg with the next five ingredients. Spread 1 cup sausage mixture in a greased 13x9-inch baking dish. Top with spaghetti and remaining sausage mixture. Layer with egg mixture and mozzarella cheese.

3. Cover and bake 45 minutes. Uncover; bake until lightly browned and heated through, about 15 minutes longer. Let stand 15 minutes before cutting.

NUTRITIONAL FACTS
1 PIECE: 449 calories, 23 g fat (9 g saturated fat), 83 mg cholesterol, 1218 mg sodium, 35 g carbohydrate (10 g sugars, 4 g fiber), 25 g protein

Ham with Cranberry-Pineapple Sauce

PREP: 15 MINUTES • **COOK:** 5 HOURS • **YIELD:** 20 SERVINGS (4$\frac{1}{2}$ CUPS SAUCE)

Flag this dish for the times you crave the mouthwatering combo of cranberry, pineapple and stone-ground mustard served with thick slices of smoky boneless ham.

—*Carole Resnick, Cleveland, Ohio*

1 fully cooked boneless ham (5 to 6 pounds)	2 garlic cloves, minced
12 whole cloves	2 tablespoons stone-ground mustard
1 can (20 ounces) crushed pineapple, undrained	$\frac{1}{2}$ teaspoon coarsely ground pepper
1 can (14 ounces) whole-berry cranberry sauce	2 tablespoons cornstarch
	2 tablespoons cold water

1. Score the ham, making $\frac{1}{2}$-inch-deep diamond shapes; insert a clove in each diamond. Place ham in a 5-qt. slow cooker. In a large bowl, combine the pineapple, cranberry sauce, garlic, mustard and pepper; pour over ham.

2. Cover and cook on low for 5–6 hours or until a thermometer reads 140°. Remove meat to a cutting board and keep warm; remove and discard cloves.

3. Transfer sauce to a small saucepan. Bring to a boil. In a small bowl, combine cornstarch and water until smooth; gradually stir into pan. Bring to a boil; cook and stir for 2 minutes or until thickened. Slice ham and serve with sauce.

NUTRITIONAL FACTS
4 OUNCES HAM WITH 3 TABLESPOONS SAUCE: 176 calories, 4 g fat (1 g saturated fat), 58 mg cholesterol, 1218 mg sodium, 14 g carbohydrate (10 g sugars, 1 g fiber), 21 g protein

Pretty Penne Ham Skillet

PREP/TOTAL TIME: 30 MINUTES • **YIELD:** 6 SERVINGS

I'm a busy nurse, so fast meals are a must. This pasta is a tasty change of pace from potato-ham casseroles.

—Kathy Stephan, West Seneca, New York

- 1 package (16 ounces) penne pasta
- 1/4 cup olive oil
- 3 tablespoons butter
- 3 cups cubed fully cooked ham
- 1 large sweet red pepper, finely chopped
- 1 medium onion, chopped
- 2 garlic cloves, minced
- 1/4 cup minced fresh parsley

- 1 1/2 teaspoons minced fresh basil or 1/2 teaspoon dried basil
- 1 1/2 teaspoons minced fresh oregano or 1/2 teaspoon dried oregano
- 1 can (14 1/2 ounces) chicken broth
- 1 tablespoon lemon juice
- 1/2 cup shredded Parmesan cheese

1. Cook pasta according to package directions; drain. Meanwhile, in a large skillet, heat oil and butter over medium-high heat. Add ham, red pepper and onion; cook and stir 4–6 minutes or until ham is browned and vegetables are tender. Add garlic and herbs; cook 1–2 minutes longer.

2. Stir in broth and lemon juice. Bring to a boil. Reduce heat; simmer, uncovered, 10–15 minutes or until liquid is reduced by half. Add pasta; toss to combine. Sprinkle with cheese.

NUTRITIONAL FACTS
1 2/3 CUPS: 567 calories, 24 g fat (8 g saturated fat), 57 mg cholesterol, 1344 mg sodium, 62 g carbohydrate (5 g sugars, 4 g fiber), 27 g protein

Quick Tip
My grandma used to add some sugar to the salted water when she boiled macaroni or spaghetti. I still do this, and the pasta has much better flavor.—Judy N., Hawley, MN

Broiled Chicken & Artichokes

PREP/TOTAL TIME: 15 MINUTES ● **YIELD:** 8 SERVINGS

My wife and I first made this chicken entree as newlyweds and have been hooked ever since. We love it because it's so simple and affordable, yet delicious and healthy. Can't beat that. We make it almost weekly.

—*Chris Koon, Midlothian, Virginia*

8 boneless skinless chicken thighs (about 2 pounds)

2 jars (7½ ounces each) marinated quartered artichoke hearts, drained

2 tablespoons olive oil

1 teaspoon salt

½ teaspoon pepper

¼ cup shredded Parmesan cheese

2 tablespoons minced fresh parsley

1. Preheat broiler. In a large bowl, toss chicken and artichokes with oil, salt and pepper. Transfer to a broiler pan.

2. Broil 3 inches from heat 8–10 minutes or until a thermometer inserted in chicken reads 170°, turning chicken and artichokes halfway through cooking. Sprinkle with cheese. Broil 1–2 minutes longer or until cheese is melted. Sprinkle with parsley.

NUTRITIONAL FACTS
1 SERVING: 288 calories, 21 g fat (5 g saturated fat), 77 mg cholesterol, 584 mg sodium, 4 g carbohydrate (0 sugars, 0 fiber), 22 g protein

Quick Tip

Buying skinned and boned chicken can cut up to 15 minutes off your cooking time. Save money by buying larger packages when they're on sale, then rewrap each breast individually or in family-size portions and freeze. Pull out and thaw whenever you need a quick chicken dinner.

Teriyaki Chicken Thighs

PREP: 15 MINUTES ● **COOK:** 4 HOURS ● **YIELD:** 8 SERVINGS

Here's a real slow-cooker sensation: Asian-style chicken and rice. It always goes over big with my family.

—*Gigi Miller, Stoughton, Wisconsin*

3 pounds boneless skinless chicken thighs	$\frac{3}{4}$ teaspoon ground ginger
$\frac{3}{4}$ cup sugar	$\frac{1}{4}$ teaspoon pepper
$\frac{3}{4}$ cup reduced-sodium soy sauce	4 teaspoons cornstarch
$\frac{1}{3}$ cup cider vinegar	4 teaspoons cold water
1 garlic clove, minced	Hot cooked rice, optional

1. Place chicken in a 4- or 5-qt. slow cooker. In a small bowl, mix sugar, soy sauce, vinegar, garlic, ginger and pepper; pour over chicken. Cook, covered, on low 4–5 hours or until chicken is tender.

2. Remove chicken to a serving platter; keep warm. Transfer cooking juices to a small saucepan; skim fat. Bring cooking juices to a boil. In a small bowl, mix cornstarch and cold water until smooth; stir into cooking juices. Return to a boil; cook and stir 1–2 minutes or until thickened. Serve with chicken and, if desired, rice.

NUTRITIONAL FACTS
5 OUNCES COOKED CHICKEN WITH $\frac{1}{3}$ CUP SAUCE: 342 calories, 12 g fat (3 g saturated fat), 113 mg cholesterol, 958 mg sodium, 22 g carbohydrate (19 g sugars, 0 fiber), 33 g protein

Quick Tip **Wash the insert to your slow cooker in the dishwasher or in warm soapy water. Avoid using abrasive cleansers since they may scratch the stoneware.**

Chicken with Apple-Chardonnay Gravy

PREP: 20 MINUTES ● **COOK:** 6 HOURS ● **YIELD:** 6 SERVINGS

I create all my own recipes by experimenting with various ingredients in the kitchen. I love this savory slow-cooker chicken dish because it's easy, affordable and fills the house with awesome aromas that make your mouth water.

—*Theresa Retelle, Appleton, Wisconsin*

- 6 chicken leg quarters
- ½ teaspoon salt
- ¼ teaspoon pepper
- 2 large sweet apples, peeled and cut into wedges
- 1 large sweet onion, chopped
- 2 celery ribs, chopped
- ½ cup chardonnay
- 1 envelope brown gravy mix
- 2 large garlic cloves, minced
- 1 teaspoon each minced fresh oregano, rosemary and thyme
- Hot mashed potatoes

1. Sprinkle chicken with salt and pepper. Place half of the chicken in a 5-qt. slow cooker. In a bowl, combine the apples, onion and celery; spoon half of the mixture over chicken. Repeat layers.

2. In the same bowl, whisk wine, gravy mix, garlic and herbs until blended; pour over top. Cover and cook on low for 6–8 hours or until chicken is tender.

3. Remove chicken to a serving platter; keep warm. Cool apple mixture slightly; skim fat. In a blender, cover and process apple mixture in batches until smooth. Transfer to a saucepan and heat through over medium heat, stirring occasionally. Serve with chicken and mashed potatoes.

NUTRITIONAL FACTS
1 CHICKEN LEG QUARTER WITH ¾ CUP GRAVY (CALCULATED WITHOUT POTATOES): 356 calories, 17 g fat (4 g saturated fat), 105 mg cholesterol, 532 mg sodium, 15 g carbohydrate (10 g sugars, 2 g fiber), 32 g protein

Prosciutto Chicken Cacciatore

PREP: 30 MINUTES • **COOK:** 4 HOURS • **YIELD:** 6–8 SERVINGS

I tailored my mother's recipe so I can slow-cook this hearty entree for busy weekday nights.

—*Sandra Putnam, Gallatin Gateway, Montana*

2 pounds boneless skinless chicken thighs

1½ pounds boneless skinless chicken breast halves

½ cup all-purpose flour

1 teaspoon salt

¼ teaspoon pepper

3 tablespoons olive oil

1 can (14½ ounces) chicken broth

1 can (14½ ounces) diced tomatoes, undrained

1 cup sliced fresh mushrooms

1 medium onion, chopped

1 package (3 ounces) thinly sliced prosciutto or deli ham, coarsely chopped

1 tablespoon diced pimientos

2 garlic cloves, minced

½ teaspoon Italian seasoning

Hot cooked linguine

Grated Parmesan cheese

1. Cut chicken into serving-size pieces. In a large resealable plastic bag, combine the flour, salt and pepper. Add chicken, a few pieces at a time, and shake to coat.

2. In a large skillet, brown chicken in oil in batches. Transfer to a 5-qt. slow cooker.

3. Stir in the broth, tomatoes, mushrooms, onion, prosciutto, pimientos, garlic and Italian seasoning. Cover and cook on low for 4–4½ hours or until chicken juices run clear. Serve with a slotted spoon over linguine; sprinkle with cheese.

NUTRITIONAL FACTS

1 CUP: 375 calories, 17 g fat (4 g saturated fat), 133 mg cholesterol, 892 mg sodium, 11 g carbohydrate (3 g sugars, 2 g fiber), 43 g protein

Pan-Roasted Chicken and Vegetables

PREP: 15 MINUTES ● **BAKE:** 45 MINUTES ● **YIELD:** 6 SERVINGS

This one-dish meal tastes like it needs hours of hands-on time to put together, but it's just minutes to prep the simple ingredients. So easy.

—Sherri Melotik, Oak Creek, Wisconsin

2 pounds red potatoes (about 6 medium), cut into ¾-inch pieces

1 large onion, coarsely chopped

2 tablespoons olive oil

3 garlic cloves, minced

1¼ teaspoons salt, divided

1 teaspoon dried rosemary, crushed, divided

¾ teaspoon pepper, divided

½ teaspoon paprika

6 bone-in chicken thighs (about 2¼ pounds), skin removed

6 cups fresh baby spinach (about 6 ounces)

1. Preheat oven to 425°. In a large bowl, combine potatoes, onion, oil, garlic, ¾ teaspoon salt, ½ teaspoon rosemary and ½ teaspoon pepper; toss to coat. Transfer to a 15x10x1-inch baking pan coated with cooking spray.

2. In a small bowl, mix paprika and the remaining salt, rosemary and pepper. Sprinkle chicken with paprika mixture; arrange over vegetables. Roast until a thermometer inserted in chicken reads 170°–175° and vegetables are just tender, 35–40 minutes.

3. Remove chicken to a serving platter; keep warm. Top vegetables with spinach. Roast until vegetables are tender and spinach is wilted, 8–10 minutes longer. Stir vegetables to combine; serve with chicken.

NUTRITIONAL FACTS
1 CHICKEN THIGH WITH 1 CUP VEGETABLES: 357 calories, 14 g fat (3 g saturated fat), 87 mg cholesterol, 597 mg sodium, 28 g carbohydrate (3 g sugars, 4 g fiber), 28 g protein

Potluck Fried Chicken

PREP: 40 MINUTES • **BAKE:** 25 MINUTES • **YIELD:** 12 SERVINGS

This Sunday dinner staple is first fried and then baked to a crispy golden brown. Well-seasoned with oregano and sage, this classic is sure to satisfy diners at church potlucks or late-summer picnics, too. I love fixing it for family and friends.

—Donna Kuhaupt, Slinger, Wisconsin

1½ cups all-purpose flour	1 teaspoon pepper
½ cup cornmeal	2 large eggs
¼ cup cornstarch	¼ cup water
3 teaspoons salt	2 broiler/fryer chickens
2 teaspoons paprika	(3 to 4 pounds each), cut up
1 teaspoon dried oregano	Oil for frying
1 teaspoon rubbed sage	

1. Preheat oven to 350°. In a large resealable plastic bag, combine the flour, cornmeal, cornstarch, salt, paprika, oregano, sage and pepper. In a shallow bowl, beat eggs and water. Dip chicken in egg mixture; place in the bag, a few pieces at a time, and shake to coat.

2. In an electric skillet, heat 1 inch of oil to 375°. Fry chicken, a few pieces at a time, for 3–5 minutes on each side or until golden and crispy.

3. Place in two ungreased 15x10x1-inch baking pans. Bake, uncovered, for 25–30 minutes or until juices run clear.

NUTRITIONAL FACTS
1 SERVING: 497 calories, 29 g fat (6 g saturated fat), 135 mg cholesterol, 693 mg sodium, 20 g carbohydrate (0 sugars, 1 g fiber), 36 g protein

Soy-Garlic Chicken

PREP: 10 MINUTES • **COOK:** 4 HOURS • **YIELD:** 6 SERVINGS

Because I am a full-time mom and help my husband on our ranch, I'm always looking for simple yet hearty meals for the slow cooker. My family really likes this one.

—*Colleen Faber, Buffalo, Montana*

6 chicken leg quarters, skin removed	¼ cup packed brown sugar
1 can (8 ounces) tomato sauce	2 teaspoons minced garlic
½ cup reduced-sodium soy sauce	

1. With a sharp knife, cut leg quarters at the joints if desired. Place in a 4-qt. slow cooker. In a small bowl, combine the tomato sauce, soy sauce, brown sugar and garlic; pour over chicken.

2. Cover and cook on low for 4–5 hours or until chicken is tender.

NUTRITIONAL FACTS
1 EACH: 245 calories, 8 g fat (2 g saturated fat), 90 mg cholesterol, 1063 mg sodium, 12 g carbohydrate (9 g sugars, 0 fiber), 28 g protein

Freeze It **Cool chicken in sauce. Freeze in freezer containers. To use, partially thaw in refrigerator overnight. Heat through slowly in a covered skillet until a thermometer inserted in chicken reads 165°, stirring occasionally and adding a little broth or water if necessary.**

Slow-Cooked Lemon Chicken

PREP: 20 MINUTES • **COOK:** 5¼ HOURS • **YIELD:** 6 SERVINGS

Garlic, oregano and lemon juice give spark to this memorable main dish. It's easy to fix—just brown the chicken in a skillet, then let the slow cooker do the work. I like to serve this dish to company.

—*Walter Powell, Wilmington, Delaware*

6 bone-in chicken breast halves
   (12 ounces each), skin removed
1 teaspoon dried oregano
½ teaspoon seasoned salt
¼ teaspoon pepper
2 tablespoons butter

¼ cup water
3 tablespoons lemon juice
2 garlic cloves, minced
1 teaspoon chicken bouillon granules
2 teaspoons minced fresh parsley
   Hot cooked rice

1. Pat chicken dry with paper towels. In a small bowl, combine the oregano, seasoned salt and pepper; rub over chicken. In a skillet over medium heat, brown the chicken in butter; transfer to a 5-qt. slow cooker. Add water, lemon juice, garlic and bouillon to the skillet; bring to a boil, stirring to loosen browned bits. Pour over chicken.

2. Cover and cook on low for 5–6 hours. Baste chicken with cooking juices. Add parsley. Cover and cook 15–30 minutes longer or until meat juices run clear. If desired, remove chicken to a platter and keep warm; thicken cooking juices. Serve over chicken and rice.

NUTRITIONAL FACTS
1 CHICKEN BREAST HALF: 336 calories, 10 g fat (4 g saturated fat), 164 mg cholesterol, 431 mg sodium, 1 g carbohydrate (0 sugars, 0 fiber), 56 g protein

Quick Tip When I have a hands-on job like forming meatballs or skinning chicken, I wear disposable gloves to keep my hands clean.—Paul V., Whiting, NJ

Casablanca Chutney Chicken

PREP: 25 MINUTES ● **COOK:** 7 HOURS ● **YIELD:** 4 SERVINGS

If you enjoy Indian food, you'll love this dish. An array of spices and dried fruit slow cook with boneless chicken thighs for an aromatic and satisfying meal. To make it complete, serve over jasmine or basmati rice.

—*Roxanne Chan, Albany, California*

1	pound boneless skinless chicken thighs, cut into ¾-inch pieces
1	can (14½ ounces) chicken broth
⅓	cup finely chopped onion
⅓	cup chopped sweet red pepper
⅓	cup chopped carrot
⅓	cup chopped dried apricots
⅓	cup chopped dried figs
⅓	cup golden raisins
2	tablespoons orange marmalade
1	tablespoon mustard seed
2	garlic cloves, minced
½	teaspoon curry powder
¼	teaspoon crushed red pepper flakes
¼	teaspoon ground cumin
¼	teaspoon ground cinnamon
¼	teaspoon ground cloves
2	tablespoons minced fresh parsley
2	tablespoons minced fresh mint
1	tablespoon lemon juice
4	tablespoons chopped pistachios

1. In a 3-qt. slow cooker, combine the first 16 ingredients. Cover and cook on low for 7–8 hours or until chicken is tender.

2. Stir in the parsley, mint and lemon juice; heat through. Sprinkle each serving with pistachios.

NUTRITIONAL FACTS
1 CUP: 389 calories, 13 g fat (3 g saturated fat), 78 mg cholesterol, 567 mg sodium, 44 g carbohydrate (31 g sugars, 6 g fiber), 26 g protein

Parmesan Chicken

PREP: 10 MINUTES ● **BAKE:** 25 MINUTES ● **YIELD:** 6 SERVINGS

The savory coating on this chicken has the satisfying flavor of Parmesan cheese. It's easy enough to be a family weekday meal yet impressive enough to serve to guests. When I make this chicken for dinner, we never have leftovers.

—Schelby Thompson, Camden Wyoming, Delaware

½ cup butter, melted

2 teaspoons Dijon mustard

1 teaspoon Worcestershire sauce

½ teaspoon salt

1 cup dry bread crumbs

½ cup grated Parmesan cheese

6 boneless skinless chicken breast halves (7 ounces each)

1. Preheat oven to 350°. In a shallow bowl, combine butter, mustard, Worcestershire sauce and salt. Place bread crumbs and cheese in another shallow bowl. Dip chicken in butter mixture, then in bread crumb mixture, patting to help coating adhere.

2. Place in an ungreased 15x10x1-inch baking pan. Drizzle with any remaining butter mixture. Bake, uncovered, 25–30 minutes or until a thermometer reads 170°.

NUTRITIONAL FACTS

1 CHICKEN BREAST HALF: 270 calories, 16 g fat (9 g saturated fat), 82 mg cholesterol, 552 mg sodium, 10 g carbohydrate (1 g sugars, 0 fiber), 21 g protein

Creamy Garlic-Lemon Chicken

PREP: 15 MINUTES ● **COOK:** 3 HOURS ● **YIELD:** 6 SERVINGS

I needed an easy way to prepare my family's favorite meal, lemon chicken, and this recipe is it! My entire family loves this rich slow-cooker dish, and everyone who eats it asks for the recipe—it's a keeper. I serve the chicken over a bed of rice or couscous and spoon some of the creamy sauce over the top.

—*Nan Slaughter, Sammamish, Washington*

1 cup vegetable broth	6 boneless skinless chicken breast halves (6 ounces each)
1½ teaspoons grated lemon peel	
3 tablespoons lemon juice	2 tablespoons butter
2 tablespoons capers, drained	2 tablespoons all-purpose flour
3 garlic cloves, minced	½ cup heavy whipping cream
½ teaspoon pepper	Hot cooked rice

1. In a small bowl, combine the first six ingredients. Place chicken in a 5-qt. slow cooker; pour broth mixture over chicken. Cook, covered, on low 3–4 hours or until chicken is tender.

2. Remove chicken from slow cooker; keep warm. In a large saucepan, melt butter over medium heat. Stir in flour until smooth; gradually whisk in cooking juices. Bring to a boil, stirring constantly; cook and stir 1–2 minutes or until thickened. Remove from heat and stir in cream. Serve chicken and rice with sauce.

NUTRITIONAL FACTS
1 CHICKEN BREAST HALF WITH ½ CUP SAUCE (CALCULATED WITHOUT RICE): 301 calories, 15 g fat (8 g saturated fat), 127 mg cholesterol, 297 mg sodium, 4 g carbohydrate (1 g sugars, 0 fiber), 35 g protein

Slow Cooker Sizes

HOUSEHOLD SIZE	SLOW COOKER CAPACITY
1 to 2 people	2 to 3½ quarts
3 to 4 people	3½ to 4½ quarts
4 to 5 people	4½ to 5 quarts
6 or more people	5 to 7 quarts

Honey Pineapple Chicken

PREP: 15 MINUTES • **COOK:** 3 HOURS • **YIELD:** 8 SERVINGS

Sweet pineapple and salty soy sauce season a flavorful chicken dish. I adapted the recipe for my slow cooker because it's so much easier to do the preparation hours in advance, then let it simmer all day.

—*Carol Gillespie, Chambersburg, Pennsylvania*

3 pounds boneless skinless chicken breast halves

2 tablespoons canola oil

1 can (8 ounces) unsweetened crushed pineapple, undrained

1 cup packed brown sugar

$\frac{1}{2}$ cup honey

$\frac{1}{3}$ cup lemon juice

$\frac{1}{4}$ cup butter, melted

2 tablespoons prepared mustard

2 teaspoons reduced-sodium soy sauce

1. In a large skillet, brown chicken in oil in batches on both sides; transfer to a 5-qt. slow cooker. In a small bowl, combine the remaining ingredients; pour over chicken.

2. Cover and cook on low for 3–4 hours or until meat is tender. Strain cooking liquid, reserving pineapple. Serve pineapple with the chicken.

NUTRITIONAL FACTS
1 SERVING: 455 calories, 13 g fat (5 g saturated fat), 109 mg cholesterol, 226 mg sodium, 50 g carbohydrate (48 g sugars, 0 fiber), 35 g protein

Freeze It **Cool chicken mixture. Freeze in freezer containers. To use, partially thaw in refrigerator overnight. Heat through slowly in a covered skillet until a thermometer inserted in chicken reads 165°, stirring occasionally and adding a little water if necessary.**

South Carolina Chicken & Rice

PREP: 10 MINUTES • **COOK:** 50 MINUTES • **YIELD:** 12 SERVINGS

Chicken Bog is the traditional name for this South Carolina Low-Country dish. We always make a big batch the day after Thanksgiving, when we're working on our family's Christmas tree farm.
—*Jean Cochran, Lexington, South Carolina*

2½ pounds boneless skinless chicken thighs	1 large onion, finely chopped
8 cups chicken broth, divided	3 cups uncooked long-grain rice
2 packages (13 to 14 ounces each) smoked sausage, sliced	Salt and pepper to taste

1. In a 6-quart stockpot, cook chicken in 2 cups broth over medium heat until a thermometer reads 170°, turning halfway through cooking. Remove chicken; set aside to cool. Add sausage, onion and remaining broth to stockpot; bring to a boil. Add rice. Reduce heat; simmer, uncovered, 15–18 minutes or until rice is almost tender (mixture may be soupy).

2. Shred chicken; add to rice. Cook, covered, until rice is tender. Season with salt and pepper to taste.

NUTRITIONAL FACTS
1 CUP (CALCULATED WITHOUT SALT): 528 calories, 24 g fat (9 g saturated fat), 107 mg cholesterol, 1402 mg sodium, 43 g carbohydrate (3 g sugars, 1 g fiber), 31 g protein

Creamed Chicken over Beans

PREP/TOTAL TIME: 15 MINUTES ● **YIELD:** 4 SERVINGS

This simple but tasty blend will surprise you. It uses leftover chicken and frozen green beans, so it's fast to fix for a brunch or light lunch.

—Louise Martin, Denver, Pennsylvania

¼ cup butter

¼ cup all-purpose flour

½ teaspoon salt

⅛ teaspoon pepper

1½ cups water

¼ cup whole milk

1 teaspoon chicken bouillon granules

2 cups cubed cooked chicken

1 package (16 ounces) frozen cut green beans, cooked and drained

Paprika, optional

In a large saucepan, melt butter. Stir in the flour, salt and pepper until smooth. Gradually add the water, milk and bouillon. Bring to a boil; cook and stir for 2 minutes or until thickened. Add the chicken and heat through. Serve over beans. Sprinkle with paprika if desired.

NUTRITIONAL FACTS
1 CUP: 307 calories, 17 g fat (9 g saturated fat), 95 mg cholesterol, 818 mg sodium, 14 g carbohydrate (4 g sugars, 3 g fiber), 23 g protein

Quick Tip

When organizing a buffet, most folks stack the plates, eating utensils, and napkins at the front of the table. Moving the silverware and napkins to the end of the buffet, however, frees up guests' hands since they only have to balance their plates as they work their way through the line.

Slow Cooker Buffalo Chicken Lasagna

PREP: 25 MINUTES ● **COOK:** 4 HOURS + STANDING ● **YIELD:** 8 SERVINGS

When I make this tasty chicken lasagna at home, I use a whole bottle of Buffalo wing sauce because my family likes it nice and spicy. Increase the pasta sauce and use less wing sauce if you prefer.

—Heidi Pepin, Sykesville, Maryland

1½ pounds ground chicken	9 no-cook lasagna noodles
1 tablespoon olive oil	2 medium sweet red peppers, chopped
1 bottle (12 ounces) Buffalo wing sauce	½ cup crumbled blue cheese or feta cheese
1½ cups meatless spaghetti sauce	Chopped celery and additional crumbled blue cheese, optional
1 carton (15 ounces) ricotta cheese	
2 cups shredded part-skim mozzarella cheese	

1. In a Dutch oven, cook chicken in oil over medium heat until no longer pink; drain. Stir in wing sauce and spaghetti sauce. In a small bowl, mix ricotta and mozzarella cheeses.

2. Spread 1 cup sauce onto the bottom of an oval 6-qt. slow cooker. Layer with three noodles (breaking noodles to fit), 1 cup sauce, a third of the peppers and a third of the cheese mixture. Repeat layers twice. Top with remaining sauce; sprinkle with blue cheese.

3. Cover and cook on low for 4–5 hours or until noodles are tender. Let stand 15 minutes before serving. Top with celery and additional blue cheese if desired.

NUTRITIONAL FACTS
1 SERVING (CALCULATED WITHOUT OPTIONAL INGREDIENTS): 445 calories, 23 g fat (11 g saturated fat), 104 mg cholesterol, 1996 mg sodium, 28 g carbohydrate (9 g sugars, 3 g fiber), 33 g protein

Helpful Foil Handles

Layered dishes or meat loaves are easier to get out of the slow cooker using foil handles. Here's how:

● Cut three 20- x 3-inch strips of heavy-duty aluminum foil or create them by folding wider strips of regular foil. Crisscross the strips so they resemble the spokes of a wheel.

● Place the meat loaf in the center of the strips, and pull them up and bend the edges to form handles.

● Grasp the foil handles to lift the loaf and lower it into the slow cooker. Leave the foil in while you cook so you can easily lift the meat out to serve.

● For a layered dish, place the strips in the cooker and up the sides before putting in the food. Leave them in. Once the food is cooked, pull the strips together as a handle to neatly remove the food in one piece.

Chicken and Olive Mole Casserole

PREP: 50 MINUTES • **BAKE:** 40 MINUTES + STANDING • **YIELD:** 8 SERVINGS

My Southwestern chicken casserole makes the perfect party dish when you're looking for something a little out of the ordinary. The mole sauce lends an authentic flavor, and folks are always pleasantly surprised to taste a little sweetness from the chocolate.

—Barbara White, Livingston, Texas

- 2 large onions, finely chopped, divided
- 3 tablespoons olive oil
- 3 garlic cloves, minced
- 1 teaspoon salt
- 1 teaspoon dried oregano
- 1 teaspoon ground cumin
- $\frac{1}{4}$ teaspoon ground cinnamon
- 5 tablespoons chili powder
- 3 tablespoons all-purpose flour
- $4\frac{1}{2}$ cups reduced-sodium chicken broth
- $\frac{1}{2}$ ounce semisweet chocolate, coarsely chopped
- 6 cups shredded cooked chicken
- 12 corn tortillas (6 inches), warmed
- 1 cup sliced pimiento-stuffed olives
- 4 cups shredded Monterey Jack cheese

1. Preheat oven to 375°. In a large saucepan, saute 1 cup onion in oil until tender. Reduce heat to low. Add the garlic, salt, oregano, cumin and cinnamon; cover and cook for 10 minutes. Stir in chili powder and flour until blended. Gradually stir in broth. Bring to a boil. Cook until mixture is reduced to 3 cups, about 35 minutes. Remove from the heat; stir in chocolate.

2. In a large bowl, combine chicken and $\frac{1}{2}$ cup sauce. Spread $\frac{1}{2}$ cup sauce into a greased 13x9-inch baking dish. Layer with half of the tortillas, chicken mixture, remaining onion and olives. Top with 1 cup sauce and 2 cups cheese. Repeat layers.

3. Cover and bake for 30 minutes. Uncover; bake 10–15 minutes longer or until cheese is melted. Let stand for 10 minutes before serving.

NUTRITIONAL FACTS
1 SERVING: 640 calories, 36 g fat (14 g saturated fat), 144 mg cholesterol, 1483 mg sodium, 32 g carbohydrate (4 g sugars, 5 g fiber), 50 g protein

Contest-Winning Greek Pasta Bake

PREP: 20 MINUTES • **BAKE:** 25 MINUTES • **YIELD:** 8 SERVINGS

I've brought this hot dish to potlucks, and it received rave reviews. There's never a crumb left. Best of all, it's a simple, healthy and hearty supper made with easy to find ingredients.

—*Anne Taglienti, Kennett Square, Pennsylvania*

- 1 package (13¼ ounces) whole wheat penne pasta
- 4 cups cubed cooked chicken breast
- 1 can (29 ounces) tomato sauce
- 1 can (14½ ounces) diced tomatoes, drained
- 1 package (10 ounces) frozen chopped spinach, thawed and squeezed dry
- 2 cans (2¼ ounces each) sliced ripe olives, drained
- ¼ cup chopped red onion
- 2 tablespoons chopped green pepper
- 1 teaspoon dried basil
- 1 teaspoon dried oregano
- ½ cup shredded part-skim mozzarella cheese
- ½ cup crumbled feta cheese

1. Preheat oven to 400°. Cook pasta according to package directions; drain. In a large bowl, combine the pasta, chicken, tomato sauce, tomatoes, spinach, olives, onion, green pepper, basil and oregano.

2. Transfer to a 13x9-inch baking dish coated with cooking spray. Sprinkle with cheeses. Bake, uncovered, for 25–30 minutes or until heated through and cheese is melted.

NUTRITIONAL FACTS
1½ CUPS: 366 calories, 7 g fat (2 g saturated fat), 62 mg cholesterol, 847 mg sodium, 43 g carbohydrate (6 g sugars, 6 g fiber), 32 g protein

Freeze It **Cool unbaked casserole; cover and freeze. To use, partially thaw in refrigerator overnight. Remove from refrigerator 30 minutes before baking. Preheat oven to 400°. Bake casserole as directed, increasing time as necessary to heat through and for a thermometer inserted in center to read 165°.**

Potluck Cordon Bleu Casserole

PREP: 25 MINUTES ● **BAKE:** 30 MINUTES ● **YIELD:** 10 SERVINGS

Whenever I'm invited to attend a potluck, people usually ask me to bring this tempting casserole. The turkey, ham and cheese are delectable combined with the crunchy topping. When I bake a turkey, I prepare the leftovers for this dish, knowing I'll be making it again soon.

—Joyce Paul, Moose Jaw, Saskatchewan

4 cups cubed cooked turkey
3 cups cubed fully cooked ham
1 cup shredded cheddar cheese
1 cup chopped onion
¼ cup butter, cubed
⅓ cup all-purpose flour
2 cups half-and-half cream
1 teaspoon dill weed
⅛ teaspoon ground mustard
⅛ teaspoon ground nutmeg

TOPPING:
1 cup dry bread crumbs
2 tablespoons butter, melted
¼ teaspoon dill weed
¼ cup shredded cheddar cheese
¼ cup chopped walnuts

1. Preheat oven to 350°. In a large bowl, combine the turkey, ham and cheese; set aside. In a large saucepan, saute onion in butter until tender. Add flour; stir until blended. Gradually add cream, stirring constantly. Bring to a boil; cook and stir for 1–2 minutes or until thickened. Stir in the dill, mustard and nutmeg. Remove from the heat and pour over meat mixture.

2. Spoon into a greased 13x9-inch baking dish. In a small bowl, combine the bread crumbs, butter and dill. Stir in cheese and walnuts. Sprinkle over casserole.

3. Bake, uncovered, for 30 minutes or until heated through.

NUTRITIONAL FACTS
1 EACH: 421 calories, 24 g fat (13 g saturated fat), 122 mg cholesterol, 848 mg sodium, 16 g carbohydrate (3 g sugars, 1 g fiber), 32 g protein

Take-It Tip **When taking a casserole to a potluck, try setting the dish inside a clear plastic oven bag. The bag traps any spills, it doesn't melt and organizers can see what's inside. It's so easy to slide the dish in and seal it with a simple twist tie.**

Sage Turkey Thighs

PREP: 15 MINUTES • **COOK:** 6 HOURS • **YIELD:** 4 SERVINGS

I created this for my boys, who love dark meat. It's more convenient than cooking a whole turkey. It reminds me of our traditional Thanksgiving turkey and stuffing that's seasoned with sage.

—*Natalie Swanson, Catonsville, Maryland*

4 medium carrots, halved	1 tablespoon cornstarch
1 medium onion, chopped	1/4 cup cold water
1/2 cup water	1/4 teaspoon salt
2 garlic cloves, minced	1/8 teaspoon pepper
1 1/2 teaspoons rubbed sage, divided	1 teaspoon browning sauce, optional
2 turkey thighs or turkey drumsticks (2 pounds total), skin removed	

1. In a 3-qt. slow cooker, combine the carrots, onion, water, garlic and 1 teaspoon sage. Top with turkey. Sprinkle with remaining sage. Cover and cook on low for 6–8 hours or until a thermometer reads 170°–175°.

2. Remove turkey to a serving platter; keep warm. Strain broth, reserving vegetables. Skim fat from cooking juices; transfer to a small saucepan.

3. Place vegetables in a food processor; cover and process until smooth. Add to cooking juices. Bring to a boil. In a small bowl or measuring cup, combine cornstarch and water until smooth. Gradually stir into the pan. Add salt, pepper and, if desired, browning sauce. Bring to a boil; cook and stir for 2 minutes or until thickened. Serve with turkey.

NUTRITIONAL FACTS
4 OUNCES COOKED TURKEY: 277 calories, 8 g fat (3 g saturated fat), 96 mg cholesterol, 280 mg sodium, 15 g carbohydrate (0 sugars, 3 g fiber), 34 g protein

Slow Cooker Turkey Breast

PREP: 10 MINUTES ● **COOK:** 5 HOURS ● **YIELD:** 14 SERVINGS

Try this wonderfully flavored, easy-fixing, tender, slow-cooker entree when you're craving turkey.
—*Maria Juco, Milwaukee, Wisconsin*

1   bone-in turkey breast (6 to 7 pounds), skin removed
1   tablespoon olive oil
1   teaspoon dried minced garlic
1   teaspoon seasoned salt

1   teaspoon paprika
1   teaspoon Italian seasoning
1   teaspoon pepper
½   cup water

Brush turkey with oil. In a small bowl, combine the garlic, seasoned salt, paprika, Italian seasoning and pepper; rub over turkey. Transfer to a 6-qt. slow cooker; add water. Cover and cook on low for 5–6 hours or until tender.

NOTE: Lemon-Garlic Turkey Breast: Combine ¼ cup minced fresh parsley, 8 minced garlic cloves, 4 teaspoons grated lemon peel, 2 teaspoons salt-free lemon-pepper seasoning and 1½ teaspoons salt; rub over turkey breast. Add water and cook as directed.

NUTRITIONAL FACTS
4 OUNCES COOKED TURKEY: 174 calories, 2 g fat (0 saturated fat), 101 mg cholesterol, 172 mg sodium, 0 carbohydrate (0 sugars, 0 fiber), 37 g protein

Spanish Marsala Turkey Breast

PREP: 15 MINUTES + MARINATING ● **BAKE:** 35 MINUTES ● **YIELD:** 8 SERVINGS

Every home cook has a go-to party dish; this one is mine. The only prep is popping everything in to marinate before roasting. It's a lifesaver during the holidays.

—*Johnna Johnson, Scottsdale, Arizona*

2 skin-on boneless turkey breast halves (about 2 pounds each)

1 cup pitted dates, quartered

½ cup pitted green olives, halved

½ cup red wine vinegar

½ cup olive oil

1 jar (3½ ounces) capers, drained

1 whole garlic bulb, cloves separated, peeled and minced (about ¼ cup)

¼ cup dried oregano

6 bay leaves

½ teaspoon salt

1 cup packed brown sugar

1 cup Marsala wine

1. Cut each turkey breast half crosswise in half; place in a 2-gal. resealable plastic bag. Add dates, olives, vinegar, oil, capers, garlic, oregano, bay leaves and salt. Seal bag and turn to coat; refrigerate 3–4 hours.

2. Preheat oven to 350°. Place turkey in a single layer in a large shallow roasting pan; top with marinade mixture. Sprinkle brown sugar over turkey. Pour wine around turkey. Bake, uncovered, 35–45 minutes or until a thermometer inserted in turkey reads 165°, basting turkey occasionally with pan juices.

3. Remove from oven; let turkey stand 5 minutes before slicing. Discard bay leaves. Serve turkey with date-olive mixture and pan juices.

NOTE: If skin-on boneless turkey breast halves are not available, you may ask your butcher to debone a 5-pound bone-in turkey breast, leaving the skin attached.

NUTRITIONAL FACTS
8 OUNCES COOKED TURKEY WITH 2 TABLESPOONS OLIVE MIXTURE AND ¼ CUP PAN JUICES: 661 calories, 29 g fat (6 g saturated fat), 132 mg cholesterol, 793 mg sodium, 47 g carbohydrate (39 g sugars, 3 g fiber), 52 g protein

Slow-Cooked Turkey with Berry Compote

PREP: 35 MINUTES • **COOK:** 3 HOURS • **YIELD:** 12 SERVINGS (3¼ CUPS COMPOTE)

We love to eat turkey at our house, and this delicious dish is a great way to get all that yummy flavor without heating up the house; the berries make the perfect summer chutney. For browner turkey, broil for a few minutes before serving.

—Margaret Bracher, Robertsdale, Alabama

1 teaspoon salt
½ teaspoon garlic powder
½ teaspoon dried thyme
½ teaspoon pepper
2 boneless turkey breast halves (2 pounds each)
⅓ cup water

COMPOTE:

2 medium apples, peeled and finely chopped
2 cups fresh raspberries
2 cups fresh blueberries
1 cup white grape juice
¼ teaspoon crushed red pepper flakes
¼ teaspoon ground ginger

1. In a small bowl, mix salt, garlic powder, thyme and pepper; rub over turkey breasts. Place in a 5- or 6-qt. slow cooker. Pour water around turkey. Cook, covered, on low 3–4 hours (a thermometer inserted in turkey should read at least 165°).

2. Remove turkey from slow cooker; tent with foil. Let stand 10 minutes before slicing.

3. Meanwhile, in a large saucepan, combine compote ingredients. Bring to a boil. Reduce heat to medium; cook, uncovered, 15–20 minutes or until slightly thickened and apples are tender, stirring occasionally. Serve turkey with compote.

NUTRITIONAL FACTS
5 OUNCES COOKED TURKEY WITH ¼ CUP COMPOTE: 215 calories, 1 g fat (0 saturated fat), 94 mg cholesterol, 272 mg sodium, 12 g carbohydrate (8 g sugars, 2 g fiber), 38 g protein

Quick Tip Removable stoneware inserts make cleanup a breeze. Be sure to cool the insert before rinsing or cleaning with water to avoid cracking. Do not immerse the metal base unit in water. Clean it with a damp sponge.

Stuffed Turkey with Mojo Sauce

PREP: 30 MINUTES ● **COOK:** 5 HOURS + STANDING ● **YIELD:** 8 SERVINGS (ABOUT 1 CUP SAUCE)

I love Latin food, so I created this recipe that combines wonderful spices and fresh ingredients. This is a traditional turkey recipe with a healthier twist because it uses chicken sausage instead of chorizo.

—Melissa Lauer, San Antonio, Texas

1 medium green pepper, finely chopped
1 medium onion, finely chopped
2 garlic cloves, minced
2 teaspoons ground coriander
1 teaspoon ground cumin
$\frac{1}{8}$ teaspoon cayenne pepper
1 pound uncooked chicken sausage links, casings removed
1 fresh boneless turkey breast (4 pounds)
$\frac{1}{4}$ teaspoon salt
$\frac{1}{4}$ teaspoon pepper

MOJO SAUCE:

1 cup orange juice
$\frac{1}{2}$ cup fresh cilantro leaves
$\frac{1}{4}$ cup minced fresh oregano or 4 teaspoons dried oregano
$\frac{1}{4}$ cup lime juice
4 garlic cloves, minced
1 teaspoon ground cumin
$\frac{1}{2}$ teaspoon pepper
$\frac{1}{4}$ teaspoon salt
$\frac{1}{8}$ teaspoon cayenne pepper
1 cup olive oil

1. In a bowl, combine the first six ingredients. Crumble sausage over mixture and mix well.

2. With skin side down, pound turkey breast with a meat mallet to $\frac{1}{2}$-inch thickness. Sprinkle with salt and pepper. Spread sausage mixture over turkey to within 1 inch of edges. Roll up jelly-roll style, starting with a short side; tie at $1\frac{1}{2}$-inch to 2-inch intervals with kitchen string. Place in a 5-qt. oval slow cooker.

3. In a blender, combine the first nine sauce ingredients; cover and process until blended. While processing, gradually add oil in a steady stream. Pour over turkey.

4. Cover and cook on low for 5 hours or until a thermometer inserted in center reads 165°. Remove from slow cooker; cover and let stand for 10 minutes before slicing. Discard string.

5. Meanwhile, skim fat from cooking juices; transfer juices to a small saucepan. Bring to a boil; cook until liquid is reduced by half. Serve with turkey.

NOTE: To bake in oven, place turkey roll in a 13x9-inch baking dish. Pour sauce over top. Bake, uncovered, at 400° for 70–80 minutes or until a thermometer inserted in center of stuffing reads 165°. (Cover loosely with foil during the last 20 minutes if turkey browns too quickly.) Remove from oven; cover and let stand for 10 minutes before slicing. Discard string. Skim fat from cooking juices; serve juices with turkey.

NUTRITIONAL FACTS
1 SLICE WITH 2 TABLESPOONS SAUCE: 719 calories, 46 g fat (9 g saturated fat), 174 mg cholesterol, 515 mg sodium, 7 g carbohydrate (4 g sugars, 1 g fiber), 66 g protein

Classic Turkey Tetrazzini

PREP: 30 MINUTES ● **BAKE:** 30 MINUTES ● **YIELD:** 12 SERVINGS

This classic casserole is so easy to make and works well with either leftover turkey or fresh turkey cutlets. You can also substitute flavored bread crumbs for the plain ones and jarred, roasted red pepper for the fresh variety.

—*Shannon Weddle, Berryville, Virginia*

1 package (16 ounces) spaghetti
2 medium onions, chopped
9 tablespoons butter, divided
1 pound sliced fresh mushrooms
1 large sweet red pepper, chopped
½ cup all-purpose flour
1 teaspoon salt

6 cups 2% milk
1 tablespoon chicken bouillon granules
6 cups cubed cooked turkey breast
1 cup grated Parmesan cheese
1½ cups dry bread crumbs
4 teaspoons minced fresh parsley

1. Preheat oven to 350°. Cook spaghetti according to package directions. Meanwhile, in a Dutch oven, saute onions in 6 tablespoons butter until tender. Add mushrooms and red pepper; saute 4–5 minutes longer or until vegetables are tender.

2. Stir in flour and salt until blended. Gradually whisk in milk and bouillon. Bring to a boil; cook and stir for 2 minutes or until thickened. Stir in turkey and cheese; heat through. Remove from the heat.

3. Drain spaghetti; add to turkey mixture and mix well. Transfer to one greased 13x9-inch baking dish and one greased 11x7-inch baking dish.

4. Melt remaining butter; toss with bread crumbs. Sprinkle over casseroles. Bake, uncovered, for 30–35 minutes or until heated through. Sprinkle with parsley.

NUTRITIONAL FACTS
1⅓ CUPS: 499 calories, 15 g fat (9 g saturated fat), 98 mg cholesterol, 773 mg sodium, 53 g carbohydrate (10 g sugars, 3 g fiber), 37 g protein

Turkey Taco Macaroni

PREP: 15 MINUTES • **COOK:** 3 HOURS + STANDING • **YIELD:** 10 SERVINGS

This is a nice little twist on a classic dish. If you love cheese, feel free to add more, and green peppers are a great taste if you want some vegetables.

—*Barb Kondolf, Hamlin, New York*

2   tablespoons canola oil, divided
4   cups uncooked elbow macaroni
2   pounds ground turkey
1   medium onion, chopped
4   cans (8 ounces each) tomato sauce

1   cup water
1   cup salsa
1   envelope taco seasoning
2   cups shredded cheddar cheese

1. In a large skillet, heat 1 tablespoon oil over medium heat. Add pasta; cook and stir 2–3 minutes or until pasta is toasted. Transfer to a 5-qt. slow cooker. In same skillet, heat remaining oil over medium-high heat. Add turkey and onion; cook 6–8 minutes or until meat is no longer pink, breaking into crumbles.

2. Transfer to slow cooker. Stir in tomato sauce, water, salsa and taco seasoning. Cook, covered, 3–4 hours or until pasta is tender.

3. Remove insert; top with cheese. Let stand, covered, 15 minutes.

NUTRITIONAL FACTS
1 CUP: 402 calories, 19 g fat (6 g saturated fat), 83 mg cholesterol, 1063 mg sodium, 32 g carbohydrate (4 g sugars, 3 g fiber), 29 g protein

Quick Tip   If you don't like chopping fresh onions or would like to streamline your cooking prep time, try using frozen chopped onions, which are available in the frozen vegetable section of supermarkets. A small onion yields about $\frac{1}{3}$ cup chopped; a medium onion about $\frac{1}{2}$ cup chopped; and a large onion 1 to $1\frac{1}{4}$ cups chopped.

Forgotten Jambalaya

PREP: 35 MINUTES ● **COOK:** 4¼ HOURS ● **YIELD:** 11 SERVINGS

During chilly months, I fix this jambalaya at least once a month. It's so easy! I just chop the vegetables, dump everything in the slow cooker and forget it! Even my sons, who are picky about spicy things, like this dish.

—*Cindi Coss, Coppell, Texas*

- 1 can (14½ ounces) diced tomatoes, undrained
- 1 can (14½ ounces) beef or chicken broth
- 1 can (6 ounces) tomato paste
- 3 celery ribs, chopped
- 2 medium green peppers, chopped
- 1 medium onion, chopped
- 5 garlic cloves, minced
- 3 teaspoons dried parsley flakes
- 2 teaspoons dried basil
- 1½ teaspoons dried oregano
- 1¼ teaspoons salt
- ½ teaspoon cayenne pepper
- ½ teaspoon hot pepper sauce
- 1 pound boneless skinless chicken breasts, cut into 1-inch cubes
- 1 pound smoked sausage, halved and cut into ¼-inch slices
- ½ pound uncooked medium shrimp, peeled and deveined
  Hot cooked rice

1. In a 5-qt. slow cooker, combine the tomatoes, broth and tomato paste. Stir in the celery, green peppers, onion, garlic and seasonings. Stir in chicken and sausage.

2. Cover and cook on low for 4–6 hours or until chicken is no longer pink. Stir in shrimp. Cover and cook 15–30 minutes longer or until shrimp turn pink. Serve with rice.

NUTRITIONAL FACTS
1 CUP: 230 calories, 13 g fat (5 g saturated fat), 75 mg cholesterol, 1016 mg sodium, 9 g carbohydrate (5 g sugars, 2 g fiber), 20 g protein

Freeze It **Place individual portions of cooled stew in freezer containers and freeze. To use, partially thaw in refrigerator overnight. Heat through in a saucepan, stirring occasionally and adding a little water if necessary.**

Spicy Seafood Stew

PREP: 30 MINUTES • **COOK:** $4\frac{3}{4}$ HOURS • **YIELD:** 9 SERVINGS

This zippy stew is very easy and quick to prepare. The hardest part is peeling and dicing the potatoes, and even that can be done the night before. Just place the potatoes in water and store them in the refrigerator overnight to speed up assembly the next day.

—*Bonnie Marlow, Ottoville, Ohio*

2 pounds potatoes, peeled and diced
1 pound carrots, sliced
1 jar (26 ounces) spaghetti sauce
2 jars (6 ounces each) sliced mushrooms, drained
$1\frac{1}{2}$ teaspoons ground turmeric
$1\frac{1}{2}$ teaspoons minced garlic

1 teaspoon cayenne pepper
$\frac{3}{4}$ teaspoon salt
$1\frac{1}{2}$ cups water
1 pound sea scallops
1 pound uncooked medium shrimp, peeled and deveined

1. In a 5-qt. slow cooker, combine the first eight ingredients. Cover and cook on low for $4\frac{1}{2}$–5 hours or until potatoes are tender.

2. Stir in the water, scallops and shrimp. Cover and cook for 15–20 minutes or until scallops are opaque and shrimp turn pink.

NUTRITIONAL FACTS
1 CUP: 261 calories, 4 g fat (1 g saturated fat), 93 mg cholesterol, 958 mg sodium, 35 g carbohydrate (10 g sugars, 5 g fiber), 22 g protein

Take-It Tip

Whenever you're bringing a stew, soup or chili to a potluck, you'll find it can be easily transported in a 5-quart slow cooker.—Charlene Spelock, Apollo, PA

Tilapia with Tomato-Orange Relish

PREP/TOTAL TIME: 25 MINUTES ● **YIELD:** 6 SERVINGS

The mild flavor and tender texture of tilapia goes beautifully with this colorful, garden-fresh relish. It makes a big impression with little effort.

—*Helen Conwell, Portland, Oregon*

6 tilapia fillets (6 ounces each)
3 tablespoons butter, melted
½ teaspoon salt, divided
½ teaspoon lemon-pepper seasoning
1 medium tomato, seeded and chopped

1 medium orange, peeled, sectioned and chopped
⅓ cup finely chopped red onion
1 tablespoon capers, drained
1½ tablespoons brown sugar
1 tablespoon red wine vinegar

1. Preheat oven to 425° Place fish in a greased 15x10x1-inch baking pan. Drizzle with butter; sprinkle with ¼ teaspoon salt and the lemon-pepper. Bake for 10 minutes or until fish flakes easily with a fork.

2. In a small bowl, combine the tomato, orange, onion, capers, brown sugar, vinegar and remaining salt. Serve with fish.

NUTRITIONAL FACTS
1 EACH: 219 calories, 7 g fat (4 g saturated fat), 98 mg cholesterol, 381 mg sodium, 7 g carbohydrate (6 g sugars, 1 g fiber), 32 g protein

Salmon with Brown Sugar Glaze

PREP: 15 MINUTES ● **BAKE:** 20 MINUTES ● **YIELD:** 8 SERVINGS

I was not a salmon lover until I tried this recipe. Now it is one of my favorite dishes to serve friends.

—*Rachel Garcia, Arlington, Virginia*

1	tablespoon brown sugar	1	tablespoon reduced-sodium soy sauce
2	teaspoons butter	½ to ¾	teaspoon salt
1	teaspoon honey	¼	teaspoon pepper
1	tablespoon olive oil	1	salmon fillet (2½ pounds)
1	tablespoon Dijon mustard		

1. Preheat oven to 350°. In a small saucepan over medium heat, cook and stir the brown sugar, butter and honey until melted. Remove from the heat; whisk in the oil, mustard, soy sauce, salt and pepper. Cool for 5 minutes.

2. Place salmon in a large foil-lined baking pan; spoon brown sugar mixture over top. Bake, uncovered, for 20–25 minutes or until fish flakes easily with a fork.

NUTRITIONAL FACTS
1 EACH: 295 calories, 18 g fat (3 g saturated fat), 84 mg cholesterol, 403 mg sodium, 3 g carbohydrate (2 g sugars, 0 fiber), 28 g protein

Salmon with Creamy Dill Sauce

PREP/TOTAL TIME: 30 MINUTES • **YIELD:** 6 SERVINGS

There's nothing like fresh salmon, and my mom bakes it just right so it nearly melts in your mouth. The sour cream sauce is subtly seasoned with dill and horseradish so that it doesn't overpower the delicate salmon flavor.

—*Susan Emery, Everett, Washington*

1	salmon fillet (about 2 pounds)
1 to 1½	teaspoons lemon-pepper seasoning
1	teaspoon onion salt
1	small onion, sliced and separated into rings
6	lemon slices
¼	cup butter, cubed

DILL SAUCE:

⅓	cup sour cream
⅓	cup mayonnaise
1	tablespoon finely chopped onion
1	teaspoon lemon juice
1	teaspoon prepared horseradish
¾	teaspoon dill weed
¼	teaspoon garlic salt
	Pepper to taste

1. Preheat oven to 350°. Line a 15x10x1-inch baking pan with heavy-duty foil; grease lightly. Place salmon skin side down on foil. Sprinkle with lemon-pepper and onion salt. Top with onion and lemon. Dot with butter. Fold foil around salmon; seal tightly.

2. Bake for 20 minutes. Open foil carefully, allowing steam to escape. Broil 4–6 inches from the heat for 8–12 minutes or until the fish flakes easily with a fork.

3. Combine the sauce ingredients until smooth. Serve with salmon.

NUTRITIONAL FACTS
4 OUNCES COOKED SALMON WITH ABOUT 2 TABLESPOONS SAUCE: 418 calories, 33 g fat (11 g saturated fat), 100 mg cholesterol, 643 mg sodium, 3 g carbohydrate (1 g sugars, 0 fiber), 26 g protein

Quick Tip **When buying salmon, look for fillets that have a fresh-cut appearance with no discoloration or browning around the edges. Prepackaged fish should be tightly wrapped with no air space between the fish and the wrapping. There should be no liquid in the package.—Taste of Home Test Kitchen**

Honey-Pecan Baked Cod

PREP/TOTAL TIME: 30 MINUTES ● **YIELD:** 6 SERVINGS

One night at dinner, while vacationing in the Blue Ridge Mountains, we tried a pecan-encrusted trout that we've tried to re-create. We enjoy this tasty version with fresh or frozen cod often.

—Lana German, Lenoir, North Carolina

3 tablespoons honey	$\frac{1}{2}$ teaspoon paprika
2 tablespoons butter, melted	$\frac{1}{4}$ teaspoon seasoned salt
1 tablespoon reduced-sodium soy sauce	$1\frac{1}{2}$ cups finely chopped pecans
$1\frac{1}{2}$ teaspoons lemon-pepper seasoning	6 cod fillets (6 ounces each)
$\frac{1}{2}$ teaspoon garlic powder	

1. Preheat oven to 400°. In a shallow bowl, combine first seven ingredients. Place pecans in another shallow bowl. Dip fillets in honey mixture, then coat with pecans.

2. Place in a greased 13x9-inch baking dish. Bake, uncovered, 15–20 minutes or until fish flakes easily with a fork.

NUTRITIONAL FACTS
1 FILLET: 330 calories, 19 g fat (4 g saturated fat), 75 mg cholesterol, 398 mg sodium, 12 g carbohydrate (10 g sugars, 2 g fiber), 29 g protein

Parsley-Crusted Cod

PREP/TOTAL TIME: 30 MINUTES ● **YIELD:** 4 SERVINGS

Struggling to increase your family's fish servings? You'll appreciate this easy cod with staple ingredients. The flavors are mild and delicious, so even picky eaters won't complain.

—*Judy Grebetz, Racine, Wisconsin*

¾ cup dry bread crumbs	¼ teaspoon kosher salt
1 tablespoon minced fresh parsley	¼ teaspoon pepper
2 teaspoons grated lemon peel	2 tablespoons olive oil
1 garlic clove, minced	4 cod fillets (6 ounces each)

1. Preheat oven to 400°. In a shallow bowl, combine the first six ingredients. Brush oil over one side of fillets; gently press into crumb mixture.

2. Place crumb side up in a 13x9-inch baking dish coated with cooking spray. Bake for 15–20 minutes or until fish flakes easily with a fork.

NUTRITIONAL FACTS
1 FILLET: 215 calories, 8 g fat (1 g saturated fat), 65 mg cholesterol, 194 mg sodium, 6 g carbohydrate (1 g sugars, 0 fiber), 28 g protein

Crab Cake–Stuffed Portobellos

PREP/TOTAL TIME: 30 MINUTES • **YIELD:** 6 SERVINGS

Served as an hors d'oeuvre or a light main dish, these stuffed mushrooms are pretty and delicious. Canned crabmeat becomes absolutely elegant.

—*Jennifer Coduto, Kent, Ohio*

- 6 large portobello mushrooms
- ¾ cup finely chopped sweet onion
- 2 tablespoons olive oil, divided
- 1 package (8 ounces) cream cheese, softened
- 1 large egg
- ½ cup seasoned bread crumbs
- ½ cup plus 1 teaspoon grated Parmesan cheese, divided
- 1 teaspoon seafood seasoning
- 2 cans (6½ ounces each) lump crabmeat, drained
- ¼ teaspoon paprika

1. Preheat oven to 400°. Remove stems from mushrooms (discard or save for another use); set caps aside. In a small skillet, saute onion in 1 tablespoon oil until tender. In a small bowl, combine the cream cheese, egg, bread crumbs, ½ cup cheese and seafood seasoning. Gently stir in crab and onion.

2. Spoon ½ cup crab mixture into each mushroom cap; drizzle with remaining oil. Sprinkle with paprika and remaining cheese. Place in a greased 15x10x1-inch baking pan.

3. Bake, uncovered, for 15–20 minutes or until mushrooms are tender.

NUTRITIONAL FACTS
1 EACH: 346 calories, 22 g fat (11 g saturated fat), 138 mg cholesterol, 695 mg sodium, 14 g carbohydrate (3 g sugars, 2 g fiber), 23 g protein

Shrimp Monterey

PREP/TOTAL TIME: 25 MINUTES ● **YIELD:** 6 SERVINGS

For a special occasion or when company's coming, this delicious seafood dish makes a lasting impression. You'll be surprised at how fast you can prepare it. A mild, fresh-tasting sauce and the Monterey Jack cheese nicely complement the shrimp. I serve it over pasta or rice.

—*Jane Birch, Edison, New Jersey*

2 garlic cloves, minced

2 tablespoons butter

2 pounds uncooked medium shrimp, peeled and deveined

$\frac{1}{2}$ cup white wine or chicken broth

2 cups shredded Monterey Jack cheese

2 tablespoons minced fresh parsley

1. Preheat oven to 350°. In a skillet over medium heat, saute garlic in butter for 1 minute. Add shrimp; cook for 4–5 minutes or until pink. Using a slotted spoon, transfer shrimp to a greased 11x7-inch baking dish; set aside and keep warm.

2. Add wine to the skillet; bring to a boil. Cook and stir for 5 minutes or until sauce is reduced. Pour over shrimp; top with cheese and parsley. Bake, uncovered, for 10 minutes or until cheese is melted.

NUTRITIONAL FACTS
1 CUP: 303 calories, 16 g fat (10 g saturated fat), 268 mg cholesterol, 500 mg sodium, 1 g carbohydrate (0 sugars, 0 fiber), 33 g protein

Italian Shrimp 'n' Pasta

PREP: 20 MINUTES • **COOK:** 7½ HOURS • **YIELD:** 6 SERVINGS

This dish will remind you a bit of classic Shrimp Creole, but it has a surprise Italian twist. Slow cooking gives it hands-off ease—perfect for company.

—*Karen Edwards, Sanford, Maine*

1 pound boneless skinless chicken thighs, cut into 2x1-inch strips
2 tablespoons canola oil
1 can (28 ounces) crushed tomatoes
2 celery ribs, chopped
1 medium green pepper, cut into 1-inch pieces
1 medium onion, coarsely chopped
2 garlic cloves, minced

1 tablespoon sugar
½ teaspoon salt
½ teaspoon Italian seasoning
⅛ to ¼ teaspoon cayenne pepper
1 bay leaf
1 cup uncooked orzo or other small pasta
1 pound cooked medium shrimp, peeled and deveined

1. In a large skillet, brown chicken in oil; transfer to a 3-qt. slow cooker. Stir in tomatoes, celery, pepper, onion, garlic, sugar and seasonings. Cook, covered, on low 7–8 hours or until chicken is just tender.

2. Discard bay leaf. Stir in pasta; cook, covered, on high 15 minutes or until pasta is tender. Stir in shrimp; cook, covered, 5 minutes longer or until heated through.

NUTRITIONAL FACTS
1½ CUPS: 418 calories, 12 g fat (2 g saturated fat), 165 mg cholesterol, 611 mg sodium, 40 g carbohydrate (10 g sugars, 4 g fiber), 36 g protein

Quick Tip
To remove mineral stains on a crockery insert, fill the cooker with hot water and 1 cup white vinegar; cover. Turn heat control to high for 2 hours. Then empty. When cool, wash with hot sudsy water and a cloth or sponge. Rinse well and dry with a towel.

Sweet Potato Lentil Stew

PREP: 15 MINUTES ● **COOK:** 5 HOURS ● **YIELD:** 6 SERVINGS

I fell in love with the spice in this slow-cooked lentil stew. Add ingredients as the spirit moves you, like zucchini, spinach, kale and corn.
—*Heather Gray, Little Rock, Arkansas*

1¼ pounds sweet potatoes (about 2 medium), peeled and cut into 1-inch pieces
1½ cups dried lentils, rinsed
3 medium carrots, cut into 1-inch pieces
1 medium onion, chopped
4 garlic cloves, minced

½ teaspoon ground cumin
¼ teaspoon ground ginger
¼ teaspoon cayenne pepper
1 carton (32 ounces) vegetable broth
¼ cup minced fresh cilantro

In a 3-qt. slow cooker, combine the first nine ingredients. Cook, covered, on low 5–6 hours or until vegetables and lentils are tender. Stir in cilantro.

NUTRITIONAL FACTS
1⅓ CUPS: 290 calories, 1 g fat (0 saturated fat), 0 cholesterol, 662 mg sodium, 58 g carbohydrate (16 g sugars, 15 g fiber), 15 g protein

Peppered Portobello Penne

PREP/TOTAL TIME: 30 MINUTES • **YIELD:** 4 SERVINGS

Meaty mushrooms and a kickin' hot cheese sauce take this simple pasta toss from drab to fab! My family loves that it tastes like a restaurant dish, but it's made at home.

—*Veronica Callaghan, Glastonbury, Connecticut*

2 cups uncooked penne pasta

4 large portobello mushrooms, stems removed, halved and thinly sliced

2 tablespoons olive oil

$^1/_2$ cup heavy whipping cream

$^3/_4$ teaspoon salt

$^1/_4$ teaspoon pepper

1 cup shredded pepper jack cheese

1. Cook pasta according to package directions.

2. Meanwhile, in a large skillet, saute mushrooms in oil until tender. Stir in the cream, salt and pepper; heat through. Stir in cheese until melted. Drain pasta. Add to skillet and toss to coat.

NUTRITIONAL FACTS
1 CUP: 503 calories, 28 g fat (13 g saturated fat), 71 mg cholesterol, 632 mg sodium, 48 g carbohydrate (3 g sugars, 3 g fiber), 17 g protein

Vegetarian Stuffed Peppers

PREP: 30 MINUTES ● **COOK:** 3$\frac{1}{2}$ HOURS ● **YIELD:** 6 SERVINGS

These filling and flavorful peppers are an updated version of my mom's stuffed peppers, which were a favorite when I was growing up in upstate New York. Whenever I make them, I'm reminded of home.

—*Melissa McCabe, Long Beach, California*

2	cups cooked brown rice	4	fresh basil leaves, thinly sliced
3	small tomatoes, chopped	3	garlic cloves, minced
1	cup frozen corn, thawed	1	teaspoon salt
1	small sweet onion, chopped	$\frac{1}{2}$	teaspoon pepper
$\frac{3}{4}$	cup cubed Monterey Jack cheese	6	large sweet peppers
$\frac{1}{3}$	cup chopped ripe olives	$\frac{3}{4}$	cup meatless spaghetti sauce
$\frac{1}{3}$	cup canned black beans, rinsed and drained	$\frac{1}{2}$	cup water
$\frac{1}{3}$	cup canned red beans, rinsed and drained	4	tablespoons grated Parmesan cheese, divided

1. Place the first 12 ingredients in a large bowl; mix lightly to combine. Cut and discard tops from sweet peppers; remove seeds. Fill peppers with rice mixture.

2. In a small bowl, mix spaghetti sauce and water; pour half of the mixture into an oval 5-qt. slow cooker. Add filled peppers. Top with remaining sauce. Sprinkle with 2 tablespoons Parmesan cheese.

3. Cook, covered, on low 3$\frac{1}{2}$–4 hours or until heated through and peppers are tender. Sprinkle with remaining Parmesan cheese.

NUTRITIONAL FACTS
1 STUFFED PEPPER: 261 calories, 8 g fat (4 g saturated fat), 18 mg cholesterol, 815 mg sodium, 39 g carbohydrate (9 g sugars, 7 g fiber), 11 g protein

Artichoke & Lemon Pasta

PREP: 20 MINUTES • **COOK:** 20 MINUTES • **YIELD:** 6 SERVINGS

While sailing in the Mediterranean, we tasted a lemony pasta. I developed my own version of it that our guests love. Try it with shrimp, kalamatas and asparagus.

—*Peter Halferty, Corpus Christi, Texas*

2½ teaspoons salt, divided
½ pound fresh asparagus, trimmed and cut into 1½-inch pieces
4 cups uncooked bow tie pasta (about 12 ounces)
3 tablespoons olive oil, divided
1 can (14 ounces) water-packed quartered artichoke hearts, well drained

2 garlic cloves, minced
1 cup crumbled goat cheese
2 tablespoons minced fresh parsley
1 tablespoon grated lemon peel
2 to 3 tablespoons lemon juice
⅓ cup grated Parmesan cheese

1. Fill a 6-qt. stockpot three-fourths full with water; add 2 teaspoons salt and bring to a boil. Add asparagus; cook, uncovered, 1–2 minutes or just until crisp-tender. Remove asparagus and immediately drop into ice water. Drain and pat dry.

2. In same pot of water, cook pasta according to package directions for al dente. Drain, reserving 1 cup pasta water. Return pasta to pot.

3. Meanwhile, in a large skillet, heat 1 tablespoon oil over medium-high heat. Add artichoke hearts; cook and stir 3–4 minutes or until lightly browned. Add garlic; cook 1 minute longer. Add to pasta.

4. Add asparagus, goat cheese, parsley, lemon peel, lemon juice and the remaining salt and oil; toss to combine, adding enough reserved pasta water to coat. Heat through. Serve with Parmesan cheese.

NUTRITIONAL FACTS
1¼ CUPS: 343 calories, 14 g fat (5 g saturated fat), 27 mg cholesterol, 919 mg sodium, 43 g carbohydrate (2 g sugars, 3 g fiber), 14 g protein

Italian Three-Cheese Macaroni

PREP: 30 MINUTES ● **BAKE:** 50 MINUTES ● **YIELD:** 12 SERVINGS

My husband is a self-proclaimed mac-and-cheese connoisseur and says that this is his favorite version. The Italian seasoning and tomatoes really complement the pasta and cheeses.

—Adriane Mummert, Lancaster, Pennsylvania

- 4 cups uncooked elbow macaroni
- 1/2 cup butter, cubed
- 1/4 cup all-purpose flour
- 2 teaspoons Italian seasoning
- 1 teaspoon salt
- 1 teaspoon pepper
- 4 cups 2% milk
- 2 cups shredded cheddar cheese
- 1/2 cup grated Parmesan cheese
- 2 cans (14 1/2 ounces each) diced tomatoes, undrained
- 2 cups shredded part-skim mozzarella cheese
- 1/2 cup dry bread crumbs
- 2 tablespoons butter, melted

1. Cook macaroni according to package directions.

2. Meanwhile, preheat oven to 350°. In a small saucepan, melt butter. Stir in flour, Italian seasoning, salt and pepper until smooth; gradually add milk. Bring to a boil; cook and stir 2 minutes or until thickened. Remove from the heat; stir in cheddar and Parmesan cheeses until melted. Drain macaroni.

3. Spread 1 cup cheese sauce in a greased 13x9-inch baking pan. Layer with half of macaroni, tomatoes and cheese sauce. Repeat layers. Sprinkle with mozzarella cheese. Combine bread crumbs and butter; sprinkle over top.

4. Cover and bake 40 minutes. Uncover and bake 10–15 minutes longer or until golden brown and bubbly. Let stand 5 minutes before serving.

NUTRITIONAL FACTS
1 CUP: 402 calories, 23 g fat (13 g saturated fat), 66 mg cholesterol, 763 mg sodium, 33 g carbohydrate (8 g sugars, 2 g fiber), 17 g protein

Quick Tip

I store all my pastas in canning jars rather than the opened boxes. The pasta stays fresher, and the jars stack nicely, too, conserving pantry space. When I'm preparing my grocery list, I can see what I need at a glance.—Laurie S., Gettysburg, PA

Tortellini Spinach Casserole

PREP: 20 MINUTES ● **BAKE:** 20 MINUTES ● **YIELD:** 12 SERVINGS

Spinach gives this popular casserole a fresh taste that will delight even those who say they don't like spinach. In fact, people are often surprised at just how good it is! Whenever I bring it to a gathering, it doesn't sit around long.
—*Barbara Kellen, Antioch, Illinois*

1 package (19 ounces) frozen cheese tortellini
1 pound sliced fresh mushrooms
1 teaspoon garlic powder
¼ teaspoon onion powder
¼ teaspoon pepper

½ cup butter, divided
1 can (12 ounces) evaporated milk
½ pound brick cheese, cubed
3 packages (10 ounces each) frozen chopped spinach, thawed and squeezed dry
2 cups shredded part-skim mozzarella cheese

1. Preheat oven to 350°. Cook tortellini according to package directions.

2. Meanwhile, in a large skillet, saute mushrooms, garlic powder, onion powder and pepper in ¼ cup butter until mushrooms are tender. Remove and keep warm.

3. In same skillet, combine milk and remaining butter. Bring to a gentle boil; stir in brick cheese until smooth. Drain tortellini; place in a large bowl. Stir in mushroom mixture and spinach. Add cheese sauce and toss to coat.

4. Transfer to a greased 13x9-inch baking dish; sprinkle with mozzarella cheese. Cover and bake 15 minutes. Uncover; bake 5–10 minutes longer or until heated through and cheese is melted.

NUTRITIONAL FACTS
1 CUP: 281 calories, 19 g fat (12 g saturated fat), 64 mg cholesterol, 378 mg sodium, 13 g carbohydrate (4 g sugars, 1 g fiber), 15 g protein

Quick Tip Freezing meals for future use is a great idea for family cooks, particularly those who like to contribute to church suppers and charity potlucks but don't have time to do so. Most casseroles can be frozen for up to 3 months, but always check the recipes for freezer guidelines. When freezing a casserole, consider using a disposable aluminum baking pan so your good casserole dishes aren't sitting in the freezer for months. Be sure to use heavy-duty foil to cover the pan, or use foil specifically meant to protect against freezer burn. Defrost casseroles in the refrigerator the day before baking.

Satisfying Sides

Fast Italian Vegetable Skillet

PREP/TOTAL TIME: 20 MINUTES • **YIELD:** 6 SERVINGS

This colorful blend of sauteed vegetables is as pretty as it is tasty. A dear friend gave me the recipe, and it's become a family favorite. It's a quick summer side from our garden.

—Sue Spencer, Coarsegold, California

1 medium onion, halved and sliced	1 large tomato, chopped
1 medium sweet red pepper, chopped	2 teaspoons minced fresh basil
1 tablespoon olive oil	½ teaspoon salt
3 medium zucchini, thinly sliced	½ teaspoon Italian seasoning
1 garlic clove, minced	¼ cup shredded Parmesan cheese
1½ cups frozen corn, thawed	

1. In a large nonstick skillet, saute onion and red pepper in oil for 2 minutes. Add zucchini; saute 4–5 minutes or until vegetables are crisp-tender. Add garlic; cook 1 minute longer.

2. Stir in the corn, tomato, basil, salt and Italian seasoning; cook and stir until heated through. Sprinkle with cheese. Serve immediately.

NUTRITIONAL FACTS
1 CUP: 93 calories, 4 g fat (1 g saturated fat), 3 mg cholesterol, 266 mg sodium, 14 g carbohydrate (4 g sugars, 3 g fiber), 4 g protein

Thymed Zucchini Saute

PREP/TOTAL TIME: 15 MINUTES ● **YIELD:** 4 SERVINGS

Simple and flavorful, this recipe is a tasty and healthy way to use up all those zucchini that are taking over your garden. It's ready in no time!

—*Bobby Taylor, Ulster Park, New York*

- 1 tablespoon olive oil
- 1 pound medium zucchini, quartered lengthwise and halved
- ¼ cup finely chopped onion
- ½ vegetable bouillon cube, crushed
- 2 tablespoons minced fresh parsley
- 1 teaspoon minced fresh thyme or ¼ teaspoon dried thyme

In a large skillet, heat oil over medium-high heat. Add zucchini, onion and bouillon; cook and stir 4–5 minutes or until zucchini is crisp-tender. Sprinkle with herbs.

NOTE: This recipe was prepared with Knorr vegetable bouillon.

NUTRITIONAL FACTS
¾ CUP: 53 calories, 4 g fat (1 g saturated fat), 0 cholesterol, 135 mg sodium, 5 g carbohydrate (2 g sugars, 2g fiber), 2 g protein

Quick Tip
When there's no time to chop onions, onion powder is one option. Substitute 1 tablespoon of onion powder for one medium chopped onion. For the best onion flavor, however, use frozen chopped onions or dried minced onion. One tablespoon of dried minced onion equals ¼ cup minced raw onion.

Almond Vegetable Stir-Fry

PREP/TOTAL TIME: 20 MINUTES • **YIELD:** 5 SERVINGS

While broccoli florets and chunks of red pepper give this dish plenty of color, it's the fresh gingerroot, garlic, soy sauce and sesame oil that round out the flavor.

—Mary Relyea, Canastota, New York

- 1 teaspoon cornstarch
- 1 teaspoon sugar
- 3 tablespoons cold water
- 2 tablespoons reduced-sodium soy sauce
- 1 teaspoon sesame oil
- 4 cups fresh broccoli florets
- 2 tablespoons canola oil
- 1 large sweet red pepper, cut into 1-inch chunks
- 1 small onion, cut into thin wedges
- 2 garlic cloves, minced
- 1 tablespoon minced fresh gingerroot
- ¼ cup slivered almonds, toasted

1. In a small bowl, combine cornstarch and sugar. Stir in water, soy sauce and sesame oil until smooth; set aside.

2. In a large nonstick wok or skillet, stir-fry broccoli in hot oil 3 minutes. Add pepper, onion, garlic and ginger; stir-fry 2 minutes. Reduce heat. Stir soy sauce mixture; stir into vegetables with nuts. Cook and stir 2 minutes or until thickened.

NUTRITIONAL FACTS
¾ CUP: 143 calories, 10 g fat (1 g saturated fat), 0 cholesterol, 260 mg sodium, 11 g carbohydrate (0 sugars, 3 g fiber), 4 g protein

Brussels Sprouts with Bacon & Garlic

PREP/TOTAL TIME: 30 MINUTES ● **YIELD:** 12 SERVINGS

When we have company, these sprouts are my go-to side dish because they look and taste fantastic. Fancy them up a notch with pancetta instead of bacon.

—*Mandy Rivers, Lexington, South Carolina*

2 pounds fresh Brussels sprouts (about 10 cups)

8 bacon strips, coarsely chopped

3 garlic cloves, minced

¾ cup chicken broth

½ teaspoon salt

¼ teaspoon pepper

1. Trim Brussels sprouts. Cut sprouts lengthwise in half; cut crosswise into thin slices. In a 6-qt. stockpot, cook bacon over medium heat until crisp, stirring occasionally. Add garlic; cook 30 seconds longer. Remove with a slotted spoon; drain on paper towels.

2. Add Brussels sprouts to bacon drippings; cook and stir 4–6 minutes or until sprouts begin to brown lightly. Stir in broth, salt and pepper; cook, covered, 4–6 minutes longer or until Brussels sprouts are tender. Stir in bacon mixture.

NUTRITIONAL FACTS
¾ CUP: 109 calories, 8 g fat (3 g saturated fat), 13 mg cholesterol, 300 mg sodium, 7 g carbohydrate (2 g sugars, 3 g fiber), 5 g protein

Parmesan Asparagus

PREP/TOTAL TIME: 20 MINUTES ● **YIELD:** 12 SERVINGS

Nothing could be more simple than this side dish. With just four ingredients, I assemble it in no time, then pop it in the oven for about 15 minutes. It turns out perfect every time.

—*Mary Ann Marino, West Pittsburgh, Pennsylvania*

4 pounds fresh asparagus, trimmed

¼ pound butter, melted

2 cups shredded Parmesan cheese

½ teaspoon pepper

1. Preheat oven to 350°. In a large saucepan, bring ½ inch of water to a boil. Add asparagus; cover and boil for 3 minutes or until crisp-tender. Drain.

2. Arrange asparagus in a greased 13x9-inch baking dish. Drizzle with butter; sprinkle with Parmesan cheese and pepper. Bake, uncovered, for 10–15 minutes or until cheese is melted.

NUTRITIONAL FACTS
6 OUNCES: 107 calories, 8 g fat (5 g saturated fat), 20 mg cholesterol, 273 mg sodium, 4 g carbohydrate (2 g sugars, 1 g fiber), 7 g protein

Marmalade-Glazed Carrots

PREP: 10 MINUTES • **COOK:** 5½ HOURS • **YIELD:** 6 SERVINGS

This side dish is ideal when you'd like to serve your vegetables in a different way for a special dinner. Cinnamon and nutmeg season carrots that are simmered with orange marmalade and brown sugar.

—Barb Rudyk, Vermilion, Alberta

2 pounds fresh carrots, halved lengthwise and cut into 2-inch pieces	½ teaspoon ground cinnamon
½ cup orange marmalade	¼ teaspoon salt
3 tablespoons cold water, divided	¼ teaspoon ground nutmeg
2 tablespoons brown sugar	⅛ teaspoon pepper
1 tablespoon butter, melted	1 tablespoon cornstarch

1. In a 3-qt. slow cooker, combine the carrots, marmalade, 1 tablespoon water, brown sugar, butter and seasonings. Cover and cook on low for 5–6 hours or until carrots are tender.

2. In a small bowl, combine cornstarch and remaining water until smooth; stir into carrot mixture. Cover and cook on high for 30 minutes or until thickened. Serve with a slotted spoon.

NUTRITIONAL FACTS
1 EACH: 159 calories, 2 g fat (1 g saturated fat), 5 mg cholesterol, 252 mg sodium, 36 g carbohydrate (29 g sugars, 3 g fiber), 1 g protein

Spiced Red Cabbage

PREP: 10 MINUTES • **COOK:** 1 HOUR • **YIELD:** 6 SERVINGS

When it comes to vegetable dishes, this traditional one is at the top of my list. The wonderful sweet-sour aroma and taste remind me of home. Plus, it looks so pretty on the table.

—*Karin Cousineau, Burlington, North Carolina*

$\frac{1}{2}$ medium head red cabbage, diced	1 tablespoon sugar
1 tablespoon canola oil	1 bay leaf
$\frac{1}{2}$ cup chopped onion	1 teaspoon salt, optional
1 medium tart apple, quartered	$\frac{1}{4}$ teaspoon pepper
3 tablespoons tarragon vinegar	$\frac{1}{8}$ teaspoon ground cloves

In a large saucepan, bring 1 inch of water and cabbage to a boil. Reduce heat; cover and simmer for 3–5 minutes or until crisp-tender; drain. Return to pan; stir in remaining ingredients. Cover and simmer for 1 hour or until cabbage is tender. Remove bay leaf.

NUTRITIONAL FACTS
$\frac{1}{2}$ CUP: 78 calories, 3 g fat (0 saturated fat), 0 cholesterol, 23 mg sodium, 14 g carbohydrate (0 sugars, 0 fiber), 2 g protein

German-Style Cabbage and Beans

PREP/TOTAL TIME: 30 MINUTES • **YIELD:** 6 SERVINGS

This is one of my greatest hits as a potluck dish at church suppers. If you use some red cabbage, it will have very festive colors, light pink with green. It looks so pretty.

—*Winifred Winch, Wetmore, Michigan*

1 pound fresh green beans, cut into 1$\frac{1}{2}$-inch pieces	3 tablespoons chopped onion
3 bacon strips, cut into 1-inch pieces	$\frac{1}{2}$ teaspoon salt
$\frac{1}{2}$ cup cider vinegar	$\frac{1}{4}$ teaspoon pepper
$\frac{1}{4}$ cup sugar	3 cups shredded red cabbage

1. Place 1 inch of water in a large saucepan; add beans. Bring to a boil. Reduce heat; cover and simmer for 8–10 minutes or until crisp-tender. Drain and set aside.

2. In a large skillet, cook bacon over medium heat until crisp. Remove to paper towels; drain, reserving 2 tablespoons drippings. Add the vinegar, sugar, onion, salt and pepper to the drippings. Bring to a boil.

3. Add cabbage. Reduce heat; cover and simmer for 5 minutes. Add beans; cook 3–5 minutes longer or until heated through. Stir in bacon.

NUTRITIONAL FACTS
$\frac{3}{4}$ CUP: 87 calories, 1 g fat (0 saturated fat), 3 mg cholesterol, 284 mg sodium, 16 g carbohydrate (12 g sugars, 3 g fiber), 3 g protein

Garlic Green Beans with Gorgonzola

PREP: 20 MINUTES • **COOK:** 3 HOURS • **YIELD:** 10 SERVINGS

I updated this green bean holiday side dish by adding a touch of white wine, fresh thyme and green onions. It's delicious and easy to make, and my family loves it!

—*Nancy Heishman, Las Vegas, Nevada*

- 2 pounds fresh green beans, trimmed and halved
- 1 can (8 ounces) sliced water chestnuts, drained
- 4 green onions, chopped
- 5 bacon strips, cooked and crumbled, divided

- $1/3$ cup white wine or chicken broth
- 2 tablespoons minced fresh thyme or 2 teaspoons dried thyme
- 4 garlic cloves, minced
- $1\frac{1}{2}$ teaspoons seasoned salt
- 1 cup (8 ounces) sour cream
- $3/4$ cup crumbled Gorgonzola cheese

1. Place green beans, water chestnuts, green onions and $1/4$ cup cooked bacon in a 4-qt. slow cooker. In a small bowl, mix wine, thyme, garlic and seasoned salt; pour over top. Cook, covered, on low 3–4 hours or until green beans are crisp-tender. Drain liquid from beans.

2. Just before serving, stir in sour cream; sprinkle with cheese and remaining bacon.

NUTRITIONAL FACTS
$3/4$ **CUP:** 142 calories, 9 g fat (5 g saturated fat), 17 mg cholesterol, 431 mg sodium, 11 g carbohydrate (4 g sugars, 4 g fiber), 6 g protein

Cheddar Creamed Corn

PREP: 10 MINUTES • **COOK:** 3 HOURS • **YIELD:** 9 SERVINGS

I brought this super-easy recipe to a school potluck once, and it was gone in no time. I've been asked to bring it to every function since.

—*Jessica Maxwell, Omaha, Nebraska*

2 packages (one 16 ounces, one 12 ounces) frozen corn, thawed
1 package (8 ounces) cream cheese, cubed
$\frac{3}{4}$ cup shredded cheddar cheese

$\frac{1}{4}$ cup butter, melted
$\frac{1}{4}$ cup heavy whipping cream
$\frac{1}{2}$ teaspoon salt
$\frac{1}{4}$ teaspoon pepper

In a 3- or 4-qt. slow cooker, combine all ingredients. Cook, covered, on low 3–3$\frac{1}{2}$ hours or until cheese is melted and corn is tender. Stir just before serving.

NUTRITIONAL FACTS
$\frac{1}{2}$ **CUP:** 272 calories, 20 g fat (12 g saturated fat), 56 mg cholesterol, 317 mg sodium, 20 g carbohydrate (3 g sugars, 2 g fiber), 7 g protein

Slow Cooker Temperature Check

To be considered safe, a slow cooker must be able to cook slowly enough that it can be left unattended, yet it must be fast enough to keep the food at a proper temperature. Here's how to check your slow cooker.

1. Fill the slow cooker $\frac{1}{2}$ to $\frac{2}{3}$ full with room temperature water.

2. Cover and heat on low for 8 hours.

3. Using a thermometer, check the temperature of the water quickly since the temperature can drop once the lid is removed.

4. The temperature should be at least 185°. If it's too hot, a meal cooked for 8 hours would likely be overdone. If the temperature is below 185°, the slow cooker is not safe to use and should be discarded.

Southwest Corn and Tomatoes

PREP: 20 MINUTES ● **BAKE:** 20 MINUTES ● **YIELD:** 6 SERVINGS

I came up with this recipe to use an overabundance of corn from the garden one year. Everyone liked it so much that I substituted frozen corn so I could make it all year.

—*Trisha Kruse, Eagle, Idaho*

- 1 package (16 ounces) frozen corn, thawed
- 5 plum tomatoes, seeded and coarsely chopped
- 1 large onion, chopped
- 2 jalapeno peppers, seeded and finely chopped
- 3 garlic cloves, minced
- 2 tablespoons olive oil
- ¼ cup minced fresh cilantro
- ½ teaspoon salt

1. Preheat oven to 425°. In a large bowl, combine the corn, tomatoes, onion, jalapenos and garlic. Drizzle with oil; toss to coat. Transfer to a 15x10x1-inch baking pan coated with cooking spray.

2. Bake for 20–25 minutes or until onion is tender, stirring twice. Spoon into a bowl. Stir in cilantro and salt. Serve warm.

NOTE: Wear disposable gloves when cutting hot peppers; the oils can burn skin. Avoid touching your face.

NUTRITIONAL FACTS
⅔ CUP: 130 calories, 5 g fat (1 g saturated fat), 0 cholesterol, 205 mg sodium, 21 g carbohydrate (4 g sugars, 3 g fiber), 3 g protein

Roasted Brussels Sprouts with Hazelnuts

PREP/TOTAL TIME: 20 MINUTES • **YIELD:** 4 SERVINGS

What I love about this recipe is the mix of Brussels sprouts and hazelnuts. This flavorful combo is festive enough for a special occasion yet homey and easy enough for every day.

—*Gail Prather, Hastings, Nebraska*

3 tablespoons butter

$\frac{1}{2}$ to 1 teaspoon pepper

$\frac{1}{2}$ teaspoon salt

$1\frac{1}{2}$ pounds fresh Brussels sprouts, trimmed and quartered

$\frac{1}{3}$ cup chopped hazelnuts

1. Preheat oven to 450°. In a small heavy saucepan, melt butter over medium heat. Heat 2–3 minutes or until golden brown, stirring constantly. Remove from heat; stir in pepper and salt.

2. Place Brussels sprouts and hazelnuts in a 15x10x1-inch baking pan coated with cooking spray. Drizzle with butter mixture; toss to coat. Roast 10–15 minutes or until Brussels sprouts are tender, stirring occasionally.

NUTRITIONAL FACTS
$\frac{3}{4}$ CUP: 209 calories, 15 g fat (6 g saturated fat), 23 mg cholesterol, 398 mg sodium, 17 g carbohydrate (4 g sugars, 7 g fiber), 7 g protein

Roasted Vegetables with Sage

PREP: 20 MINUTES ● **BAKE:** 35 MINUTES ● **YIELD:** 8 SERVINGS

When I can't decide what vegetable to serve at dinner, I turn to this oven-roasted medley that features Brussels sprouts, potatoes, carrots and butternut squash. It pleases everyone around the table.

—*Betty Fulks, Onia, Arkansas*

5 cups cubed peeled butternut squash
½ pound fingerling potatoes (about 2 cups)
1 cup fresh Brussels sprouts, halved
1 cup fresh baby carrots
3 tablespoons butter

1 tablespoon minced fresh sage or 1 teaspoon dried sage leaves
1 garlic clove, minced
½ teaspoon salt

1. Preheat oven to 425°. Place vegetables in a large bowl. In a microwave, melt butter; stir in remaining ingredients. Add to vegetables and toss to coat.

2. Transfer to a greased 15x10x1-inch baking pan. Roast 35–45 minutes or until tender, stirring occasionally.

NUTRITIONAL FACTS
¾ CUP: 122 calories, 5 g fat (3 g saturated fat), 11 mg cholesterol, 206 mg sodium, 20 g carbohydrate (4 g sugars, 3 g fiber), 2 g protein

Roasted Green Beans with Lemon & Walnuts

PREP/TOTAL TIME: 25 MINUTES • **YIELD:** 8 SERVINGS

I first tasted roasted green beans in a Chinese restaurant and fell in love with the texture and flavor. This is my Americanized version, and it's always a big hit at our holiday table.

—*Lily Julow, Lawrenceville, Georgia*

2 pounds fresh green beans, trimmed
2 shallots, thinly sliced
6 garlic cloves, crushed
2 tablespoons olive oil
¾ teaspoon salt
¼ teaspoon pepper
2 teaspoons grated lemon peel
½ cup chopped walnuts, toasted

1. Preheat oven to 425°. In a large bowl, combine green beans, shallots and garlic; drizzle with oil and sprinkle with salt and pepper. Transfer to two 15x10x1-inch baking pans coated with cooking spray.

2. Roast 15–20 minutes or until tender and lightly browned, stirring occasionally. Remove from oven; stir in 1 teaspoon lemon peel. Sprinkle with walnuts and remaining lemon peel.

NOTE: To toast nuts, bake in a shallow pan in a 350° oven for 5–10 minutes or cook in a skillet over low heat until lightly browned, stirring occasionally.

NUTRITIONAL FACTS
1 SERVING: 119 calories, 8 g fat (1 g saturated fat), 0 cholesterol, 229 mg sodium, 11 g carbohydrate (3 g sugars, 4 g fiber), 3 g protein

Easy Beans & Potatoes with Bacon

PREP: 15 MINUTES • **COOK:** 6 HOURS • **YIELD:** 10 SERVINGS

I love the combination of green beans with bacon, so I created this recipe. It's great for when you have company, because you can start the side dish in the slow cooker and continue preparing the rest of your dinner.

—*Barbara Brittain, Santee, California*

8 bacon strips, chopped	1 small onion, halved and sliced
$1\frac{1}{2}$ pounds fresh green beans, trimmed and cut into 2-inch pieces (about 4 cups)	$\frac{1}{4}$ cup reduced-sodium chicken broth
4 medium potatoes, peeled and cut into $\frac{1}{2}$-inch cubes	$\frac{1}{2}$ teaspoon salt
	$\frac{1}{4}$ teaspoon pepper

1. In a large skillet, cook bacon over medium heat until crisp, stirring occasionally. Remove to paper towels with a slotted spoon; drain, reserving 1 tablespoon drippings. Cover and refrigerate bacon until serving.

2. In a 5-qt. slow cooker, combine the remaining ingredients; stir in reserved drippings. Cover and cook on low for 6–8 hours or until potatoes are tender. Stir in bacon; heat through.

NUTRITIONAL FACTS
$\frac{3}{4}$ CUP: 116 calories, 4 g fat (1 g saturated fat), 8 mg cholesterol, 256 mg sodium, 17 g carbohydrate (3 g sugars, 3 g fiber), 5 g protein

Baked Parmesan Broccoli

PREP: 30 MINUTES • **BAKE:** 15 MINUTES • **YIELD:** 12 SERVINGS

I began making this creamy side dish years ago as a way to get my kids to eat broccoli. They've since grown up, but they still request this satisfying dish. It's truly a family favorite.

—*Barbara Uhl, Wesley Chapel, Florida*

4 bunches broccoli, cut into florets	1 large egg yolk, beaten
6 tablespoons butter, divided	1 cup grated Parmesan cheese
1 small onion, finely chopped	½ teaspoon salt
1 garlic clove, minced	⅛ teaspoon pepper
¼ cup all-purpose flour	½ cup seasoned bread crumbs
2 cups 2% milk	

1. Preheat oven to 400°. Place half of broccoli in a steamer basket; place in a large saucepan over 1 inch of water. Bring to a boil; cover and steam 3–4 minutes or until crisp-tender. Place in a greased 13x9-inch baking dish; repeat with remaining broccoli.

2. Meanwhile, in a small saucepan over medium heat, melt 4 tablespoons butter. Add onion; cook and stir until tender. Add garlic; cook 1 minute longer.

3. Stir in flour until blended; gradually add milk. Bring to a boil; cook and stir 2 minutes or until thickened. Stir a small amount of hot mixture into egg yolk; return all to the pan, stirring constantly. Cook and stir 1 minute longer. Remove from heat; stir in the cheese, salt and pepper.

4. Pour over broccoli. In a small skillet, cook bread crumbs in remaining butter until golden brown; sprinkle over the top.

5. Bake, uncovered, 15–18 minutes or until heated through.

NUTRITIONAL FACTS
¾ CUP: 191 calories, 10 g fat (5 g saturated fat), 41 mg cholesterol, 388 mg sodium, 19 g carbohydrate (7 g sugars, 6 g fiber), 11 g protein

Creamy Parmesan Spinach Bake

PREP: 35 MINUTES • **BAKE:** 20 MINUTES • **YIELD:** 12 SERVINGS

This creamy, comforting side dish wonderfully rounds out Thanksgiving dinner. Just a little of this rich casserole goes a long way.

—*Jennifer Bley, Austin, Texas*

3 packages (9 ounces each) fresh baby spinach
1 small red onion, chopped
1 tablespoon butter
1 package (8 ounces) cream cheese, cubed
1 cup (8 ounces) sour cream
$\frac{1}{2}$ cup half-and-half cream
$\frac{1}{3}$ cup plus 3 tablespoons grated Parmesan cheese, divided

3 garlic cloves, minced
$\frac{1}{8}$ teaspoon pepper
2 cans (14 ounces each) water-packed artichoke hearts, rinsed, drained and chopped
1 tablespoon snipped fresh dill
$\frac{1}{4}$ teaspoon seasoned salt
8 butter-flavored crackers, coarsely crushed

1. Preheat oven to 350°. Place half of the spinach in a steamer basket; place in a large saucepan over 1 inch of water. Bring to a boil; cover and steam for 3–4 minutes or just until wilted. Transfer to a large bowl. Repeat with remaining spinach; set aside.

2. In a large saucepan, saute onion in butter until tender. Reduce heat to low; stir in the cream cheese, sour cream, half-and-half, $\frac{1}{3}$ cup Parmesan cheese, garlic and pepper. Cook and stir until cream cheese is melted. Stir in the artichokes, dill, seasoned salt and spinach.

3. Transfer to an ungreased 2-qt. baking dish. Sprinkle with cracker crumbs and remaining Parmesan cheese. Bake, uncovered, for 20–25 minutes or until edges are bubbly.

NUTRITIONAL FACTS
$\frac{1}{2}$ **CUP:** 196 calories, 14 g fat (8 g saturated fat), 45 mg cholesterol, 394 mg sodium, 10 g carbohydrate (2 g sugars, 2 g fiber), 7 g protein

Oven-Baked Vegetables

PREP: 10 MINUTES • **BAKE:** 40 MINUTES • **YIELD:** 6 SERVINGS

Mom made this easy side with fresh vegetables from our garden. Knowing that we kids helped plant, nurture and pick the veggies made it even more tasty!

—Joann Jensen, Lowell, Indiana

  6 small red potatoes, quartered
 16 baby carrots, halved lengthwise
  1 small onion, cut into wedges
 ½ cup chicken broth

 1¼ teaspoons seasoned salt, divided
  2 medium zucchini, chopped
  2 tablespoons minced fresh parsley

1. Preheat oven to 400°. In a greased 2-qt. baking dish, combine the potatoes, carrots, onion, broth and 1 teaspoon seasoned salt.

2. Cover and bake for 30 minutes. Stir in zucchini and remaining seasoned salt. Bake 10–15 minutes longer or until vegetables are tender. Sprinkle with parsley.

NUTRITIONAL FACTS
¾ CUP: 59 calories, 0 fat (0 saturated fat), 0 cholesterol, 424 mg sodium, 13 g carbohydrate (3 g sugars, 2 g fiber), 2 g protein

Tomato Mozzarella Bake

PREP: 30 MINUTES • **BAKE:** 30 MINUTES • **YIELD:** 8 SERVINGS

You don't often think of casseroles to serve in summertime, but this one is scrumptious with fresh-from-the-garden tomatoes.

—Elaine Seip, Medicine Hat, Alberta

3 tablespoons butter, softened, divided
8 slices French bread (1 inch thick)
⅔ cup chopped green pepper
⅓ cup chopped onion
2 garlic cloves, minced
4 large eggs
4 bacon strips, cooked and crumbled

2 teaspoons sugar
1 teaspoon salt
1 teaspoon dried oregano
½ teaspoon pepper
2 medium tomatoes
1 cup shredded part-skim mozzarella cheese

1. Preheat oven to 400°. Spread 2 tablespoons butter over both sides of bread. Place on a baking sheet; bake for about 3 minutes on each side or until lightly toasted. Cut into 1-inch cubes. Reduce heat to 350°.

2. In a large skillet, saute green pepper, onion and garlic in remaining butter until tender. In a large bowl, lightly beat the eggs. Stir in bread cubes, vegetable mixture, bacon, sugar, salt, oregano and pepper.

3. Transfer to a greased 11x7-inch baking dish. Cut each tomato into four thick slices; arrange over the top. Sprinkle with cheese. Bake, uncovered, for 30–35 minutes or until a knife inserted near the center comes out clean.

NUTRITIONAL FACTS
1 PIECE: 211 calories, 11 g fat (6 g saturated fat), 129 mg cholesterol, 629 mg sodium, 17 g carbohydrate (4 g sugars, 2 g fiber), 10 g protein

Vegetable Strata

PREP: 40 MINUTES + CHILLING ● **BAKE:** 40 MINUTES + STANDING ● **YIELD:** 12 SERVINGS

We always serve food at our Bunco games, and since one of us is a vegetarian, we're always coming up with fun meatless dishes we can all enjoy. This strata can easily be doubled and tastes fantastic hot or at room temperature.

—Doris Mancini, Port Orchard, Washington

3 teaspoons olive oil, divided	½ teaspoon salt
1 pound fresh asparagus, trimmed and cut into 2-inch pieces	½ teaspoon pepper
2 medium zucchini, quartered and sliced	1 loaf (1 pound) Italian bread, cut into 1-inch cubes
1 cup fresh or frozen corn	3 cups shredded Gruyere or Swiss cheese
2 shallots, chopped	5 large eggs
3 garlic cloves, minced	1¾ cups 2% milk
4 teaspoons each minced fresh sage, basil and parsley	½ cup chopped pecans

1. Preheat oven to 350°. In a large skillet, heat 1 teaspoon oil over medium-high heat. Add asparagus; cook and stir until crisp-tender. Transfer to a large bowl.

2. Repeat with an additional 1 teaspoon oil and zucchini; add to asparagus. In same pan, cook and stir corn, shallots and garlic in remaining oil until shallots are tender; stir in herbs, salt and pepper. Add to asparagus mixture; stir in bread cubes.

3. Place half of mixture in a greased 13x9-inch baking dish. Sprinkle with 1½ cups cheese. Repeat layers. In another bowl, whisk eggs and milk; pour over casserole. Sprinkle with pecans. Refrigerate, covered, at least 1 hour.

4. Bake, uncovered, 40–50 minutes or until a knife inserted near the center comes out clean. Let stand 10 minutes before serving.

NUTRITIONAL FACTS
1 PIECE: 677 calories, 36 g fat (15 g saturated fat), 244 mg cholesterol, 940 mg sodium, 55 g carbohydrate (8 g sugars, 5 g fiber), 35 g protein

Freeze It

After assembling, cover and freeze. To use, partially thaw in refrigerator overnight. Remove from refrigerator 30 minutes before baking. Preheat oven to 350°. Bake strata, covered, 45 minutes. Uncover; bake 10–15 minutes longer or until a knife inserted near the center comes out clean. Let stand 10 minutes before serving.

Creamy Carrot Casserole

PREP: 15 MINUTES • **BAKE:** 30 MINUTES • **YIELD:** 8 SERVINGS

My mom and I developed this recipe to see if there was a carrot dish that even people who don't care for carrots would enjoy. So far, I haven't met anyone who hasn't liked this casserole.

—*Laurie Heward, Fillmore, Utah*

$1\frac{1}{2}$ pounds carrots, sliced, or 1 package (20 ounces) frozen sliced carrots, thawed

1 cup mayonnaise

1 tablespoon grated onion

1 tablespoon prepared horseradish

$\frac{1}{4}$ cup shredded cheddar cheese

2 tablespoons crushed butter-flavored crackers

1. Preheat oven to 350°. Place 1 inch of water in a large saucepan; add carrots. Bring to a boil. Reduce heat; cover and simmer for 7–9 minutes or until crisp-tender. Drain, reserving $\frac{1}{4}$ cup cooking liquid. Transfer carrots to a $1\frac{1}{2}$-qt. baking dish.

2. In a small bowl, combine the mayonnaise, onion, horseradish and reserved cooking liquid; spread evenly over carrots. Sprinkle with cheese; top with cracker crumbs. Bake, uncovered, for 30 minutes.

NUTRITIONAL FACTS

$\frac{3}{4}$ **CUP:** 238 calories, 22 g fat (4 g saturated fat), 6 mg cholesterol, 241 mg sodium, 10 g carbohydrate (4 g sugars, 2 g fiber), 2 g protein

Take-It Tip

When I transport hot dishes, I use a gym bag or a bag large enough to hold a 13x9-inch dish. I wrap the dish in newspaper, then line the bag with a large bath towel and wrap the towel around the dish. Everything stays warm, and it is easy to transport.—Virginia Lytle, Salem, WI

Corn Casserole with Jalapenos

PREP: 15 MINUTES • **BAKE:** 35 MINUTES • **YIELD:** 10 SERVINGS

Jalapenos give this creamy corn dish a subtle, spicy flavor. It makes an appearance on my table at Thanksgiving and Christmas, which makes my husband happy!

—*Anita Anderson, Mesquite, Texas*

2 cans (15¼ ounces each) whole kernel corn, drained

1 to 2 jalapeno peppers, sliced and seeded

1 tablespoon butter

1 tablespoon all-purpose flour

1 cup milk

1 package (8 ounces) cream cheese, softened and cubed

1. Preheat oven to 350°. Place half of corn in a greased 8-inch square baking dish. Top with jalapeno slices and remaining corn. In a small saucepan, melt butter. Whisk in flour until smooth. Gradually add milk. Bring to a boil; cook and stir for 1–2 minutes or until thickened and bubbly.

2. Stir in cream cheese just until melted. Pour over corn. Bake, uncovered, for 35–40 minutes or until lightly browned.

NOTE: Wear disposable gloves when cutting hot peppers; the oils can burn skin. Avoid touching your face.

NUTRITIONAL FACTS
¾ CUP: 169 calories, 11 g fat (6 g saturated fat), 30 mg cholesterol, 320 mg sodium, 12 g carbohydrate (5 g sugars, 1 g fiber), 4 g protein

Noodle Pudding

PREP: 20 MINUTES ● **BAKE:** 25 MINUTES ● **YIELD:** 9 SERVINGS

Whenever I bring this creamy dish to gatherings, it always prompts recipe requests. The surprising sweetness comes from apricot nectar, and everyone enjoys the golden buttery topping.

—*Eileen Meyers, Scott Township, Pennsylvania*

7½ cups uncooked wide egg noodles
1 package (8 ounces) cream cheese, softened
6 tablespoons butter, softened
½ cup sugar
3 large eggs
1 cup 2% milk
1 cup apricot nectar

TOPPING:
1 cup cornflake crumbs
½ cup sugar
6 tablespoons butter, melted
½ teaspoon ground cinnamon

1. Preheat oven to 350°. Cook noodles according to package directions. Meanwhile, in a large bowl, beat the cream cheese, butter and sugar until smooth. Beat in eggs. Gradually stir in milk and apricot nectar.

2. Drain noodles; place in a large bowl. Add cream cheese mixture and toss to coat. Transfer to a greased 13x9-inch baking dish.

3. Combine the topping ingredients; sprinkle over noodles. Bake, uncovered, for 25–30 minutes or until a thermometer reads 160°.

NUTRITIONAL FACTS
¾ CUP: 521 calories, 28 g fat (16 g saturated fat), 173 mg cholesterol, 342 mg sodium, 59 g carbohydrate (29 g sugars, 1 g fiber), 10 g protein

Parsnip Pancakes

PREP/TOTAL TIME: 30 MINUTES ● **YIELD:** 6 SERVINGS

Instead of rice or potatoes with her meal, Mom chose these delicate pancakes that are crispy on the outside and tender inside. The parsnips have a pleasant sweetness, while the chives add a hint of onion flavor.

—*Lois Frazee, Gardnerville, Nevada*

2 pounds parsnips, peeled	1 egg, lightly beaten
1 teaspoon salt	1 tablespoon minced chives
½ cup chopped onion	2 to 4 tablespoons canola oil
¼ cup all-purpose flour	

1. Place parsnips in a large saucepan and cover with water; add salt. Bring to a boil over medium-high heat. Reduce heat; cover and cook for 15–20 minutes or until tender.

2. Drain and place parsnips in a large bowl; mash. Stir in the onion, flour, egg and chives.

3. Heat 2 tablespoons oil in a large nonstick skillet over medium heat. Drop batter by ¼ cupfuls into oil. Fry in batches until golden brown on both sides, using remaining oil as needed. Drain on paper towels.

NUTRITIONAL FACTS
2 EACH: 159 calories, 1 g fat (0 saturated fat), 35 mg cholesterol, 419 mg sodium, 35 g carbohydrate (9 g sugars, 6 g fiber), 4 g protein

International Potato Cake

PREP: 40 MINUTES • BAKE: 35 MINUTES + COOLING • YIELD: 12 SERVINGS

Over the years, I've made this potato cake with lamb, ham and hard salami. It's a perfect side for a lunch or dinner party.

—*Judy Batson, Tampa, Florida*

¼ cup seasoned bread crumbs	¼ teaspoon lemon-pepper seasoning
3 pounds potatoes (about 9 medium), peeled and cubed	¼ pound thinly sliced fontina cheese
½ cup heavy whipping cream	¼ pound thinly sliced hard salami, coarsely chopped
¼ cup butter, cubed	
3 large eggs, beaten	**TOPPING:**
1 teaspoon Greek seasoning	⅓ cup grated Parmesan cheese
¼ teaspoon garlic salt	1 tablespoon seasoned bread crumbs
	1 tablespoon butter, melted

1. Sprinkle bread crumbs onto the bottom of a greased 9-inch springform pan; set aside.

2. Place potatoes in a large saucepan and cover with water. Bring to a boil. Reduce heat; cover and simmer 10–15 minutes or until tender. Drain; transfer to a large bowl. Mash potatoes with cream, butter, eggs and seasonings.

3. Preheat oven to 350°. Spoon half the potatoes into prepared pan. Layer with cheese and salami; top with remaining potatoes. Combine topping ingredients; spoon over potatoes.

4. Cover and bake 30 minutes. Uncover; bake 5–10 minutes longer or until topping is golden brown and a thermometer reads 160°. Cool on a wire rack 10 minutes. Carefully run a knife around edge of pan to loosen; remove sides of pan. Serve warm.

NUTRITIONAL FACTS
1 SLICE: 252 calories, 16 g fat (9 g saturated fat), 101 mg cholesterol, 526 mg sodium, 18 g carbohydrate (2 g sugars, 1 g fiber), 9 g protein

Potato Stuffing Casserole

PREP: 20 MINUTES ● **BAKE:** 30 MINUTES ● **YIELD:** 8 SERVINGS

I adapted this recipe from a Pennsylvania Dutch cookbook, and it's indicative of the fine German cooking found in this area. If you're looking for an alternative to mashed potatoes, try this dish.

—Elsa Kerschner, Kunkletown, Pennsylvania

¼ cup chopped celery	¼ cup chopped fresh parsley
1 onion, chopped	½ teaspoon salt
4 tablespoons butter, divided	¼ teaspoon pepper
3 slices bread, cubed	1 cup hot whole milk
4 or 5 large potatoes, peeled, cooked and mashed	1 large egg, beaten
	Additional parsley

1. Preheat oven to 350°. In a medium skillet, saute celery and onion in 2 tablespoons of butter until tender. Add bread cubes and stir until lightly browned. Stir in potatoes, parsley, salt, pepper, milk and egg; mix well.

2. Spoon into a greased 1½-qt. baking dish. Dot with remaining butter. Bake, uncovered, for 30–40 minutes or until lightly browned. Garnish with additional parsley.

NUTRITIONAL FACTS
¾ **CUP:** 258 calories, 8 g fat (4 g saturated fat), 46 mg cholesterol, 295 mg sodium, 41 g carbohydrate (6 g sugars, 4 g fiber), 7 g protein

Slow Cooker Loaded Mashed Potatoes

PREP: 25 MINUTES + CHILLING • **COOK:** 3 HOURS • **YIELD:** 10 SERVINGS

Every year my mom made cream cheese mashed potatoes for Thanksgiving. I tailored the recipe to my family's taste and carried on the tradition. I make them a day ahead and use my slow cooker to free up oven space for other dishes.

—Ann Nolte, Tampa, Florida

3 pounds cubed peeled potatoes (about 9 medium)

1 package (8 ounces) cream cheese, softened

1 cup (8 ounces) sour cream

$\frac{1}{2}$ cup butter, cubed

$\frac{1}{4}$ cup 2% milk

$\frac{1}{2}$ pound bacon strips, cooked and crumbled

$1\frac{1}{2}$ cups shredded cheddar cheese

$1\frac{1}{2}$ cups shredded pepper jack cheese

4 green onions, thinly sliced

$\frac{1}{2}$ teaspoon onion powder

$\frac{1}{2}$ teaspoon garlic powder

Salt and pepper to taste

1. Place potatoes in a Dutch oven, adding water to cover. Bring to a boil; reduce heat and simmer, uncovered, until tender, 10–15 minutes. Drain; return to pan. Mash with cream cheese, sour cream, butter and milk. Stir in bacon, cheeses, onions and seasonings. Cover; refrigerate overnight.

2. Transfer to a greased 3- or 4-quart slow cooker. Cook, covered, on low 3–3$\frac{1}{2}$ hours.

NUTRITIONAL FACTS

$\frac{3}{4}$ CUP: 505 calories, 36 g fat (20 g saturated fat), 109 mg cholesterol, 530 mg sodium, 31 g carbohydrate (3 g sugars, 3 g fiber), 16 g protein

Mashed Potatoes with Garlic-Olive Oil

PREP/TOTAL TIME: 30 MINUTES • **YIELD:** 12 SERVINGS

Garlic mashed potatoes are high on our love list. To intensify the flavor, I combine garlic and olive oil in the food processor and drizzle it on top of the potatoes.

—Emory Doty, Jasper, Georgia

4 pounds red potatoes, quartered	2 teaspoons salt
½ cup olive oil	½ teaspoon pepper
2 garlic cloves	⅔ to ¾ cup whole milk
⅔ cup heavy whipping cream	3 green onions, chopped
¼ cup butter, softened	¾ cup grated Parmesan cheese, optional

1. Place potatoes in a Dutch oven; add water to cover. Bring to a boil. Reduce heat; cook, uncovered, for 15–20 minutes or until tender. Meanwhile, place oil and garlic in a small food processor; process until blended.

2. Drain potatoes; return to pan. Mash potatoes, gradually adding cream, butter, salt, pepper and enough milk to reach desired consistency. Stir in green onions. Serve with garlic olive oil and, if desired, cheese.

NOTE: For food safety purposes, prepare garlic olive oil just before serving; do not store leftover oil mixture.

NUTRITIONAL FACTS
¾ CUP MASHED POTATOES WITH 1 TABLESPOON CHEESE AND ABOUT 2 TEASPOONS OIL MIXTURE: 299 calories, 20 g fat (8 g saturated fat), 31 mg cholesterol, 533 mg sodium, 26 g carbohydrate (3 g sugars, 3 g fiber), 5 g protein

Triple Mash with Horseradish Bread Crumbs

PREP/TOTAL TIME: 30 MINUTES • **YIELD:** 12 SERVINGS

Why settle for traditional mashed potatoes when you can enjoy three times the flavor? Combine spuds with rutabaga and parsnips, along with the zip of horseradish, for a taste treat.

—*Lily Julow, Lawrenceville, Georgia*

- 1¾ pounds Yukon Gold potatoes, peeled and cubed
- 4 medium parsnips (about 1¼ pounds), peeled and cubed
- 2½ cups cubed peeled rutabaga
- 2 teaspoons salt
- ½ cup butter, divided
- 1 cup soft bread crumbs
- 2 tablespoons prepared horseradish
- 1 cup whole milk
- ¼ teaspoon pepper

1. Place potatoes, parsnips, rutabaga and salt in a 6-qt. stockpot; add water to cover. Bring to a boil. Reduce heat; cook, uncovered, 15–20 minutes or until tender.

2. Meanwhile, in a skillet, heat ¼ cup butter over medium heat. Add bread crumbs; cook and stir 3–5 minutes or until toasted. Stir in horseradish; remove from heat.

3. Drain vegetables; return to pot. Mash vegetables over low heat, gradually adding milk, pepper and remaining butter. Transfer to a serving dish; sprinkle with bread crumbs.

NUTRITIONAL FACTS
⅔ CUP: 199 calories, 9 g fat (5 g saturated fat), 22 mg cholesterol, 240 mg sodium, 28 g carbohydrate (6 g sugars, 4 g fiber), 4 g protein

Crispy Smashed Herbed Potatoes

PREP: 25 MINUTES ● **BAKE:** 20 MINUTES ● **YIELD:** 4 SERVINGS

Golden brown and buttery, these spuds live up to their tantalizing name. A sprinkle of fresh herbs when they're hot out of the oven maximizes the flavor—and they're pretty.

—Althea Dye, Howard, Ohio

12 small red potatoes (about 1½ pounds)	¼ teaspoon pepper
3 tablespoons olive oil	3 tablespoons minced fresh chives
¼ cup butter, melted	1 tablespoon minced fresh parsley
¾ teaspoon salt	

1. Preheat oven to 450°. Place potatoes in a large saucepan; add water to cover. Bring to a boil. Reduce heat; cook, uncovered, 15–20 minutes or until tender. Drain.

2. Drizzle oil over the bottom of a 15x10x1-inch baking pan; arrange potatoes over oil. Using a potato masher, flatten potatoes to ½-inch thickness. Brush potatoes with butter; sprinkle with salt and pepper.

3. Roast 20–25 minutes or until golden brown. Sprinkle with chives and parsley.

NUTRITIONAL FACTS
3 SMASHED POTATOES: 292 calories, 22 g fat (9 g saturated fat), 31 mg cholesterol, 543 mg sodium, 22 g carbohydrate (1 g sugars, 2 g fiber), 3 g protein

Quick Tip
Since chives don't seem to keep long in the refrigerator, I mince them and store them in a plastic container in the freezer. Every time I want chives, I just take a few out.—Jennifer W., Pearland, TX

Twice-Baked Cheddar Potato Casserole

PREP: 70 MINUTES ● **BAKE:** 15 MINUTES ● **YIELD:** 12 SERVINGS

Bacon, cheddar and sour cream turn ordinary potatoes into an extraordinary casserole. It's one of our family's beloved standards for the holidays.

—*Kyle Cox, Scottsdale, Arizona*

 8 medium baking potatoes
    (about 8 ounces each)
 1/2 cup butter, cubed
 2/3 cup sour cream
 2/3 cup 2% milk
 1 teaspoon salt

 3/4 teaspoon pepper
 10 bacon strips, cooked and
    crumbled, divided
 2 cups shredded cheddar cheese, divided
 4 green onions, chopped, divided

1. Preheat oven to 425°. Scrub potatoes; pierce several times with a fork. Bake 45–60 minutes or until tender. Remove from oven; reduce oven setting to 350°.

2. When potatoes are cool enough to handle, cut each potato lengthwise in half. Scoop out pulp and place in a large bowl; discard shells. Mash pulp with butter; stir in sour cream, milk, salt and pepper.

3. Reserve 1/4 cup crumbled bacon for topping. Gently fold remaining bacon, 1 cup cheese and half of the green onions into potato mixture (do not overmix).

4. Transfer to a greased 11x7-inch baking dish. Top with the remaining cheese and green onions; sprinkle with reserved bacon. Bake 15–20 minutes or until heated through and cheese is melted.

NUTRITIONAL FACTS
2/3 CUP: 301 calories, 19 g fat (11 g saturated fat), 57 mg cholesterol, 517 mg sodium, 22 g carbohydrate (3 g sugars, 2 g fiber), 10 g protein

Party Potatoes

PREP: 15 MINUTES ● **BAKE:** 50 MINUTES ● **YIELD:** 12 SERVINGS

These creamy, tasty potatoes can be made the day before and stored in the refrigerator until you're ready to pop them in the oven (I often do that). The garlic powder and chives add zip, and the shredded cheese adds color.

—*Sharon Mensing, Greenfield, Iowa*

- 4 cups mashed potatoes (about 8 to 10 large) or 4 cups prepared instant potatoes
- 1 cup (8 ounces) sour cream
- 1 package (8 ounces) cream cheese, softened
- 1 teaspoon minced chives
- ¼ teaspoon garlic powder
- ¼ cup dry bread crumbs
- 1 tablespoon butter, melted
- ½ cup shredded cheddar cheese

1. Preheat oven to 350°. In a large bowl, combine potatoes, sour cream, cream cheese, chives and garlic powder. Turn into a greased 2-qt. casserole. Combine bread crumbs with butter; sprinkle over potatoes.

2. Bake for 50 to 60 minutes. Top with cheese and serve immediately.

NUTRITIONAL FACTS
¾ CUP: 207 calories, 13 g fat (8 g saturated fat), 43 mg cholesterol, 305 mg sodium, 16 g carbohydrate (1 g sugars, 0 fiber), 5 g protein

Lemon Roasted Fingerlings and Brussels Sprouts

PREP: 15 MINUTES • **BAKE:** 20 MINUTES • **YIELD:** 8 SERVINGS

My trick to roasting veggies is to choose ones that cook in the same amount of time. Try pairing up cauliflower florets with baby carrots or okra with cherry tomatoes.

—Courtney Gaylord, Columbus, Indiana

1 pound fingerling potatoes, halved
1 pound Brussels sprouts, trimmed and halved
6 tablespoons olive oil, divided
¾ teaspoon salt, divided
¼ teaspoon pepper
3 tablespoons lemon juice
1 garlic clove, minced
1 teaspoon Dijon mustard
1 teaspoon honey

1. Preheat oven to 425°. Place potatoes and Brussels sprouts in a greased 15x10x1-inch baking pan. Drizzle with 2 tablespoons oil; sprinkle with ½ teaspoon salt and pepper. Toss to coat. Roast 20–25 minutes or until tender, stirring once.

2. In a small bowl, whisk lemon juice, garlic, mustard, honey and remaining oil and salt until blended. Transfer vegetables to a large bowl; drizzle with vinaigrette and toss to coat. Serve warm.

NUTRITIONAL FACTS
¾ CUP: 167 calories, 10 g fat (1 g saturated fat), 0 cholesterol, 256 mg sodium, 17 g carbohydrate (3 g sugars, 3 g fiber), 3 g protein

Coconut Twice-Baked Sweet Potatoes

PREP: 30 MINUTES ● **BAKE:** 20 MINUTES ● **YIELD:** 8 SERVINGS

Hungry for a taste of the tropics? These pretty twice-baked potatoes definitely fill the bill and taste just as delicious as they look!

—*Nancy Sobel, Bay Shore, New York*

4 medium sweet potatoes	1 teaspoon adobo sauce
½ cup coconut milk	½ teaspoon salt
1 tablespoon maple syrup	¼ cup chopped pecans
1 teaspoon minced fresh gingerroot	¼ cup flaked coconut

1. Preheat oven to 350°. Scrub and pierce potatoes; place on a microwave-safe plate. Microwave, uncovered, on high for 10–12 minutes or until tender, turning once.

2. When cool enough to handle, cut each potato in half lengthwise. Scoop out the pulp, leaving thin shells. In a large bowl, mash the pulp with coconut milk. Stir in the syrup, ginger, adobo sauce and salt. Spoon into potato shells.

3. Place on a baking sheet. Sprinkle with pecans and coconut. Bake for 20–25 minutes or until heated through.

NUTRITIONAL FACTS
1 EACH: 137 calories, 7 g fat (4 g saturated fat), 0 cholesterol, 175 mg sodium, 18 g carbohydrate (8 g sugars, 2 g fiber), 2 g protein

Potluck Candied Sweet Potatoes

PREP: 20 MINUTES • **COOK:** 5 HOURS • **YIELD:** 12 SERVINGS

To make it easier to bring this traditional Southern staple to a potluck or gathering, I updated it so that it can be cooked in a slow cooker. It's hard to go wrong with candied sweet potatoes when it comes to pleasing a crowd.

—Deirdre Cox, Kansas City, Missouri

1 cup packed brown sugar

1 cup sugar

8 medium sweet potatoes, peeled and cut into ½-inch slices

¼ cup butter, melted

2 teaspoons vanilla extract

¼ teaspoon salt

2 tablespoons cornstarch

2 tablespoons cold water

Minced fresh parsley, optional

1. In a small bowl, combine sugars. In a greased 5-qt. slow cooker, layer a third of the sweet potatoes; sprinkle with a third of the sugar mixture. Repeat layers twice. In a small bowl, combine the butter, vanilla and salt; drizzle over potatoes. Cover and cook on low for 5–6 hours or until sweet potatoes are tender.

2. Using a slotted spoon, transfer potatoes to a serving dish; keep warm. Pour cooking juices into a small saucepan; bring to a boil. In a small bowl, combine cornstarch and water until smooth; stir into pan. Return to a boil, stirring constantly; cook and stir for 1–2 minutes or until thickened. Spoon over sweet potatoes.

3. Sprinkle with parsley if desired.

NUTRITIONAL FACTS
¾ CUP SWEET POTATO WITH ¼ CUP SAUCE: 252 calories, 4 g fat (2 g saturated fat), 10 mg cholesterol, 91 mg sodium, 54 g carbohydrate (42 g sugars, 2 g fiber), 1 g protein

Chipotle Shredded Sweet Potatoes with Bacon

PREP: 30 MINUTES ● **COOK:** 4 HOURS ● **YIELD:** 10 SERVINGS

I crave a little heat with my sweet spuds, so I mix in chipotle pepper. The smoky flavor blends perfectly with this creamy, cheesy side dish.

—*Kathi Jones-DelMonte, Rochester, New York*

- 2 tablespoons olive oil
- 1 large sweet onion, finely chopped
- 2 shallots, finely chopped
- ¼ cup minced fresh parsley
- 2 teaspoons ground chipotle pepper
- 1 teaspoon coarsely ground pepper
- ½ teaspoon kosher salt
- 3 pounds large sweet potatoes (about 4 large), peeled and shredded
- 1 package (8 ounces) cream cheese, softened

- 2 cups shredded Manchego or Monterey Jack cheese
- 2 cups shredded Muenster cheese
- 1 package (16 ounces) applewood smoked bacon, cooked and chopped
- ½ teaspoon paprika

TOPPING:

- 1 cup sour cream
- 2 tablespoons maple syrup
- ¼ teaspoon ground chipotle pepper

1. In a large skillet, heat oil over medium heat. Add onion and shallots; cook and stir 4–6 minutes or until softened.

2. Transfer onion mixture to a large bowl; stir in parsley and seasonings. Add sweet potatoes and cheeses, mixing well. Fold in chopped bacon.

3. Transfer mixture to a greased 5- or 6-qt. slow cooker. Sprinkle with paprika. Cook, covered, on low 4–5 hours or until potatoes are tender.

4. In a small bowl, mix topping ingredients. Serve with sweet potatoes.

NUTRITIONAL FACTS
¾ CUP: 491 calories, 28 g fat (14 g saturated fat), 64 mg cholesterol, 708 mg sodium, 42 g carbohydrate (19 g sugars, 5 g fiber), 20 g protein

Pecan-Stuffed Butternut Squash

PREP: 10 MINUTES • **BAKE:** 1¼ HOURS • **YIELD:** 8 SERVINGS

I love autumn, when butternut squash is at its peak. This is one of my favorite ways to prepare it. The squash is tender, and the creamy pecan filling is fabulous.

—*Sheryl Little, Sherwood, Arkansas*

2 medium butternut squash (about 3 pounds each)
¾ teaspoon salt
Pepper, optional

4 ounces cream cheese, softened
¼ cup butter, softened
3 tablespoons brown sugar
½ cup chopped pecans

1. Preheat oven to 350°. Cut each squash in half lengthwise; discard seeds. Place squash cut side down in two 13x9-inch baking dishes; add ½-inch water. Bake, uncovered, for 1 hour.

2. Turn squash over; sprinkle with salt and pepper if desired. In a small bowl, beat the cream cheese, butter and brown sugar until light and fluffy; stir in pecans. Spoon into squash cavities.

3. Bake 15–20 minutes longer or until filling is lightly browned and squash is tender.

NUTRITIONAL FACTS
¼ STUFFED SQUASH: 299 calories, 16 g fat (7 g saturated fat), 31 mg cholesterol, 317 mg sodium, 40 g carbohydrate (13 g sugars, 10 g fiber), 5 g protein

Butternut Squash with Whole Grains

PREP: 15 MINUTES • **COOK:** 4 HOURS • **YIELD:** 12 SERVINGS

Fresh thyme really shines in this hearty slow-cooked side dish featuring tender butternut squash, nutritious whole grain pilaf and vitamin-packed baby spinach.
—Taste of Home Test Kitchen

1 medium butternut squash (about 3 pounds), cut into $\frac{1}{2}$-inch cubes	2 teaspoons minced fresh thyme or $\frac{1}{2}$ teaspoon dried thyme
1 cup uncooked whole grain brown and red rice blend	$\frac{1}{2}$ teaspoon salt
1 medium onion, chopped	$\frac{1}{4}$ teaspoon pepper
$\frac{1}{2}$ cup water	1 can (14$\frac{1}{2}$ ounces) vegetable broth
3 garlic cloves, minced	1 package (6 ounces) fresh baby spinach

1. In a 4-qt. slow cooker, combine the first eight ingredients. Stir in broth.

2. Cook, covered, on low 4–5 hours or until grains are tender. Stir in spinach before serving.

NOTE: This recipe was tested with RiceSelect Royal Blend Whole Grain Texmati Brown & Red Rice with Barley and Rye. Look for it in the rice aisle.

NUTRITIONAL FACTS
$\frac{3}{4}$ CUP: 97 calories, 1 g fat (0 saturated fat), 0 cholesterol, 252 mg sodium, 22 g carbohydrate (3 g sugars, 4 g fiber), 3 g protein

Quinoa Squash Pilaf

PREP: 30 MINUTES • **COOK:** 20 MINUTES • **YIELD:** 8 SERVINGS

This is a wonderful recipe with different flavors and plenty of good-for-you ingredients.

—Annette Spiegler, Arlington Heights, Illinois

- 1 cup quinoa, rinsed
- 1 can (14$\frac{1}{2}$ ounces) vegetable broth
- $\frac{1}{4}$ cup water
- 2 medium zucchini, halved lengthwise and sliced
- 1 medium yellow summer squash, halved lengthwise and sliced
- 1 cup chopped leeks (white portion only)
- 1 tablespoon olive oil
- 2 garlic cloves, minced

- 1 large tomato, chopped
- 1 tablespoon minced fresh cilantro
- $\frac{1}{2}$ teaspoon salt
- $\frac{1}{2}$ teaspoon dried oregano
- $\frac{1}{2}$ teaspoon ground cumin
- $\frac{1}{2}$ teaspoon chili powder
- $\frac{1}{4}$ teaspoon pepper
- $\frac{1}{8}$ teaspoon crushed red pepper flakes
- 2 cups fresh baby spinach, chopped

1. In a large nonstick skillet coated with cooking spray, toast the quinoa over medium heat until lightly browned, stirring occasionally.

2. In a small saucepan, bring broth and water to a boil. Add quinoa. Reduce heat; cover and simmer for 12–15 minutes or until liquid is absorbed.

3. In a large nonstick skillet, saute the zucchini, yellow squash and leeks in oil until vegetables are tender. Add garlic; cook 1 minute longer. Stir in the tomato, cilantro, seasonings and quinoa; heat through. Add spinach; cook and stir until spinach is wilted.

NOTE: Look for quinoa in the cereal, rice or organic food aisle.

NUTRITIONAL FACTS
$\frac{3}{4}$ CUP: 126 calories, 3 g fat (0 saturated fat), 0 cholesterol, 377 mg sodium, 21 g carbohydrate (3 g sugars, 3 g fiber), 5 g protein

Zucchini Stuffing

PREP: 25 MINUTES ● **BAKE:** 40 MINUTES ● **YIELD:** 12 SERVINGS

I have been serving this dish for years and always receive compliments on it. If you don't have day-old bread in your pantry, simply slice fresh bread and bake it at 300° for 10 minutes.

—*Mary Ann Dell, Phoenixville, Pennsylvania*

1 small onion, chopped	1 teaspoon poultry seasoning
1 celery rib, chopped	½ cup canned pumpkin
3 tablespoons butter	2 large eggs
1 cup all-purpose flour	⅓ cup 2% milk
2 tablespoons sugar	¼ cup butter, melted
1 teaspoon baking powder	4 cups day-old cubed bread
1 teaspoon salt	3 medium zucchini, chopped
1 teaspoon ground cinnamon	½ cup shredded cheddar cheese

1. Preheat oven to 325°. In a small skillet, saute onion and celery in butter until tender; set aside.

2. In a large bowl, combine the flour, sugar, baking powder, salt, cinnamon and poultry seasoning. In a small bowl, whisk the pumpkin, eggs, milk and butter; stir into dry ingredients just until moistened. Fold in the bread cubes, zucchini, cheese and onion mixture.

3. Transfer to a greased 13x9-inch baking dish. Cover and bake for 30 minutes. Uncover; bake 10–15 minutes longer or until lightly browned.

NUTRITIONAL FACTS
¾ CUP: 182 calories, 10 g fat (6 g saturated fat), 58 mg cholesterol, 408 mg sodium, 20 g carbohydrate (5 g sugars, 2 g fiber), 5 g protein

Take-It Tip

When organizing a large, covered-dish get-together, consider the following: Ask everyone to bring their contribution in a disposable container. This will make cleaning up a snap. Purchase some resealable storage bags that guests can use to take home leftovers. This way you won't be swamped with extra food. Ask everyone to bring a few copies of their recipes so they can share it with others.

Moist Poultry Dressing

PREP: 20 MINUTES • **COOK:** 4 HOURS • **YIELD:** 16 SERVINGS

Tasty mushrooms and onions complement the big herb flavor in this stuffing. The dressing stays so moist when cooked this way.

—Ruth Ann Stelfox, Raymond, Alberta

2 jars (4½ ounces each) sliced mushrooms, drained
4 celery ribs, chopped
2 medium onions, chopped
¼ cup minced fresh parsley
¾ cup butter, cubed
1½ pounds day-old bread, crusts removed and cubed (about 13 cups)

1½ teaspoons salt
1½ teaspoons rubbed sage
1 teaspoon poultry seasoning
1 teaspoon dried thyme
½ teaspoon pepper
2 large eggs
1 can (14½ ounces) chicken broth or 14½ ounces vegetable broth

1. In a large skillet, saute the mushrooms, celery, onions and parsley in butter until the vegetables are tender. In a large bowl, toss the bread cubes with salt, sage, poultry seasoning, thyme and pepper. Add the mushroom mixture. Combine eggs and broth; add to the bread mixture and toss.

2. Transfer to 5-qt. slow cooker. Cover and cook on low for 4–5 hours or until a thermometer reads 160°.

NUTRITIONAL FACTS
¾ CUP: 212 calories, 11 g fat (6 g saturated fat), 50 mg cholesterol, 694 mg sodium, 24 g carbohydrate (3 g sugars, 2 g fiber), 5 g protein

Fruited Goat Cheese Stuffing

PREP: 20 MINUTES ● **BAKE:** 30 MINUTES ● **YIELD:** 10 SERVINGS

This sweet and savory side dish incorporates creamy goat cheese for an unexpected twist on a seasonal favorite. Your guests will be impressed!

—Jennifer Coduto, Kent, Ohio

- 1 pound whole wheat bread, cubed
- 1 cup chopped dates
- 1 medium onion, chopped
- $\frac{1}{4}$ cup minced fresh sage
- 1 tablespoon minced fresh rosemary or 1 teaspoon dried rosemary, crushed
- 1 teaspoon minced fresh marjoram or $\frac{1}{4}$ teaspoon dried marjoram

- 2 tablespoons butter
- 1 cup dried cherries, chopped
- $\frac{1}{4}$ teaspoon salt
- $\frac{1}{4}$ teaspoon pepper
- 3 cups reduced-sodium chicken broth
- $\frac{3}{4}$ cup crumbled goat cheese

1. Preheat oven to 350°. Place bread cubes in an ungreased 15x10x1-inch baking pan. Bake for 10 minutes or until toasted; set aside to cool. Meanwhile, in a large skillet, saute the dates, onion, sage, rosemary and marjoram in butter until onion is tender. Remove from the heat.

2. Place bread cubes in a large bowl. Stir in the onion mixture, cherries, salt and pepper. Add broth; toss to coat. Sprinkle with cheese; toss gently.

3. Transfer to a 13x9-inch baking dish coated with cooking spray. Bake, uncovered, 30–35 minutes or until top is lightly browned.

NUTRITIONAL FACTS
$\frac{3}{4}$ **CUP:** 299 calories, 10 g fat (6 g saturated fat), 29 mg cholesterol, 665 mg sodium, 44 g carbohydrate (23 g sugars, 6 g fiber), 10 g protein

Zucchini & Sweet Corn Souffle

PREP: 40 MINUTES + STANDING • **BAKE:** 45 MINUTES • **YIELD:** 10 SERVINGS

As novice gardeners, my husband and I sowed zucchini seeds—15 hills' worth! Happily, my family requests this side dish often, so it's a keeper.
—*Carol Ellerbroek, Gladstone, Illinois*

2 medium zucchini (about 1½ pounds), shredded	2 green onions, chopped
2½ teaspoons salt, divided	6 tablespoons all-purpose flour
6 large eggs	¼ teaspoon pepper
2 medium ears sweet corn, husks removed	1¼ cups 2% milk
6 tablespoons butter	½ cup shredded Swiss cheese

1. Place zucchini in a colander over a plate; sprinkle with 1 teaspoon salt and toss. Let stand 30 minutes. Rinse and drain well; blot dry with paper towels. Meanwhile, separate eggs; let stand at room temperature 30 minutes. Grease a 2½-qt. souffle dish; dust lightly with flour.

2. Preheat oven to 350°. Place corn in a large saucepan; add water to cover. Bring to a boil. Reduce heat; cook, covered, 3–5 minutes or until crisp-tender; drain. Cool slightly. Cut corn from cobs and place in a large bowl.

3. In a large skillet, heat butter over medium-high heat. Add green onions and zucchini; cook and stir until tender. Stir in flour, pepper and remaining salt until blended; gradually stir in milk. Bring to a boil, stirring constantly; cook and stir 1–2 minutes or until sauce is thickened. Add to corn; stir in cheese.

4. Stir a small amount of hot zucchini mixture into egg yolks; return all to bowl, stirring constantly. Cool slightly.

5. In a large bowl, beat egg whites on high speed until stiff but not dry. With a rubber spatula, gently stir a fourth of the egg whites into zucchini mixture. Fold in remaining egg whites. Transfer to prepared dish.

6. Bake 45–50 minutes or until top is puffed and center appears set. Serve immediately.

NUTRITIONAL FACTS
1 SERVING: 178 calories, 12 g fat (7 g saturated fat), 152 mg cholesterol, 599 mg sodium, 10 g carbohydrate (3 g sugars, 1 g fiber), 8 g protein

Hearty Maple Beans

PREP: 15 MINUTES • **BAKE:** 25 MINUTES • **YIELD:** 10 SERVINGS

I modified this recipe to suit my family's taste. It's a great side dish for a backyard barbecue with hamburgers and hot dogs. It can be made in advance and kept warm in a slow cooker without losing any flavor.

—*Marge Glassic, Easton, Pennsylvania*

- 6 bacon strips, diced
- ½ pound smoked kielbasa or Polish sausage, sliced
- 1 small onion, chopped
- 1 can (15 ounces) pork and beans
- 1 can (16 ounces) kidney beans, rinsed and drained
- 1 can (16 ounces) butter beans, rinsed and drained
- ½ cup maple syrup
- 3 tablespoons white vinegar
- 3 tablespoons ketchup
- 3 tablespoons prepared mustard

1. Preheat oven to 350°. In a large skillet, cook bacon over medium heat until crisp. Using a slotted spoon, remove to paper towels. Drain, reserving 1 tablespoon drippings. In drippings, cook sausage and onion over medium-high heat until sausage is lightly browned. Stir in bacon and remaining ingredients.

2. Transfer to an ungreased 2-qt. baking dish. Bake, uncovered, 25–30 minutes or until bubbly.

NUTRITIONAL FACTS
¾ **CUP:** 294 calories, 13 g fat (4 g saturated fat), 26 mg cholesterol, 673 mg sodium, 35 g carbohydrate (15 g sugars, 6 g fiber), 12 g protein

Smoky Baked Beans

PREP: 25 MINUTES • **COOK:** 7 HOURS • **YIELD:** 16 SERVINGS

They'll be standing in line for this saucy bean recipe, full of campfire flavor. A variation on colorful calico beans, it makes a great side dish with all your cookout favorites.

—*Lynne German, Cumming, Georgia*

- 1 pound bulk spicy pork sausage
- 1 medium onion, chopped
- 2 cans (15 ounces each) pork and beans
- 1 can (16 ounces) kidney beans, rinsed and drained
- 1 can (16 ounces) butter beans, rinsed and drained
- 1 can (15½ ounces) navy beans, rinsed and drained
- 1 can (15 ounces) black beans, rinsed and drained
- 1 can (10 ounces) diced tomatoes and green chilies, drained
- ½ cup hickory smoke–flavored barbecue sauce
- ½ cup ketchup
- ½ cup packed brown sugar
- 1 teaspoon ground mustard
- 1 teaspoon steak seasoning
- 1 teaspoon liquid smoke, optional

1. In a large skillet, cook sausage and onion over medium heat until meat is no longer pink; drain.

2. In a 5-qt. slow cooker, combine the beans, tomatoes and sausage mixture. In a small bowl, combine the barbecue sauce, ketchup, brown sugar, mustard, steak seasoning and liquid smoke if desired. Stir into bean mixture.

3. Cover and cook on low for 7–8 hours or until heated through.

NOTE: This recipe was tested with McCormick's Montreal Steak Seasoning. Look for it in the spice aisle.

NUTRITIONAL FACTS
¾ CUP: 244 calories, 6 g fat (2 g saturated fat), 10 mg cholesterol, 896 mg sodium, 39 g carbohydrate (15 g sugars, 8 g fiber), 11 g protein

Great Grain Salad

PREP: 15 MINUTES • **COOK:** 1 HOUR + CHILLING • **YIELD:** 12 SERVINGS

I can't think of a better dish to round out a meal. My grain salad features all my favorite nuts, seeds and fruits. Try adding grilled chicken to make it a meal on its own.

—*Rachel Dueker, Gervais, Oregon*

3 cups water
½ cup medium pearl barley
½ cup uncooked wild rice
⅔ cup uncooked basmati rice
½ cup slivered almonds
½ cup sunflower kernels
½ cup salted pumpkin seeds or pepitas
½ cup each golden raisins, chopped dried apricots and dried cranberries

⅓ cup minced fresh parsley
4 teaspoons grated orange peel

VINAIGRETTE:
⅔ cup walnut oil
⅔ cup raspberry vinegar
2 teaspoons orange juice
2 teaspoons pepper
1 teaspoon salt

1. In a large saucepan, bring water to a boil. Add barley and wild rice. Reduce heat; cover and simmer for 55–65 minutes or until tender. Meanwhile, cook basmati rice according to package directions. Cool barley and rices to room temperature.

2. In a large bowl, combine the almonds, sunflower kernels, pumpkin seeds, dried fruit, parsley and orange peel; add barley and rices.

3. In a small bowl, whisk the vinaigrette ingredients. Pour over salad and toss to coat. Cover and refrigerate for at least 2 hours.

NUTRITIONAL FACTS
¾ CUP: 368 calories, 22 g fat (3 g saturated fat), 0 cholesterol, 281 mg sodium, 39 g carbohydrate (11 g sugars, 4 g fiber), 8 g protein

Take-It Tip **Rice side dishes and chilled rice salads make great contributions to church suppers. Not only is the variety of rice recipes endless, but they complement most entrees and travel well. In addition, many can be made in advance and can be served cold or at room temperature.**

Lemon Mushroom Orzo

PREP/TOTAL TIME: 25 MINUTES ● **YIELD:** 12 SERVINGS

Sometimes I serve this side dish chilled; sometimes I serve it hot. It has a very lovely appearance and goes well with almost any entree.

—*Shelly Nelson, Akeley, Minnesota*

1   package (16 ounces) orzo pasta
3   tablespoons olive oil, divided
¾   pound sliced fresh mushrooms
¾   cup chopped pecans, toasted
½   cup minced fresh parsley

1   teaspoon grated lemon peel
3   tablespoons lemon juice
1   teaspoon salt
½   teaspoon pepper

1. Cook orzo according to package directions. Meanwhile, in a large skillet, heat 2 tablespoons oil over medium-high heat. Add mushrooms; cook and stir until tender and lightly browned. Drain orzo.

2. In a large bowl, place orzo, mushroom mixture, pecans, parsley, lemon peel, lemon juice, salt, pepper and remaining oil; toss to combine.

NUTRITIONAL FACTS
¾ **CUP:** 225 calories, 9 g fat (1 g saturated fat), 0 cholesterol, 202 mg sodium, 31 g carbohydrate (2 g sugars, 2 g fiber), 6 g protein

Creamed Garden Potatoes and Peas

PREP/TOTAL TIME: 25 MINUTES ● **YIELD:** 12 SERVINGS

New potatoes and peas are treated to a creamy sauce for this special side.

—Jane Uphoff, Cunningham, Kansas

2	pounds small red potatoes, quartered	1½	teaspoons salt
3	cups fresh or frozen peas	¼	teaspoon pepper
1	cup water	2	cups 2% milk
2	tablespoons chopped onion	1	cup half-and-half cream
2	tablespoons butter		
3	tablespoons plus 1 teaspoon all-purpose flour		

1. Place potatoes in a large saucepan and cover with water. Bring to a boil. Reduce heat; cover and simmer for 8–12 minutes or until tender. Drain.

2. Meanwhile, place peas and water in a small saucepan. Bring to a boil. Reduce heat; cover and simmer for 3–5 minutes or until tender. Drain.

3. In a large saucepan, saute onion in butter until tender. Stir in the flour, salt and pepper until blended; gradually add milk and cream. Bring to a boil; cook and stir for 2 minutes or until thickened. Stir in potatoes and peas; heat through.

NUTRITIONAL FACTS
⅔ CUP: 156 calories, 5 g fat (3 g saturated fat), 18 mg cholesterol, 345 mg sodium, 22 g carbohydrate (6 g sugars, 3 g fiber), 6 g protein

Lemon Vinaigrette Potato Salad

PREP: 25 MINUTES ● **COOK:** 15 MINUTES ● **YIELD:** 12 SERVINGS

I developed this recipe for a friend who needed a potato salad that could withstand Fourth of July weather. The vinaigrette was a safe and delicious alternative to traditional mayonnaise-based potato salads. I've also substituted fresh thyme for the basil. Any fresh herbs would be great!

—*Melanie Cloyd, Mullica Hill, New Jersey*

3 pounds red potatoes, cut into 1-inch cubes
$\frac{1}{2}$ cup olive oil
3 tablespoons lemon juice
2 tablespoons minced fresh basil
2 tablespoons minced fresh parsley

1 tablespoon red wine vinegar
1 teaspoon grated lemon peel
$\frac{3}{4}$ teaspoon salt
$\frac{1}{2}$ teaspoon pepper
1 small onion, finely chopped

1. Place potatoes in a large saucepan and cover with water. Bring to a boil. Reduce heat; cover and simmer for 10–15 minutes or until tender. Meanwhile, in a small bowl, whisk the oil, lemon juice, herbs, vinegar, lemon peel, salt and pepper.

2. Drain potatoes. Place in a large bowl; add onion. Drizzle with vinaigrette; toss to coat. Serve warm or chill until serving.

NUTRITIONAL FACTS
$\frac{3}{4}$ **CUP:** 165 calories, 9 g fat (1 g saturated fat), 0 cholesterol, 155 mg sodium, 19 g carbohydrate (1 g sugars, 2 g fiber), 2 g protein

Make It Ahead **While you can enjoy a pasta, rice or potato salad right after tossing it together, you'll find tastier results if it chills a bit in the refrigerator and the flavors have blended.**

California Pasta Salad

PREP: 15 MINUTES + CHILLING • **YIELD:** 15 SERVINGS

Not only does this salad travel well to get-togethers such as picnics or tailgate parties, but people absolutely love it when it gets there.

—*Jeanette Krembas, Laguna Niguel, California*

1 pound thin spaghetti, broken into 1-inch pieces
3 large tomatoes, diced
2 medium zucchini, diced
1 large cucumber, diced
1 medium green pepper, diced
1 sweet red pepper, diced
1 large red onion, diced
2 cans (2-1/4 ounces each) sliced ripe olives, drained

DRESSING:

1 bottle (16 ounces) Italian salad dressing
1/4 cup grated Parmesan cheese
1 tablespoon sesame seeds
2 teaspoons poppy seeds
1 teaspoon paprika
1/2 teaspoon celery seed
1/4 teaspoon garlic powder

1. Cook pasta according to package directions; Drain and rinse in cold water. Transfer to a large bowl. Add the vegetables and olives.

2. In a large bowl, whisk the dressing ingredients. Drizzle over spaghetti mixture; toss to coat. Cover and refrigerate overnight. Serve with a slotted spoon.

NUTRITIONAL FACTS
3/4 CUP: 257 calories, 13 g fat (2 g saturated fat), 1 mg cholesterol, 567 mg sodium, 30 g carbohydrate (5 g sugars, 2 g fiber), 6 g protein

Fire and Ice Tomatoes

PREP: 10 MINUTES • **COOK:** 5 MINUTES + CHILLING • **YIELD:** 8 SERVINGS

You won't miss the salt in this refreshing tomato salad! It's well-seasoned with cayenne pepper, mustard seed and vinegar but not the least bit spicy. This dish is always a hit at potlucks.

—Nan Rickey, Yuma, Arizona

5 large tomatoes, cut into wedges	$\frac{1}{4}$ cup water
1 medium onion, sliced	3 teaspoons mustard seed
$\frac{3}{4}$ cup white vinegar	$\frac{1}{4}$ teaspoon cayenne pepper
6 tablespoons sugar	1 large cucumber, sliced

1. Place tomatoes and onion in a large heatproof nonreactive bowl. In a small saucepan, combine vinegar, sugar, water, mustard seed and cayenne; bring to a boil. Cook 1 minute, stirring to dissolve sugar; pour carefully over tomato mixture. Cool completely.

2. Stir in cucumber. Refrigerate, covered, overnight.

NUTRITIONAL FACTS
$\frac{3}{4}$ **CUP:** 72 calories, 1 g fat (0 saturated fat), 0 cholesterol, 11 mg sodium, 17 g carbohydrate (0 sugars, 2 g fiber), 2 g protein

Broccoli Salad Supreme

PREP/TOTAL TIME: 10 MINUTES • **YIELD:** ABOUT 20 SERVINGS

People can't get enough of the sweet grapes and crunchy broccoli in this colorful salad. I appreciate its make-ahead convenience.

> —*Terri Twyman, Bonanza, Oregon*

10 cups broccoli florets (about 3½ pounds)	⅔ cup sugar
6 cups seedless red grapes (about 3 pounds)	2 tablespoons cider vinegar
1 cup sliced celery	1 pound sliced bacon, cooked and crumbled
6 green onions, sliced	1⅓ cups slivered almonds, toasted
2 cups mayonnaise	

1. In a large salad bowl, combine the broccoli, grapes, celery and onions. In a small bowl, combine the mayonnaise, sugar and vinegar. Pour over broccoli mixture and toss to coat.

2. Cover and refrigerate for at least 4 hours or overnight. Just before serving, gently stir in bacon and almonds.

NUTRITIONAL FACTS
1 CUP: 344 calories, 26 g fat (4 g saturated fat), 14 mg cholesterol, 268 mg sodium, 25 g carbohydrate (20 g sugars, 4 g fiber), 7 g protein

Take-It Tip Perishable foods such as mayonnaise-based salads should be stored below 45° for food safety concerns. These items should never be left at room temperature for more than 2 hours. One way to keep salads cold is to nestle the serving dish in a large bowl filled with ice cubes. Sealing the cubes in storage bags prevents a mess as the ice melts.

Carrot Raisin Salad

PREP/TOTAL TIME: 10 MINUTES • **YIELD:** 8 SERVINGS

This colorful traditional salad is one of my mother-in-law's favorites. It's fun to eat because of its crunchy texture, and the raisins give a slightly sweet flavor. Plus, it's easy to prepare.

> —*Denise Baumert, Dalhart, Texas*

4 cups shredded carrots	2 tablespoons sugar
¾ to 1½ cups raisins	2 to 3 tablespoons 2% milk
¼ cup mayonnaise	

Place carrots and raisins in a large bowl. In a small bowl, combine the mayonnaise, sugar and enough milk to achieve dressing consistency. Pour over carrot mixture; toss to coat.

NUTRITIONAL FACTS
½ CUP: 122 calories, 5 g fat (1 g saturated fat), 1 mg cholesterol, 76 mg sodium, 19 g carbohydrate (14 g sugars, 3 g fiber), 1 g protein

Corn Salad with Tamale Croutons

PREP: 30 MINUTES ● **BAKE:** 25 MINUTES ● **YIELD:** 12 SERVINGS

This recipe is special because I was able to take a delectable, but somewhat complicated, appetizer recipe and turn it into a salad that's easy to make and transport. Adjust the jalapeno and chipotles to suit your spiciness level.

—Richi Reynolds, Scottsboro, Alabama

TAMALE CROUTONS:

- 3 cups frozen corn, divided
- 2/3 cup butter, softened
- 1/3 cup sugar
- 1/4 teaspoon salt
- 1 cup masa harina
- 1/4 cup all-purpose flour

CHIPOTLE RANCH DRESSING:

- 1/4 cup buttermilk
- 1/4 cup mayonnaise
- 1 teaspoon buttermilk ranch salad dressing mix
- 1 teaspoon minced chipotle peppers in adobo sauce

SALAD:

- 6 cans (7 ounces each) white or shoepeg corn, drained
- 2 cups grape tomatoes, chopped
- 1 can (10 ounces) diced tomatoes and green chilies, well drained
- 1 small red onion, chopped
- 1/2 cup chopped peeled jicama
- 1/4 cup minced fresh cilantro
- 1/4 cup lime juice
- 1 jalapeno pepper, seeded and minced
- 4 medium ripe avocados, peeled and cubed
- 3/4 cup shredded Mexican cheese blend

1. Preheat oven to 400°. Place 2 cups corn in food processor; cover and process until finely chopped. Add the butter, sugar and salt; cover and process until blended. Stir in masa harina and flour until a soft dough forms; fold in remaining corn. Using wet hands, press dough into a greased 15x10x1-inch baking pan.

2. Bake for 20 minutes. Score the dough into 1-inch squares. Bake 4–6 minutes longer or until golden brown. Immediately cut along the scored lines; cool in pan on a wire rack.

3. In a small bowl, combine the dressing ingredients. In a large bowl, combine the corn, tomatoes, onion, jicama, cilantro, lime juice and jalapeno. Pour dressing over salad and toss to coat; gently stir in avocados. Sprinkle with cheese and croutons. Serve immediately.

NOTE: Wear disposable gloves when cutting hot peppers; the oils can burn skin. Avoid touching your face.

NUTRITIONAL FACTS
3/4 CUP WITH 1/3 CUP CROUTONS AND 1 TABLESPOON CHEESE: 449 calories, 26 g fat (10 g saturated fat), 35 mg cholesterol, 638 mg sodium, 53 g carbohydrate (11 g sugars, 9 g fiber), 8 g protein

Quick Tip
When you entertain, keep a record of the date, guests and recipes used. Make a note of which dishes were most popular and received the most comments. That way, you can serve a variety of new recipes along with everyone's favorites at the next party.

No-Fail Desserts

Pineapple Sheet Cake

PREP: 15 MINUTES • **BAKE:** 35 MINUTES + COOLING • **YIELD:** ABOUT 24 SERVINGS

This cake is perfect for serving to a crowd. It keeps so well that you can easily prepare it a day ahead and it will stay moist. I often take this to potluck meals at our church, and I have yet to take much of it home.

—Kim Miller Spiek, Sarasota, Florida

2 cups all-purpose flour
2 cups sugar
2 large eggs
1 cup chopped nuts
2 teaspoons baking soda
$\frac{1}{2}$ teaspoon salt
1 teaspoon vanilla extract
1 can (20 ounces) crushed pineapple, undrained

CREAM CHEESE ICING:

1 package (8 ounces) cream cheese, softened
$\frac{1}{2}$ cup butter, softened
$3\frac{3}{4}$ cups confectioners' sugar
1 teaspoon vanilla extract
$\frac{1}{2}$ cup chopped nuts

1. Preheat oven to 350°. In a large bowl, combine cake ingredients; beat until smooth. Pour into a greased 15x10x1-inch baking pan. Bake for 35 minutes. Cool.

2. For icing, in a small bowl, combine the cream cheese, butter, confectioners' sugar and vanilla until smooth. Spread over cake and sprinkle with nuts.

NUTRITIONAL FACTS
1 PIECE: 315 calories, 12 g fat (5 g saturated fat), 38 mg cholesterol, 227 mg sodium, 49 g carbohydrate (39 g sugars, 1 g fiber), 4 g protein

Double Chocolate Sheet Cake

PREP: 25 MINUTES • **BAKE:** 25 MINUTES + COOLING • **YIELD:** 24 SERVINGS

Here's a great dessert for a big family or to bring to the potluck or church supper. The tender, moist cake and chocolaty frosting is every sweet tooth's dream come true.

—*Barbara Walsh, Murdock, Nebraska*

½ cup butter, softened
2 cups sugar
2 large eggs
3 teaspoons vanilla extract
2 cups all-purpose flour
1 teaspoon baking soda
½ teaspoon salt
1 cup water

½ cup 2% milk
2 ounces unsweetened chocolate, melted and cooled

FROSTING:
1 cup sugar
½ cup 2% milk
½ cup butter, cubed
2 tablespoons baking cocoa

1. Preheat oven to 325°. In a large bowl, cream butter and sugar until crumbly. Add eggs, one at a time, beating well after each addition. Beat in vanilla. In a small bowl, combine the flour, baking soda and salt; add to creamed mixture alternately with water and milk. Beat in chocolate until combined.

2. Pour into a greased 15x10x1-inch baking pan. Bake for 25–30 minutes or until a toothpick inserted near the center comes out clean. Cool on a wire rack.

3. For frosting, in a small saucepan, combine the sugar, milk, butter and cocoa. Bring to a boil; cook and stir for 1 minute. Remove from the heat. Transfer to a bowl; stir occasionally until completely cooled. Beat until smooth; spread over cake.

NUTRITIONAL FACTS
1 SLICE: 227 calories, 10 g fat (6 g saturated fat), 38 mg cholesterol, 164 mg sodium, 34 g carbohydrate (26 g sugars, 1 g fiber), 2 g protein

Best Coconut Chocolate Cake

PREP: 35 MINUTES ● **BAKE:** 20 MINUTES ● **YIELD:** 35 SERVINGS

I hope other families enjoy this coconut chocolate cake as much as my family does. I've given almost 100 copies of this recipe to others who have tried the cake and liked it.

—*Dorothy West, Nacogdoches, Texas*

2 cups all-purpose flour
2 cups sugar
1 teaspoon baking soda
$\frac{1}{2}$ teaspoon salt
1 cup butter, cubed
1 cup water
$\frac{1}{4}$ cup baking cocoa
2 large eggs
$\frac{1}{2}$ cup buttermilk
1 teaspoon vanilla extract

TOPPING:

1 can (12 ounces) evaporated milk, divided
$1\frac{1}{4}$ cups sugar, divided
20 large marshmallows
1 package (14 ounces) coconut
2 cups slivered almonds, toasted, divided
$\frac{1}{2}$ cup butter, cubed
1 cup semisweet chocolate chips

1. Preheat oven to 350°. In a large bowl, combine the flour, sugar, baking soda and salt. In a small saucepan, combine the butter, water and cocoa. Cook and stir until butter is melted; add to dry ingredients. In a small bowl, combine the eggs, buttermilk and vanilla; add to chocolate mixture and mix well.

2. Pour into a greased 15x10x1-inch baking pan. Bake for 20–25 minutes or until a toothpick inserted near the center comes out clean.

3. Meanwhile, in a large saucepan, combine 1 cup evaporated milk, $\frac{3}{4}$ cup sugar and marshmallows; cook and stir until marshmallows are melted. Remove from heat; stir in coconut. Immediately sprinkle 1 cup almonds over cake. Spread coconut mixture over top. Sprinkle with remaining almonds (pan will be full).

4. In a small saucepan, combine butter with remaining milk and sugar. Cook and stir until butter is melted. Remove from the heat; stir in chocolate chips until melted. Drizzle over almonds. Cool on a wire rack.

NUTRITIONAL FACTS
1 PIECE: 317 calories, 18 g fat (10 g saturated fat), 37 mg cholesterol, 199 mg sodium, 39 g carbohydrate (29 g sugars, 2 g fiber), 4 g protein

Spiced Pudding Cake

PREP: 25 MINUTES • **BAKE:** 35 MINUTES + COOLING • **YIELD:** 15 SERVINGS

I came across this recipe years ago and made a few changes. It's very popular. My mom's church group serves it for dessert quite regularly.

—*Kelly Kirby, Westville, Nova Scotia*

½ cup butter, softened	½ teaspoon ground allspice
½ cup sugar	¼ teaspoon ground nutmeg
1 large egg	¼ teaspoon salt
1 cup molasses	2½ cups water, divided
2½ cups all-purpose flour	⅔ cup packed brown sugar
1½ teaspoons baking soda	¼ cup butter, cubed
1½ teaspoons ground cinnamon	Whipped cream and
1¼ teaspoons ground ginger	ground cinnamon, optional

1. Preheat oven to 350°. In a large bowl, cream butter and sugar until light and fluffy. Add egg; beat well. Beat in molasses. In a medium bowl, combine the flour, baking soda, spices and salt; add to the creamed mixture alternately with 1 cup water, beating well after each addition.

2. Transfer to an ungreased 13x9-inch baking pan; sprinkle with brown sugar. In a microwave, heat butter and remaining water until butter is melted; carefully pour over batter.

3. Bake for 35–40 minutes or until a toothpick inserted near the center comes out clean. Cool on a wire rack. Serve warm. Garnish with whipped cream and cinnamon if desired.

NUTRITIONAL FACTS
1 PIECE (CALCULATED WITHOUT WHIPPED CREAM): 287 calories, 10 g fat (6 g saturated fat), 38 mg cholesterol, 247 mg sodium, 48 g carbohydrate (28 g sugars, 1 g fiber), 3 g protein

Contest-Winning Moist Chocolate Cake

PREP: 15 MINUTES ● **BAKE:** 45 MINUTES + COOLING ● **YIELD:** 12 SERVINGS

You don't have to spend a lot of time to serve an elegant and delicious dessert. You can quickly mix up the batter in one bowl, bake your cake and serve a crowd.

—*Christa Hageman, Telford, Pennsylvania*

2 cups sugar	2 large eggs
1¾ cups all-purpose flour	1 cup strong brewed coffee
¾ cup baking cocoa	1 cup buttermilk
2 teaspoons baking soda	½ cup canola oil
1 teaspoon baking powder	1 teaspoon vanilla extract
1 teaspoon salt	1 tablespoon confectioners' sugar

1. Preheat oven to 350°. In a large bowl, combine the first six ingredients. Add the eggs, coffee, buttermilk, oil and vanilla; beat on medium speed for 2 minutes (batter will be thin). Pour into a greased and floured 10-inch fluted tube pan.

2. Bake for 45–50 minutes or until a toothpick inserted near the center comes out clean. Cool for 10 minutes before removing from pan to a wire rack to cool completely. Dust with confectioners' sugar.

NUTRITIONAL FACTS
1 SLICE: 315 calories, 11 g fat (2 g saturated fat), 36 mg cholesterol, 473 mg sodium, 52 g carbohydrate (34 g sugars, 1 g fiber), 5 g protein

Cranberry Pineapple Upside-Down Cake

PREP: 20 MINUTES • **BAKE:** 50 MINUTES + COOLING • **YIELD:** 15 SERVINGS

Both kids and grown-ups like this gorgeous dessert. It will keep a few days and is actually better the second day, so you can make it a day ahead.

—*Sherry Conley, Noel Hants County, Nova Scotia*

1 cup packed brown sugar
½ cup butter, melted
1 can (20 ounces) sliced pineapple, drained
1 cup fresh or frozen cranberries

CAKE:
1 cup butter, softened
1¼ cups sugar
2 large eggs
1 teaspoon vanilla extract
2 cups all-purpose flour
2 teaspoons baking powder
1 teaspoon salt
1 teaspoon ground cinnamon
½ teaspoon ground allspice
¾ cup sour cream
1 cup fresh or frozen cranberries, halved
Sweetened whipped cream, optional

1. Preheat oven to 350°. In a small bowl, mix brown sugar and butter; spread onto the bottom of a greased 13x9-inch baking pan. Top with pineapple slices. Place a whole cranberry in the center of each pineapple; sprinkle remaining cranberries around pineapple.

2. For cake, in a large bowl, cream butter and sugar until light and fluffy. Add eggs, one at a time, beating well after each addition. Beat in vanilla. In another bowl, whisk flour, baking powder, salt, cinnamon and allspice; add to creamed mixture alternately with sour cream, beating well after each addition. Fold in cranberries; spoon over pineapple.

3. Bake 50–60 minutes or until a toothpick inserted in center comes out clean. Cool 10 minutes; invert onto a serving plate. Serve warm; if desired, top with whipped cream.

NUTRITIONAL FACTS
1 PIECE (CALCULATED WITHOUT WHIPPED CREAM): 402 calories, 21 g fat (13 g saturated fat), 84 mg cholesterol, 363 mg sodium, 51 g carbohydrate (36 g sugars, 1 g fiber), 3 g protein

Flourless Dark Chocolate Cake

PREP: 25 MINUTES • **BAKE:** 30 MINUTES + COOLING • **YIELD:** 12 SERVINGS

Here's a simple cake that's rich, elegant and over-the-top chocolaty. For finishing touches, add powdered sugar, cocoa or liqueur-flavored whipped cream.

—*Marie Parker, Milwaukee, Wisconsin*

4 large eggs, separated
3 tablespoons butter
8 ounces dark baking chocolate, chopped
$\frac{1}{3}$ cup plus $\frac{1}{4}$ cup sugar, divided

1 container ($2\frac{1}{2}$ ounces) prune baby food
$1\frac{1}{2}$ teaspoons vanilla extract
Confectioners' sugar

1. Place egg whites in a small bowl; let stand at room temperature 30 minutes. Preheat oven to 350°. Coat a 9-inch springform pan with cooking spray; place on a baking sheet.

2. In a small saucepan, melt butter and chocolate over low heat, stirring constantly. Remove from heat; cool slightly. In a large bowl, beat egg yolks on high speed 3 minutes or until slightly thickened. Gradually add $\frac{1}{3}$ cup sugar, beating until thick and lemon-colored. Beat in baby food, vanilla and chocolate mixture.

3. With clean beaters, beat egg whites on medium speed until soft peaks form. Gradually add remaining sugar, 1 tablespoon at a time, beating on high after each addition until sugar is dissolved. Continue beating until stiff glossy peaks form. Fold a fourth of the whites into chocolate mixture, then fold in remaining whites.

4. Pour into prepared pan. Bake 30–35 minutes or until a toothpick inserted in center comes out with moist crumbs. Cool on a wire rack 20 minutes. Loosen sides from pan with a knife; remove rim from pan. Cool cake completely. Dust with confectioners' sugar before serving.

NUTRITIONAL FACTS
1 SLICE: 188 calories, 11 g fat (6 g saturated fat), 78 mg cholesterol, 50 mg sodium, 22 g carbohydrate (18 g sugars, 2 g fiber), 4 g protein

Chocolate Chiffon Cake

PREP: 25 MINUTES + COOLING ● BAKE: 1 HOUR + COOLING ● YIELD: 20 SERVINGS

If you want to offer family and friends a dessert that really stands out from the rest, this is the cake to make. Beautiful, rich sponge cake is drizzled with a succulent chocolate glaze.

—Erma Fox, Memphis, Missouri

7	large eggs, separated
½	cup baking cocoa
¾	cup boiling water
1¾	cups cake flour
1¾	cups sugar
1½	teaspoons baking soda
1	teaspoon salt
½	cup canola oil
2	teaspoons vanilla extract
¼	teaspoon cream of tartar

ICING:

⅓	cup butter
2	cups confectioners' sugar
2	ounces unsweetened chocolate, melted and cooled
1½	teaspoons vanilla extract
3 to 4	tablespoons hot water
	Chopped nuts, optional

1. Let eggs stand at room temperature for 30 minutes. In a bowl, combine cocoa and water until smooth; cool for 20 minutes. Preheat oven to 325°. In a large bowl, combine flour, sugar, baking soda and salt. In a bowl, whisk the egg yolks, oil and vanilla; add to dry ingredients along with the cocoa mixture. Beat until well blended. In another large bowl and with clean beaters, beat egg whites and cream of tartar on high speed until stiff peaks form. Gradually fold into egg yolk mixture.

2. Gently spoon batter into an ungreased 10-inch tube pan. Cut through the batter with a knife to remove air pockets. Bake on lowest rack for 60–65 minutes or until top springs back when lightly touched. Immediately invert pan; cool completely. Run a knife around sides and center tube of pan. Invert cake onto a serving plate.

3. For icing, melt butter in a saucepan. Remove from the heat; stir in the confectioners' sugar, chocolate, vanilla and water. Drizzle over cake. Sprinkle with nuts if desired.

NUTRITIONAL FACTS
1 PIECE: 268 calories, 11 g fat (3 g saturated fat), 73 mg cholesterol, 262 mg sodium, 40 g carbohydrate (30 g sugars, 1 g fiber), 4 g protein

Fudgy Peanut Butter Cake

PREP: 10 MINUTES • **COOK:** 1½ HOURS • **YIELD:** 4 SERVINGS

I clipped this cake recipe from a newspaper years ago. The house smells great while it's cooking. My husband and son enjoy this slow-cooked dessert with vanilla ice cream and nuts on top.

—*Bonnie Evans, Norcross, Georgia*

⅓ cup whole milk	½ cup all-purpose flour
¼ cup peanut butter	¾ teaspoon baking powder
1 tablespoon canola oil	2 tablespoons baking cocoa
½ teaspoon vanilla extract	1 cup boiling water
¾ cup sugar, divided	Vanilla ice cream

1. In a large bowl, beat the milk, peanut butter, oil and vanilla until well blended. In a small bowl, combine ¼ cup sugar, flour and baking powder; gradually beat into milk mixture until blended. Spread into a 1½-qt. slow cooker coated with cooking spray.

2. In a small bowl, combine cocoa and remaining sugar; stir in boiling water. Pour into slow cooker (do not stir).

3. Cover and cook on high for 1½–2 hours or until a toothpick inserted near the center comes out clean. Serve warm with ice cream.

NOTE: Reduced-fat peanut butter is not recommended for this recipe.

NUTRITIONAL FACTS
1 PIECE: 348 calories, 13 g fat (3 g saturated fat), 3 mg cholesterol, 160 mg sodium, 55 g carbohydrate (39 g sugars, 2 g fiber), 7 g protein

Molten Mocha Cake

PREP: 10 MINUTES ● **COOK:** 2½ HOURS ● **YIELD:** 4 SERVINGS

When I first made my slow cooker chocolate cake, my husband and daughter *loved* it. My daughter claims it's one of her "*most* favorite" desserts! I also shared the cake with my next- door neighbor's son, who liked it so much that he ate the whole thing without telling anyone about it!

—*Aimee Fortney, Fairview, Tennessee*

4 large eggs	½ cup baking cocoa
1½ cups sugar	1 tablespoon instant coffee granules
½ cup butter, melted	¼ teaspoon salt
3 teaspoons vanilla extract	Fresh raspberries or sliced fresh strawberries and vanilla ice cream, optional
1 cup all-purpose flour	

1. In a large bowl, beat eggs, sugar, butter and vanilla until blended. In another bowl, whisk flour, cocoa, coffee granules and salt; gradually beat into egg mixture.

2. Transfer to a greased 1½-qt. slow cooker. Cook, covered, on low 2½–3 hours or until a toothpick comes out with moist crumbs. If desired, serve warm cake with berries and ice cream.

NUTRITIONAL FACTS
1 CUP (CALCULATED WITHOUT OPTIONAL INGREDIENTS): 723 calories, 29 g fat (16 g saturated fat), 247 mg cholesterol, 403 mg sodium, 107 g carbohydrate (76 g sugars, 3 g fiber), 12 g protein

Blue-Ribbon Butter Cake

PREP: 20 MINUTES ● **BAKE:** 65 MINUTES + COOLING ● **YIELD:** 16 SERVINGS

I found this recipe in an old cookbook I bought at a garage sale and couldn't wait to try it. I knew it had been someone's favorite because of the well-worn page.
—*Joan F. Gertz, Palmetto, Florida*

1 cup butter, softened
2 cups sugar
4 large eggs
2 teaspoons vanilla extract
3 cups all-purpose flour
1 teaspoon baking powder
$\frac{1}{2}$ teaspoon baking soda
$\frac{1}{2}$ teaspoon salt
1 cup buttermilk

BUTTER SAUCE:

1 cup sugar
$\frac{1}{2}$ cup butter, cubed
$\frac{1}{4}$ cup water
$1\frac{1}{2}$ teaspoons almond extract
$1\frac{1}{2}$ teaspoons vanilla extract

1. Preheat oven to 350°. In a large bowl, cream butter and sugar until light and fluffy. Add eggs, one at a time, beating well after each addition. Beat in vanilla. In a bowl, combine the flour, baking powder, baking soda and salt; add to creamed mixture alternately with buttermilk, beating well after each addition.

2. Pour into a greased and floured 10-inch tube pan. Bake for 65–70 minutes or until a toothpick inserted in center comes out clean. Cool 10 minutes. Run a knife around edges and center tube of pan. Invert cake onto a wire rack over waxed paper.

3. For sauce, combine the sugar, butter and water in a small saucepan. Cook over medium heat just until butter is melted and sugar is dissolved. Remove from the heat; stir in extracts.

4. Poke holes in the top of the warm cake; spoon $\frac{1}{4}$ cup sauce over cake. Let stand until sauce is absorbed. Repeat twice. Poke holes into sides of cake; brush remaining sauce over sides. Cool completely.

NUTRITIONAL FACTS
1 SLICE: 410 calories, 19 g fat (11 g saturated fat), 100 mg cholesterol, 344 mg sodium, 56 g carbohydrate (38 g sugars, 1 g fiber), 5 g protein

Zucchini Chocolate Cake
with Orange Glaze

PREP: 20 MINUTES • **BAKE:** 50 MINUTES + COOLING • **YIELD:** 16 SERVINGS

This moist and mouthwatering cake has a rich chocolate flavor, a hint of orange and is chock-full of zucchini and nuts.

—*Barbara Worrel, Granbury, Texas*

½ cup butter, softened
1½ cups sugar
2 large eggs
¼ cup unsweetened applesauce
1 teaspoon vanilla extract
2½ cups all-purpose flour
½ cup baking cocoa
1¼ teaspoons baking powder
1 teaspoon salt
1 teaspoon ground cinnamon

½ teaspoon baking soda
½ cup fat-free milk
3 cups shredded zucchini
½ cup chopped walnuts
1 tablespoon grated orange peel

GLAZE:
1¼ cups confectioners' sugar
2 tablespoons orange juice
1 teaspoon vanilla extract

1. Preheat oven to 350°. Coat a 10-inch fluted tube pan with cooking spray and sprinkle with flour.

2. In a large bowl, cream butter and sugar until light and fluffy. Add eggs, one at a time, beating well after each addition. Beat in applesauce and vanilla.

3. In a medium bowl, combine the flour, cocoa, baking powder, salt, cinnamon and baking soda; add to creamed mixture alternately with milk, beating well after each addition. Fold in the zucchini, walnuts and orange peel.

4. Transfer to prepared pan. Bake for 50–60 minutes or until a toothpick inserted near the center comes out clean.

5. Cool for 10 minutes before removing from pan to a wire rack to cool completely. Combine glaze ingredients; drizzle over cake.

NUTRITIONAL FACTS
1 SLICE: 282 calories, 9 g fat (4 g saturated fat), 42 mg cholesterol, 273 mg sodium, 47 g carbohydrate (29 g sugars, 2 g fiber), 4 g protein

Quick Tip **Cakes baked in tube pans should cool for 10–15 minutes before you move them to a wire rack to cool completely. Removing a cake too soon can cause it to crack, break or stick to the pan. Leaving it in too long, however, can cause moisture to form between the cake and the pan.**

Surprise Carrot Cake

PREP: 25 MINUTES • **BAKE:** 55 MINUTES + COOLING • **YIELD:** 16 SERVINGS

A cousin gave me this carrot cake recipe. It's a wonderful potluck pleaser with its "surprise" cream cheese center. My husband and our two young children love it, too!

—*Lisa Bowen, Little Britain, Ontario*

3	cups shredded carrots
1¾	cups sugar
1	cup canola oil
3	large eggs
2	cups all-purpose flour
2	teaspoons baking soda
2	teaspoons ground cinnamon
1	teaspoon salt
½	cup chopped pecans

FILLING:

1	package (8 ounces) cream cheese, softened
¼	cup sugar
1	large egg

FROSTING:

1	package (8 ounces) cream cheese, softened
¼	cup butter, softened
2	teaspoons vanilla extract
4	cups confectioners' sugar

1. Preheat oven to 350°. In a large bowl, beat the carrots, sugar, oil and eggs until well blended. In a large bowl, combine the flour, baking soda, cinnamon and salt; gradually beat into carrot mixture until blended. Stir in the pecans. Pour 3 cups batter into a greased and floured 10-inch fluted tube pan.

2. In a small bowl, beat cream cheese and sugar until smooth. Beat in egg. Spoon over batter. Top with remaining batter.

3. Bake for 55–60 minutes or until a toothpick inserted near the center comes out clean. Cool for 10 minutes before removing from pan to a wire rack to cool completely.

4. For frosting, in a small bowl, beat the cream cheese, butter and vanilla until fluffy. Gradually add confectioners' sugar until smooth. Frost cake. Store in the refrigerator.

NUTRITIONAL FACTS
1 SLICE: 570 calories, 30 g fat (10 g saturated fat), 92 mg cholesterol, 442 mg sodium, 71 g carbohydrate (55 g sugars, 2 g fiber), 6 g protein

William Tell's Never-Miss Apple Cake

PREP: 40 MINUTES ● **BAKE:** 50 MINUTES + COOLING ● **YIELD:** 12 SERVINGS

I bake my family-favorite fall cake to usher in this abundant season. It looks so luscious that eating one piece is nearly impossible.

—*Jamie Jones, Madison, Georgia*

1 package (8 ounces) cream cheese, softened
¼ cup sugar
1 large egg

CAKE:

1¾ cups sugar
1 cup canola oil
3 large eggs
2 cups all-purpose flour
2 teaspoons baking powder
2 teaspoons ground cinnamon
1 teaspoon salt

¼ teaspoon baking soda
2 cups chopped peeled tart apples
1 cup shredded carrots
½ cup chopped pecans, toasted

PRALINE ICING:

½ cup packed brown sugar
¼ cup butter, cubed
2 tablespoons 2% milk
½ cup confectioners' sugar
½ teaspoon vanilla extract
¼ cup chopped pecans, toasted

1. Preheat oven to 350°. Grease and flour a 10-inch fluted tube pan. In a small bowl, beat cream cheese and sugar until smooth; beat in egg.

2. For cake, in a large bowl, beat sugar, oil and eggs until well blended. In another bowl, whisk flour, baking powder, cinnamon, salt and baking soda; gradually beat into sugar mixture. Stir in apples, carrots and pecans.

3. Transfer half of the batter to prepared pan; layer with cream cheese mixture, then remaining batter. Bake 50–60 minutes or until a toothpick inserted in cake portion comes out clean. Cool 10 minutes before removing to a wire rack to cool completely.

4. For icing, in a large saucepan, combine brown sugar, butter and milk; bring to a boil. Cook and stir 1 minute. Remove from heat; whisk in confectioners' sugar and vanilla until smooth. Drizzle over cake. Sprinkle with pecans.

NOTES: To remove cake easily, use solid shortening to grease plain and fluted tube pans. To toast nuts, bake in a shallow pan in a 350° oven for 5–10 minutes or cook in a skillet over low heat until lightly browned, stirring occasionally.

NUTRITIONAL FACTS
1 SLICE: 614 calories, 36 g fat (9 g saturated fat), 102 mg cholesterol, 407 mg sodium, 68 g carbohydrate (50 g sugars, 2 g fiber), 7 g protein

Lemon-Filled Coconut Cake

PREP: 35 MINUTES • **BAKE:** 25 MINUTES + COOLING • **YIELD:** 16 SERVINGS

One of my co-workers brought this cake to a luncheon almost 40 years ago. It was so delicious that I asked for the recipe. I have baked it ever since, and it's always a hit!

—Jackie Bergenheier, Wichita Falls, Texas

1 cup butter, softened
2 cups sugar
3 large eggs
2 teaspoons vanilla extract
3¼ cups all-purpose flour
3¼ teaspoons baking powder
¾ teaspoon salt
1½ cups 2% milk

FILLING:
1 cup sugar
¼ cup cornstarch

1 cup water
4 large egg yolks, lightly beaten
⅓ cup lemon juice
2 tablespoons butter

FROSTING:
1½ cups sugar
2 large egg whites
⅓ cup water
¼ teaspoon cream of tartar
1 teaspoon vanilla extract
3 cups flaked coconut

1. Preheat oven to 350°. In a large bowl, cream butter and sugar until light and fluffy. Add eggs, one at a time, beating well after each addition. Beat in vanilla. In another bowl, combine the flour, baking powder and salt; add to creamed mixture alternately with milk, beating well after each addition.

2. Transfer to three greased and floured 9-inch round baking pans. Bake for 25–30 minutes or until a toothpick inserted near the center comes out clean. Cool for 10 minutes before removing from pans to wire racks to cool completely.

3. For filling, in a small saucepan, combine the sugar, cornstarch and water until smooth. Bring to a boil; cook and stir 2 minutes longer or until thickened and bubbly. Remove from the heat.

4. Stir a small amount of hot mixture into egg yolks; return all to the pan, stirring constantly. Bring to a gentle boil; cook and stir 2 minutes longer. Remove from the heat; gently stir in lemon juice and butter. Cool to room temperature without stirring.

5. Place one cake on serving plate; spread with half of the filling. Repeat layers. Top with remaining cake.

6. For frosting, in a large heavy saucepan, combine the sugar, egg whites, water and cream of tartar. With a portable mixer, beat on low speed for 1 minute. Continue beating on low over low heat until frosting reaches 160°, about 10 minutes.

7. Transfer to a large bowl; add vanilla. Beat on high until stiff peaks form, about 7 minutes. Frost top and sides of cake. Sprinkle with coconut. Store in the refrigerator.

NUTRITIONAL FACTS
1 SLICE: 564 calories, 22 g fat (15 g saturated fat), 127 mg cholesterol, 360 mg sodium, 88 g carbohydrate (64 g sugars, 2 g fiber), 6 g protein

Marvelous Marble Cake

PREP: 45 MINUTES ● **BAKE:** 20 MINUTES + COOLING ● **YIELD:** 16 SERVINGS

Pound cake and chocolate make the best marble cake.
—Ellen Riley, Birmingham, Alabama

4 ounces bittersweet chocolate, chopped
3 tablespoons plus $1\frac{1}{4}$ cups butter, softened, divided
2 cups sugar
5 large eggs
3 teaspoons vanilla extract
$2\frac{1}{4}$ cups all-purpose flour
2 teaspoons baking powder
$\frac{1}{2}$ teaspoon salt
$\frac{1}{2}$ cup sour cream

$\frac{1}{2}$ cup miniature semisweet chocolate chips, optional

FROSTING:
$\frac{3}{4}$ cup butter, softened
$6\frac{3}{4}$ cups confectioners' sugar
2 teaspoons vanilla extract
$\frac{1}{2}$ to $\frac{2}{3}$ cup 2% milk
2 tablespoons miniature semisweet chocolate chips

1. In top of a double boiler or a metal bowl over barely simmering water, melt chocolate and 3 tablespoons butter; stir until smooth. Cool to room temperature.

2. Preheat oven to 375°. Line bottoms of three greased 8-inch round baking pans with parchment paper; grease paper.

3. In a large bowl, cream remaining butter and sugar until light and fluffy. Add eggs, one at a time, beating well after each addition. Beat in vanilla. In a medium bowl, whisk flour, baking powder and salt; add to creamed mixture alternately with sour cream, beating well after each addition.

4. Remove 2 cups batter to a small bowl; stir in cooled chocolate mixture and, if desired, chocolate chips until blended. Drop plain and chocolate batters by tablespoonfuls into prepared pans, dividing batters evenly among pans. To make batter level in pans, bang cake pans several times on counter.

5. Bake 20–25 minutes or until a toothpick inserted in center comes out clean. Cool in pans 10 minutes before removing to wire racks; remove paper. Cool completely.

6. For frosting, in a large bowl, beat butter until smooth. Gradually beat in confectioners' sugar, vanilla and enough milk to reach desired consistency.

7. If cake layers have rounded tops, trim with a serrated knife to make level. In a microwave, melt chocolate chips; stir until smooth. Cool slightly.

8. Place one cake layer on a serving plate; spread with $\frac{1}{2}$ cup frosting. Repeat layers. Top with remaining cake layer. Frost top and sides of cake.

9. Drop cooled chocolate by $\frac{1}{2}$ teaspoonfuls over frosting. Using a large offset spatula, smear chocolate to create a marble design in frosting.

NUTRITIONAL FACTS
1 SLICE: 683 calories, 33 g fat (20 g saturated fat), 138 mg cholesterol, 330 mg sodium, 97 g carbohydrate (79 g sugars, 1 g fiber), 5 g protein

Almond Brittle Torte

PREP: 35 MINUTES • **BAKE:** 50 MINUTES + COOLING • **YIELD:** 16 SERVINGS

I brought this impressive cake to my bridge club potluck—and now they want it every time we meet. Homemade brittle makes it extra special.

—Marrian Storm, Athol, Idaho

1½ cups sugar
½ cup water
½ cup light corn syrup
¼ teaspoon instant coffee granules
3 teaspoons baking soda
1 cup slivered almonds

CAKE:
8 large eggs, separated
¼ cup water
3 teaspoons lemon juice
1 teaspoon vanilla extract
1½ cups cake flour
1½ cups sugar, divided
1 teaspoon cream of tartar
1 teaspoon salt
3½ cups heavy whipping cream, whipped

1. Line a 13x9-inch baking pan with foil; butter the foil and set aside. In a saucepan, combine the sugar, water, corn syrup and coffee granules. Bring to a boil over medium-high heat, stirring constantly, until a candy thermometer reads 290°. Sprinkle with baking soda, stirring constantly (mixture will foam). Stir in the almonds. Pour into prepared pan. Cool completely.

2. Preheat oven to 350°. In a large bowl, combine the egg yolks, water, lemon juice and vanilla; mix well. In a medium bowl, combine flour and ¾ cup sugar; add to egg yolk mixture and mix well. In a large bowl, beat egg whites, cream of tartar and salt until soft peaks form. Beat in remaining sugar, 1 tablespoon at a time. Fold into the batter. Pour into an ungreased 10-inch tube pan. Bake for 50–55 minutes or until cake springs back when lightly touched. Cool on a wire rack.

3. Remove cake from pan. Split horizontally into four layers. Place bottom layer on a serving plate; spread with about ¾ cup whipped cream. Break almond brittle into small pieces; sprinkle some over cream. Repeat layers twice. Spread remaining whipped cream over top and sides of cake; sprinkle with remaining brittle. Refrigerate until serving.

NOTE: Almond brittle will melt on the whipped cream and form a syrup.

NUTRITIONAL FACTS
1 PIECE: 478 calories, 25 g fat (13 g saturated fat), 178 mg cholesterol, 448 mg sodium, 59 g carbohydrate (44 g sugars, 1 g fiber), 7 g protein

Spiced Pumpkin Tiramisu

PREP: 30 MINUTES + CHILLING • **COOK:** 5 MINUTES • **YIELD:** 12 SERVINGS

I transformed tiramisu from coffee- to pumpkin-flavored for a special holiday with my brother and parents. A new Christmas tradition was born!

—Heather Clary, Downingtown, Pennsylvania

1 cup water	1½ teaspoons ground cinnamon
1 cup brewed coffee	½ teaspoon ground nutmeg
⅔ cup sugar	¼ teaspoon ground ginger
⅔ cup hazelnut liqueur	¼ teaspoon ground allspice
	1¼ cups heavy whipping cream

PUMPKIN MIXTURE:

2 cartons (8 ounces each) mascarpone cheese

¾ cup canned pumpkin

5 tablespoons sugar, divided

ASSEMBLY:

54 crisp ladyfinger cookies (about 16 ounces)

1 tablespoon sugar

½ teaspoon ground cinnamon

1. In a small saucepan, combine water, coffee, sugar and liqueur; cook and stir over medium-low heat until sugar is dissolved, about 3 minutes. Transfer to a shallow bowl; cool completely.

2. In a large bowl, mix mascarpone cheese, pumpkin, 3 tablespoons sugar and spices just until blended. In a small bowl, beat cream until it begins to thicken. Add remaining sugar; beat until soft peaks form. Fold into mascarpone mixture.

3. Quickly dip 18 ladyfingers into coffee mixture, allowing excess to drip off. Arrange in a single layer in a 13x9-inch dish. Spread with 1⅔ cups cheese mixture. Repeat layers twice.

4. Mix sugar and cinnamon; sprinkle over top. Refrigerate, covered, at least 8 hours or overnight.

NOTE: This recipe was prepared with Alessi brand ladyfinger cookies.

NUTRITIONAL FACTS
1 PIECE: 491 calories, 28 g fat (15 g saturated fat), 121 mg cholesterol, 88 mg sodium, 52 g carbohydrate (38 g sugars, 1 g fiber), 7 g protein

Pink Grapefruit Cheesecake

PREP: 20 MINUTES • **COOK:** 2 HOURS + CHILLING • **YIELD:** 6 SERVINGS

Cheesecake from a slow cooker? It's true! I experimented a few times to turn this iconic dessert into a slow-cooker classic. Give it a try. You'll be amazed at the results!

—*Krista Lanphier, Milwaukee, Wisconsin*

¾ cup graham cracker crumbs

1 tablespoon plus ⅔ cup sugar, divided

1 teaspoon grated grapefruit peel

¼ teaspoon ground ginger

2½ tablespoons butter, melted

2 packages (8 ounces each) cream cheese, softened

½ cup sour cream

2 tablespoons pink grapefruit juice

2 large eggs, lightly beaten

1. Place a greased 6-inch springform pan on a double thickness of heavy-duty foil (about 12 inch square). Wrap foil securely around pan. Pour 1 inch water into a 6-qt. slow cooker. Layer two 24-inch pieces of foil. Starting with a long side, fold up foil to create a 1-inch-wide strip; roll into a coil. Place in slow cooker to form a rack for the cheesecake.

2. In a small bowl, mix cracker crumbs, 1 tablespoon sugar, peel and ginger; stir in butter. Press onto bottom and about 1 inch up sides of prepared pan.

3. In a large bowl, beat cream cheese and remaining sugar until smooth. Beat in sour cream and grapefruit juice. Add eggs and beat on low speed just until combined.

4. Pour into crust. Place springform pan on top of coil. Cover slow cooker with a double layer of paper towels; place lid securely over towels. Cook, covered, on high 2 hours. Do not remove lid; turn off slow cooker and let cheesecake stand, covered, in slow cooker 1 hour. Center of cheesecake will be just set and top will appear dull.

5. Remove springform pan from slow cooker; remove foil from pan. Cool cheesecake on a wire rack 1 hour. Loosen sides from pan with a knife. Refrigerate overnight, covering when completely cooled. Remove rim from pan.

CITRUS TOPPING: Top cheesecake with orange and grapefruit sections (from half an orange and half a grapefruit) and kumquat slices. Add sugared cranberries (recipe below) if desired.

SUGARED CRANBERRY TOPPING: Lightly mist ½ cup fresh cranberries with water; toss with 2 tablespoons sugar. Place over cheesecake; top with orange peel curls.

CHOCOLATE & PECAN TOPPING: Melt 2 ounces semisweet chocolate with 1 teaspoon shortening and stir until smooth; drizzle over cheesecake. Top with glazed pecans.

NOTE: Six-inch springform pans are available at wilton.com.

NUTRITIONAL FACTS
1 SLICE: 515 calories, 37 g fat (21 g saturated fat), 171 mg cholesterol, 404 mg sodium, 39 g carbohydrate (32 g sugars, 0 fiber), 8 g protein

Quick Tip **I always like to precut cheesecake by dipping the knife into hot water and wiping it on a paper towel before making another cut.—Rick Peters, Manson, IA**

Chocolate Chip Cookie Dough Cheesecake

PREP: 25 MINUTES ● **BAKE:** 45 MINUTES + CHILLING ● **YIELD:** 14 SERVINGS

I created this recipe to combine two of my all-time favorites: cheesecake for the grown-up in me and chocolate chip cookie dough for the little girl in me. Sour cream offsets the sweetness and adds a nice tang. Everyone who tries this scrumptious treat loves it.

—*Julie Craig, Kewaskum, Wisconsin*

1¾ cups crushed chocolate chip cookies
    or chocolate wafer crumbs
¼ cup sugar
⅓ cup butter, melted

FILLING:
3 packages (8 ounces each)
    cream cheese, softened
1 cup sugar
1 cup (8 ounces) sour cream
½ teaspoon vanilla extract
3 large eggs, lightly beaten

COOKIE DOUGH:
¼ cup butter, softened
¼ cup sugar
¼ cup packed brown sugar
1 tablespoon water
1 teaspoon vanilla extract
½ cup all-purpose flour
1½ cups miniature semisweet
    chocolate chips, divided

1. Preheat oven to 350°. In a small bowl, combine cookie crumbs and sugar; stir in butter. Press onto the bottom and 1 inch up the sides of a greased 9-inch springform pan.

2. In a large bowl, beat cream cheese and sugar until smooth. Beat in sour cream and vanilla. Add eggs; beat on low speed just until combined. Pour over crust; set aside.

3. In another bowl, cream butter and sugars until light and fluffy. Add water and vanilla. Gradually add flour and mix well. Stir in 1 cup chocolate chips.

4. Drop dough by teaspoonfuls over filling, gently pushing dough below surface (dough should be completely covered by filling). Place pan on a baking sheet.

5. Bake for 45–55 minutes or until center is almost set. Cool on a wire rack for 10 minutes. Carefully run a knife around edge of pan to loosen; cool 1 hour longer. Refrigerate overnight.

6. Remove sides of pan. Sprinkle with remaining chips. Refrigerate leftovers.

NUTRITIONAL FACTS
1 SLICE: 551 calories, 36 g fat (22 g saturated fat), 131 mg cholesterol, 328 mg sodium, 52 g carbohydrate (37 g sugars, 2 g fiber), 8 g protein

Peanut-Filled Devil's Food Cupcakes

PREP: 30 MINUTES • **BAKE:** 15 MINUTES + COOLING • **YIELD:** 2 DOZEN

My cupcakes have a luscious peanut butter filling surrounded with devil's food and iced with a rich layer of ganache. They're to die for!

—*Mary Lou Timpson, Colorado City, Arizona*

- ½ cup plus 2 tablespoons butter, softened
- 1½ cups sugar
- 3 large eggs
- 1 teaspoon vanilla extract
- 1¼ cups cake flour
- ½ cup baking cocoa
- 1 teaspoon baking soda
- ½ teaspoon salt
- ¼ teaspoon baking powder
- ½ cup buttermilk
- ½ cup strong brewed coffee

FILLING:
- 1 cup creamy peanut butter
- ½ cup butter, softened
- 1¼ cups confectioners' sugar

GANACHE:
- 4 ounces semisweet chocolate, chopped
- ½ cup heavy whipping cream
- ½ cup dry roasted peanuts

1. Preheat oven to 325°. In a large bowl, beat butter and sugar until crumbly, about 2 minutes. Add eggs, one at a time, beating well after each addition. Beat in vanilla. In another bowl, combine the flour, cocoa, baking soda, salt and baking powder; add to creamed mixture alternately with buttermilk and coffee just until combined.

2. Fill paper-lined muffin cups half full. Bake for 15–20 minutes or until a toothpick inserted near the center comes out clean. Cool for 10 minutes before removing from pans to wire racks to cool completely.

3. For filling, in a small bowl, beat peanut butter and butter until fluffy. Gradually add confectioners' sugar; beat until smooth. Cut a small hole in the corner of a pastry or plastic bag; insert a small tip. Add filling. Push the tip through the bottom of paper liner to fill each cupcake.

4. For ganache, place chocolate in a small bowl. In a small saucepan, bring cream just to a boil. Pour over chocolate; whisk until smooth. Cool for 10 minutes or until mixture is slightly thickened.

5. Place a heaping tablespoonful of ganache on top of each cupcake; spread toward the edges. Sprinkle with peanuts. Chill for 20 minutes or until set. Refrigerate leftovers.

NUTRITIONAL FACTS
1 EACH: 294 calories, 19 g fat (8 g saturated fat), 57 mg cholesterol, 282 mg sodium, 29 g carbohydrate (20 g sugars, 1 g fiber), 6 g protein

Buttermilk Chocolate Cupcakes

PREP: 30 MINUTES • **BAKE:** 15 MINUTES + COOLING • **YIELD:** 2 DOZEN

Good any time of the year, cupcakes make a great get-up-and-go treat on busy summer days. These have been a frosted favorite with family and friends for at least 35 years. They're really popular at bake sales.

—*Ellen Moore, Springfield, New Hampshire*

½	cup butter, softened
1½	cups sugar
2	large eggs
1	teaspoon vanilla extract
1½	cups all-purpose flour
½	cup baking cocoa
1	teaspoon baking soda
¼	teaspoon salt
½	cup buttermilk
½	cup water

FROSTING:

½	cup butter, softened
3¾	cups confectioners' sugar
2	ounces unsweetened chocolate, melted
2	tablespoons evaporated milk
1	teaspoon vanilla extract
¼	teaspoon salt
	Chocolate sprinkles

1. Preheat oven to 375°. In a large bowl, cream butter and sugar until light and fluffy. Add eggs, one at a time, beating well after each addition. Beat in vanilla. In another bowl, combine flour, cocoa, baking soda and salt. Combine buttermilk and water. Add dry ingredients to creamed mixture alternately with buttermilk and water, beating well after each addition.

2. Fill paper-lined muffin cups two-thirds full. Bake 15–20 minutes or until a toothpick inserted in center comes out clean. Cool 10 minutes before removing from pans to wire racks to cool completely.

3. For frosting, in a small bowl, beat butter and confectioners' sugar until smooth. Beat in melted chocolate, milk, vanilla and salt. Frost cupcakes; garnish with chocolate sprinkles.

NUTRITIONAL FACTS
1 EACH: 239 calories, 9 g fat (5 g saturated fat), 39 mg cholesterol, 191 mg sodium, 39 g carbohydrate (30 g sugars, 1 g fiber), 2 g protein

Take-It Tip **Lightly spraying plastic wrap with nonstick cooking spray can help prevent the frosting from lifting off of your covered cakes and cupcakes. Give it a try the next time you attend a church supper. And if you're whipping up bars or brownies for a charity bake sale, why not tape a copy of the recipe outside the plastic wrap? The buyer is sure to appreciate your thoughtfulness.**

Coconut Tres Leches Cupcakes

PREP: 30 MINUTES ● **BAKE:** 20 MINUTES + CHILLING ● **YIELD:** ABOUT 1½ DOZEN

Three types of milk wonderfully moisten these cupcakes. Toasted coconut on top adds an elegant touch.
—*Taste of Home Test Kitchen*

½ cup butter, softened
1½ cups sugar
4 large egg whites
1½ teaspoons vanilla extract
2 cups all-purpose flour
1 teaspoon baking powder
½ teaspoon baking soda
¼ teaspoon salt

1⅓ cups buttermilk
1 can (14 ounces) sweetened condensed milk
⅔ cup evaporated milk
½ cup coconut milk
1 cup heavy whipping cream
3 tablespoons confectioners' sugar
Toasted flaked coconut

1. Preheat oven to 350°. In a large bowl, cream butter and sugar until light and fluffy. Add egg whites, one at a time, beating well after each addition. Beat in vanilla. In another bowl, combine the flour, baking powder, baking soda and salt; add to the creamed mixture alternately with buttermilk, beating well after each addition.

2. Fill paper-lined muffin cups two-thirds full. Bake for 18–22 minutes or until a toothpick inserted near the center comes out clean. Place pan on a wire rack; cool for 10 minutes. Remove paper liners from cupcakes; return to pan.

3. Poke holes in cupcakes with a skewer, about ½ inch apart. In a small pitcher or measuring cup with a spout, combine the sweetened condensed milk, evaporated milk and coconut milk; slowly pour over cupcakes, allowing mixture to absorb into cake. Cover and refrigerate for 2 hours.

4. In a large bowl, beat cream until it begins to thicken. Add confectioners' sugar; beat until soft peaks form. Frost cupcakes. Sprinkle with coconut. Store in the refrigerator.

NUTRITIONAL FACTS
1 EACH: 505 calories, 23 g fat (16 g saturated fat), 64 mg cholesterol, 316 mg sodium, 67 g carbohydrate (50 g sugars, 1 g fiber), 9 g protein

Quick Tip **I spray paper liners with cooking spray before filling them. The liner peels off nicely, leaving no crumbs behind.—Pamela K., Martinsburg, WV**

Zucchini Cupcakes

PREP: 20 MINUTES ● **BAKE:** 20 MINUTES + COOLING ● **YIELD:** ABOUT 1½ DOZEN

I asked my grandmother for this recipe after trying these irresistible spice cupcakes at her home. I love their creamy caramel frosting. They're such a scrumptious dessert you actually forget you're eating your vegetables, too!

—Virginia Lapierre, Greensboro Bend, Vermont

3 large eggs
1⅓ cups sugar
½ cup canola oil
½ cup orange juice
1 teaspoon almond extract
2½ cups all-purpose flour
2 teaspoons ground cinnamon
2 teaspoons baking powder
1 teaspoon baking soda

1 teaspoon salt
½ teaspoon ground cloves
1½ cups shredded zucchini

FROSTING:
1 cup packed brown sugar
½ cup butter, cubed
¼ cup 2% milk
1 teaspoon vanilla extract
1½ to 2 cups confectioners' sugar

1. Preheat oven to 350°. In a large bowl, beat first five ingredients. In another bowl, combine dry ingredients; gradually add to egg mixture and blend well. Stir in zucchini.

2. Fill paper-lined muffin cups two-thirds full. Bake until a toothpick inserted in center comes out clean, 20–25 minutes. Cool 10 minutes before removing to a wire rack.

3. For frosting, combine brown sugar, butter and milk in a large saucepan. Bring to a boil over medium heat; cook and stir until thickened, 1–2 minutes. Remove from heat; stir in vanilla. Cool to lukewarm.

4. Gradually beat in confectioners' sugar until frosting reaches spreading consistency. Frost cupcakes.

NUTRITIONAL FACTS
1 CUPCAKE: 327 calories, 12 g fat (4 g saturated fat), 45 mg cholesterol, 305 mg sodium, 52 g carbohydrate (38 g sugars, 1 g fiber), 3 g protein

Quick Tip
To quickly frost cupcakes, place frosting in a bowl. The frosting should be a soft, spreadable consistency. If it is too stiff, add milk a teaspoon at a time until it reaches desired consistency. Dip top of cupcake into the frosting, twist slightly and lift up.

Vanilla Bean Cupcakes

PREP: 30 MINUTES • **BAKE:** 20 MINUTES + COOLING • **YIELD:** 1½ DOZEN

My 3-year-old son loves these! Flecks of vanilla bean in the moist, tender cupcakes give them special-occasion status.

—Alysha Braun, St. Catharines, Ontario

¾ cup unsalted butter, softened
1¼ cups sugar
2 large eggs
2 vanilla beans
2 cups cake flour
2 teaspoons baking powder
½ teaspoon salt
⅔ cup whole milk

FROSTING:
1 package (8 ounces) cream cheese, softened
6 tablespoons unsalted butter, softened
1½ teaspoons vanilla extract
3 cups confectioners' sugar
Assorted candies and coarse sugar

1. Preheat oven to 375°. Line 18 muffin cups with paper liners.

2. In a large bowl, cream butter and sugar until light and fluffy. Add eggs, one at a time, beating well after each addition. Split vanilla beans lengthwise; using the tip of a sharp knife, scrape seeds from the center into creamed mixture. In another bowl, whisk flour, baking powder and salt; add to creamed mixture alternately with milk, beating well after each addition.

3. Fill prepared cups three-fourths full. Bake 16–18 minutes or until a toothpick inserted in center comes out clean. Cool in pans 10 minutes before removing to wire racks to cool completely.

4. In a large bowl, beat cream cheese, butter and vanilla until blended. Gradually beat in confectioners' sugar until smooth. Frost cupcakes. Decorate with candies and coarse sugar as desired. Refrigerate leftovers.

NUTRITIONAL FACTS
1 CUPCAKE (CALCULATED WITHOUT DECORATIONS): 266 calories, 13 g fat (8 g saturated fat), 56 mg cholesterol, 143 mg sodium, 36 g carbohydrate (24 g sugars, 0 fiber), 3 g protein

Freeze It **Freeze cooled cupcakes in resealable plastic freezer bags. To use, thaw at room temperature. Frost as directed.**

Shoofly Cupcakes

PREP: 15 MINUTES ● **BAKE:** 20 MINUTES + COOLING ● **YIELD:** 2 DOZEN

These moist old-fashioned molasses cupcakes were my grandmother's specialty. To keep them from disappearing too quickly, she used to store them out of sight. Somehow, we always figured out her hiding places!
—*Beth Adams, Jacksonville, Florida*

4 cups all-purpose flour	2 teaspoons baking soda
2 cups packed brown sugar	2 cups boiling water
¼ teaspoon salt	1 cup molasses
1 cup cold butter, cubed	

1. Preheat oven to 350°. In a large bowl, combine flour, brown sugar and salt. Cut in butter until crumbly. Set aside 1 cup for topping. Add baking soda to remaining crumb mixture. Stir in water and molasses.

2. Fill paper-lined muffin cups two-thirds full. Sprinkle with reserved crumb mixture. Bake 20–25 minutes or until a toothpick inserted near the center comes out clean. Cool 10 minutes before removing from pans to wire racks to cool.

NOTE: This recipe does not use eggs.

NUTRITIONAL FACTS
1 EACH: 248 calories, 8 g fat (5 g saturated fat), 20 mg cholesterol, 219 mg sodium, 43 g carbohydrate (26 g sugars, 1 g fiber), 2 g protein

Quick Tip

For easy cleanup, spritz the measuring cup with a little cooking spray before measuring sticky ingredients like honey and molasses.

Maple Carrot Cupcakes

PREP: 15 MINUTES • **BAKE:** 20 MINUTES + COOLING • **YIELD:** 1½ DOZEN

I come from a line of family cooks and have liked to cook and bake since I was young. Mother and Grandmom were always in the kitchen cooking up something delicious. These carrot cupcakes were Grandmom's specialty, and we always have them at family gatherings.

—*Lisa Ann Panzino DiNunzio, Vineland, New Jersey*

2 cups all-purpose flour
1 cup sugar
1 teaspoon baking powder
1 teaspoon baking soda
1 teaspoon ground cinnamon
½ teaspoon salt
4 large eggs
1 cup canola oil
½ cup maple syrup
3 cups grated carrots (about 6 medium)

FROSTING:

1 package (8 ounces) cream cheese, softened
¼ cup butter, softened
¼ cup maple syrup
1 teaspoon vanilla extract
Chopped walnuts, optional

1. Preheat oven to 350°. In a large bowl, combine the first six ingredients. In another bowl, beat eggs, oil and syrup. Stir into dry ingredients just until moistened. Fold in carrots.

2. Fill 18 greased or paper-lined muffin cups two-thirds full. Bake for 20–25 minutes or until a toothpick inserted near the center comes out clean. Cool for 5 minutes before removing from pans to wire racks.

3. For frosting, combine the cream cheese, butter, syrup and vanilla in a bowl; beat until smooth. Frost cooled cupcakes. Sprinkle with nuts if desired. Store in the refrigerator.

NUTRITIONAL FACTS
1 EACH: 327 calories, 20 g fat (6 g saturated fat), 68 mg cholesterol, 243 mg sodium, 33 g carbohydrate (21 g sugars, 1 g fiber), 4 g protein

Easy Coconut Cream Pie

PREP: 20 MINUTES + CHILLING • **YIELD:** 8 SERVINGS

This is my own recipe for a pie that I make often. It's been a family-favorite dessert since the '40s, when I made several of these pies to serve a threshing crew of 21 men!

—*Vera Moffitt, Oskaloosa, Kansas*

³⁄₄ cup sugar	1¹⁄₂ cups flaked coconut, toasted, divided
3 tablespoons all-purpose flour	1 tablespoon butter
¹⁄₈ teaspoon salt	1¹⁄₂ teaspoons vanilla extract
3 cups whole milk	1 pastry shell (9 inches), baked
3 large eggs, beaten	

In a medium saucepan, combine sugar, flour and salt. Stir in milk; cook and stir over medium-high heat until thickened and bubbly. Reduce heat; cook and stir 2 minutes longer. Remove from the heat; gradually stir about 1 cup of hot mixture into beaten eggs. Return all to saucepan; cook and stir over medium heat until nearly boiling. Reduce heat; cook and stir about 2 minutes more (do not boil). Remove from the heat; stir in 1 cup coconut, butter and vanilla. Pour into pie shell; sprinkle with remaining coconut. Chill for several hours before serving. Refrigerate leftovers.

NUTRITIONAL FACTS
1 PIECE: 389 calories, 20 g fat (12 g saturated fat), 101 mg cholesterol, 266 mg sodium, 47 g carbohydrate (30 g sugars, 1 g fiber), 7 g protein

Rhu-Berry Pie

PREP: 20 MINUTES • **BAKE:** 45 MINUTES • **YIELD:** 8 SERVINGS

I cook in a coffee shop, so I'm always looking for new and unique pies to serve my customers. The combination of blueberries and rhubarb in this recipe caught my eye, and it was an instant best-seller.

—*Karen Dougherty, Freeport, Illinois*

Pastry for single-crust pie (9 inches)	1 cup unsweetened apple juice
¹⁄₂ cup sugar	3¹⁄₂ cups diced fresh rhubarb
¹⁄₄ cup cornstarch	2¹⁄₂ cups fresh blueberries

1. Preheat oven to 375°. Roll out pastry to fit a 9-inch pie plate. Transfer pastry to pie plate. Trim pastry to ¹⁄₂ inch beyond edge of plate; flute edges.

2. In a large heavy saucepan, combine sugar and cornstarch. Stir in apple juice until smooth. Cook and stir over medium heat until thickened. Add rhubarb; cook and stir gently 2–3 minutes or just until heated through. Stir in blueberries. Spoon mixture into pie shell.

3. Place a foil-lined baking sheet on a rack below the pie to catch any spills. Bake for 45–50 minutes or until bubbly. Cool completely on a wire rack.

NUTRITIONAL FACTS
1 PIECE: 231 calories, 7 g fat (3 g saturated fat), 5 mg cholesterol, 104 mg sodium, 41 g carbohydrate (22 g sugars, 2 g fiber), 2 g protein

Cranberry Pear Crisp Pie

PREP: 25 MINUTES ● **BAKE:** 55 MINUTES + COOLING ● **YIELD:** 8 SERVINGS

Filled with a bubbling combination of cranberries and pears, this crumb-topped dessert is a wonderful change-of-pace from traditional pies.

—Priscilla Gilbert, Indian Harbour Beach, Florida

5 cups sliced peeled fresh pears
1 tablespoon lemon juice
1 teaspoon vanilla extract
1²⁄₃ cups fresh or frozen cranberries
½ cup packed brown sugar
⅓ cup all-purpose flour
Pastry for single-crust pie (9 inches)

TOPPING:
¼ cup all-purpose flour
¼ cup quick-cooking oats
3 tablespoons packed brown sugar
¾ teaspoon ground cinnamon
2 tablespoons cold butter

1. Preheat oven to 375°. Place the pears in a large bowl; sprinkle with lemon juice and vanilla. Add cranberries. In a small bowl, combine the brown sugar and flour; sprinkle over fruit and gently toss to coat.

2. Roll out pastry to fit a 9-inch pie plate. Transfer pastry to pie plate. Trim pastry to ½ inch beyond edge of plate; flute edges. Add filling.

3. In a small bowl, combine the flour, oats, brown sugar and cinnamon. Cut in butter until crumbly. Sprinkle over filling.

4. Cover edges of pastry loosely with foil. Bake for 30 minutes. Remove foil; bake 25–30 minutes longer or until filling is bubbly. Cool on a wire rack.

NUTRITIONAL FACTS
1 PIECE: 332 calories, 11 g fat (5 g saturated fat), 13 mg cholesterol, 137 mg sodium, 58 g carbohydrate (32 g sugars, 4 g fiber), 3 g protein

Contest-Winning Rhubarb Meringue Pie

PREP: 50 MINUTES + CHILLING • **BAKE:** 65 MINUTES + COOLING • **YIELD:** 8 SERVINGS

My husband's grandmother was a great cook and didn't always share her secrets, so we are fortunate to have her recipe for rhubarb cream pie. I added one of my favorite crusts and a never-fail meringue.
—*Elaine Sampson, Colesburg, Iowa*

$\frac{3}{4}$ cup all-purpose flour
$\frac{1}{4}$ teaspoon salt
$\frac{1}{4}$ teaspoon sugar
$\frac{1}{4}$ cup shortening
1 tablespoon beaten egg
$\frac{1}{4}$ teaspoon white vinegar
3 to $4\frac{1}{2}$ teaspoons cold water

FILLING:
3 cups chopped fresh or frozen rhubarb
1 cup sugar

2 tablespoons all-purpose flour
Dash salt
3 large egg yolks
1 cup heavy whipping cream

MERINGUE:
4 teaspoons plus $\frac{1}{3}$ cup sugar, divided
2 teaspoons cornstarch
$\frac{1}{3}$ cup water
3 large egg whites
$\frac{1}{8}$ teaspoon cream of tartar

1. In a small bowl, combine flour, salt and sugar; cut in shortening until crumbly. Combine egg and vinegar; sprinkle over crumb mixture. Gradually add water, tossing with a fork until a ball forms. Cover and chill for 1 hour or until easy to handle.

2. Preheat oven to 350°. On a lightly floured surface, roll out pastry to fit a 9-inch pie plate. Trim to $\frac{1}{2}$ inch beyond edge of plate; flute edges.

3. Place rhubarb in crust. In a bowl, whisk the sugar, flour, salt, egg yolks and cream; pour over rhubarb. Bake for 50–60 minutes or until a knife comes out clean.

4. In a small saucepan, combine 4 teaspoons sugar and cornstarch. Gradually stir in water. Bring to a boil, stirring constantly; cook for 1–2 minutes or until thickened. Cool to room temperature.

5. In a small bowl, beat egg whites and cream of tartar until frothy. Add cornstarch mixture; beat on high until soft peaks form. Gradually beat in remaining sugar, 1 tablespoon at a time, on high until stiff glossy peaks form and sugar is dissolved.

6. Spread evenly over hot filling, sealing edges to crust. Bake for 15 minutes or until meringue is golden brown. Cool on a wire rack for 1 hour. Store in the refrigerator.

NOTE: If using frozen rhubarb, measure rhubarb while still frozen, then thaw completely. Drain in a colander, but do not press liquid out.

NUTRITIONAL FACTS
1 PIECE: 388 calories, 19 g fat (9 g saturated fat), 129 mg cholesterol, 131 mg sodium, 50 g carbohydrate (37 g sugars, 1 g fiber), 5 g protein

Upside-Down Apple Pie

PREP: 30 MINUTES + CHILLING • **BAKE:** 50 MINUTES + COOLING • **YIELD:** 8 SERVINGS

This upside-down apple pie has won eight ribbons at area fairs. People say it looks and tastes like a giant apple-cinnamon bun. I take time off from work around the holidays to fill pie requests from family and friends. This recipe is everyone's favorite.

—*Susan Frisch, Germansville, Pennsylvania*

2 cups all-purpose flour
½ teaspoon salt
6 tablespoons shortening
2 tablespoons cold butter
5 to 7 tablespoons orange juice

FILLING:

6 tablespoons butter, melted, divided
½ cup packed brown sugar
½ cup chopped pecans

8 cups thinly sliced peeled tart apples (about ⅛ inch thick)
1 cup sugar
⅓ cup all-purpose flour
¾ teaspoon ground cinnamon
¼ teaspoon ground nutmeg

GLAZE:

½ cup confectioners' sugar
2 to 3 teaspoons orange juice

1. In a large bowl, combine flour and salt; cut in shortening and butter until crumbly. Gradually add orange juice, tossing with a fork until dough forms a ball. Divide dough into two balls. Wrap in plastic wrap; refrigerate for at least 30 minutes.

2. Preheat oven to 375°. Line a 9-inch deep-dish pie plate with heavy-duty foil, leaving 1½ inches beyond edge; coat the foil with cooking spray. In a small bowl, combine 4 tablespoons butter, brown sugar and pecans; spoon into prepared pie plate.

3. In a large bowl, combine the apples, sugar, flour, cinnamon, nutmeg and remaining butter; toss gently.

4. On waxed paper, roll out one ball of pastry to fit pie plate. Place pastry over nut mixture, pressing firmly against mixture and sides of plate; trim to 1 inch beyond plate edge. Fill with apple mixture.

5. Roll out remaining pastry to fit top of pie; place over filling. Trim to ¼ inch beyond plate edge. Fold bottom pastry over top pastry; seal and flute edges. Cut four 1-inch slits in top pastry.

6. Bake for 50–55 minutes or until apples are tender and crust is golden brown (cover edges with foil during the last 20 minutes to prevent overbrowning if necessary).

7. Cool for 15 minutes on a wire rack. Invert onto a serving platter; carefully remove foil. Combine glaze ingredients; drizzle over pie.

NUTRITIONAL FACTS
1 SLICE: 613 calories, 26 g fat (10 g saturated fat), 31 mg cholesterol, 270 mg sodium, 92 g carbohydrate (60 g sugars, 4 g fiber), 5 g protein

Take-It Tip Pies are an ideal item to bring to a church supper, picnic or other carry-in event. Whether featuring apples, cherries, lemon or pumpkin, these classic desserts are proven to tickle the sweet tooth of anyone who approaches the dessert table. In addition, the goodies don't need to be reheated or kept particularly cold, so food safety isn't often an issue. Best of all . . . they travel well. To make sure pies arrive in good condition, turn a foil pie plate upside down, and set it over the dessert. Use a rubber band or two to keep the plate in place.

Mom's Peach Pie

PREP: 15 MINUTES • **BAKE:** 40 MINUTES • **YIELD:** 8 SERVINGS

A delightful summertime pie, this dessert is overflowing with fresh peach flavor. Each sweet slice is packed with old-fashioned appeal. The streusel topping makes this pie a little different than the ordinary and adds homemade flair.

—Sally Holbrook, Pasadena, California

1 large egg white, lightly beaten	$\frac{1}{3}$ cup sugar
1 unbaked pastry shell (9 inches)	$\frac{1}{4}$ cup cold butter, cubed
$\frac{3}{4}$ cup all-purpose flour	6 cups sliced peeled fresh peaches
$\frac{1}{2}$ cup packed brown sugar	

1. Preheat oven to 375°. Brush egg white over pastry shell; set aside.

2. In a small bowl, combine flour and sugars; cut in butter until mixture resembles fine crumbs. Sprinkle two-thirds into pastry; top with peaches. Sprinkle with remaining crumb mixture.

3. Bake for 40–45 minutes or until filling is bubbly and peaches are tender.

NUTRITIONAL FACTS
1 SLICE: 354 calories, 13 g fat (7 g saturated fat), 20 mg cholesterol, 170 mg sodium, 58 g carbohydrate (34 g sugars, 3 g fiber), 4 g protein

Chocolate Cobbler

PREP: 10 MINUTES • **BAKE:** 40 MINUTES • **YIELD:** 8 SERVINGS

It's impossible to resist the flavorful chocolate sauce that appears when this delightful cake bakes.

—Margaret McNeil, Germantown, Tennessee

1 cup self-rising flour	3 tablespoons vegetable oil
$\frac{1}{2}$ cup sugar	1 cup packed brown sugar
2 tablespoons plus $\frac{1}{4}$ cup baking cocoa, divided	$1\frac{3}{4}$ cups hot water
$\frac{1}{2}$ cup milk	Vanilla ice cream, optional

Preheat oven to 350°. In a bowl, combine the flour, sugar and 2 tablespoons cocoa. Stir in milk and oil until smooth. Pour into a greased 8-inch square baking pan. In a small bowl, combine the brown sugar and remaining cocoa; sprinkle over batter. Pour hot water over top (do not stir). Bake for 40–45 minutes or until top of cake springs back when lightly touched. Serve warm with ice cream if desired.

NOTE: As a substitute for 1 cup of self-rising flour, place $1\frac{1}{2}$ teaspoons baking powder and $\frac{1}{2}$ teaspoon salt in a measuring cup. Add all-purpose flour to measure 1 cup.

NUTRITIONAL FACTS
1 EACH: 267 calories, 6 g fat (1 g saturated fat), 2 mg cholesterol, 198 mg sodium, 53 g carbohydrate (40 g sugars, 1 g fiber), 3 g protein

Iva's Peach Cobbler

PREP: 15 MINUTES ● **BAKE:** 45 MINUTES ● **YIELD:** 12 SERVINGS

My mother received this recipe from a friend of hers many years ago, and fortunately she shared it with me. Boise is situated right between two large fruit-producing areas in our state, so peaches are plentiful in the summer.

—Ruby Ewart, Boise, Idaho

6 to 8   large ripe peaches, peeled and sliced
2½   tablespoons cornstarch
¾ to 1   cup sugar

CRUST:
1   cup all-purpose flour
2   large egg yolks

¼   cup butter, melted
1   teaspoon baking powder
1   cup sugar
2   large egg whites, stiffly beaten

Preheat oven to 375°. In a bowl, combine peaches, cornstarch and sugar; place in a greased 13x9-inch baking dish. For crust, combine flour, egg yolks, butter, baking powder and sugar in a bowl. Gently fold in egg whites. Spread over peaches. Bake for about 45 minutes or until the fruit is bubbling around edges and top is golden.

NUTRITIONAL FACTS
½ CUP: 224 calories, 5 g fat (3 g saturated fat), 46 mg cholesterol, 83 mg sodium, 44 g carbohydrate (33 g sugars, 1 g fiber), 3 g protein

Quick Tip   **Purchase peaches that have an intense fragrance and that give slightly to palm pressure. Avoid those that are hard or have soft spots. Store ripe peaches in a plastic bag in the refrigerator for up to 5 days. To ripen peaches, place in a brown paper bag and store at room temperature for about 2 days.**

Slow-Cooked Blueberry Grunt

PREP: 20 MINUTES • **COOK:** 2½ HOURS • **YIELD:** 6 SERVINGS

If you love blueberries, then you can't go wrong with this easy slow-cooked dessert. For a special treat, serve it warm with vanilla ice cream.

—*Cleo Gonske, Redding, California*

- 4 cups fresh or frozen blueberries
- ¾ cup sugar
- ½ cup water
- 1 teaspoon almond extract

DUMPLINGS:
- 2 cups all-purpose flour
- 4 teaspoons baking powder
- 1 teaspoon sugar
- ½ teaspoon salt
- 1 tablespoon cold butter
- 1 tablespoon shortening
- ¾ cup 2% milk
  Vanilla ice cream, optional

1. Place blueberries, sugar, water and extract in a 3-qt. slow cooker; stir to combine. Cook, covered, on high 2–3 hours or until bubbly.

2. For dumplings, in a small bowl, whisk flour, baking powder, sugar and salt. Cut in butter and shortening until crumbly. Add milk; stir just until a soft dough forms.

3. Drop dough by tablespoonfuls on top of hot blueberry mixture. Cook, covered, 30 minutes longer or until a toothpick inserted in center of dumplings comes out clean. If desired, serve warm with ice cream.

NUTRITIONAL FACTS
1 CUP (CALCULATED WITHOUT ICE CREAM): 360 calories, 5 g fat (2 g saturated fat), 7 mg cholesterol, 494 mg sodium, 73 g carbohydrate (37 g sugars, 3 g fiber), 6 g protein

Cranberry Stuffed Apples

PREP: 10 MINUTES • **COOK:** 4 HOURS • **YIELD:** 5 SERVINGS

Cinnamon, nutmeg and walnuts add a homey autumn flavor to these stuffed apples, but the slow cooker does most of the work for me.

—*Graciela Sandvigen, Rochester, New York*

5 medium apples

$\frac{1}{3}$ cup fresh or frozen cranberries, chopped

$\frac{1}{4}$ cup packed brown sugar

2 tablespoons chopped walnuts

$\frac{1}{4}$ teaspoon ground cinnamon

$\frac{1}{8}$ teaspoon ground nutmeg

Whipped cream or vanilla ice cream, optional

1. Core apples, leaving bottoms intact. Peel top third of each apple; place in a 5-qt. slow cooker. In a bowl, combine the cranberries, brown sugar, walnuts, cinnamon and nutmeg; spoon into apples.

2. Cover and cook on low for 4–5 hours or until apples are tender. Serve with whipped cream or ice cream if desired.

NUTRITIONAL FACTS
1 STUFFED APPLE: 136 calories, 2 g fat (0 saturated fat), 0 cholesterol, 6 mg sodium, 31 g carbohydrate (25 g sugars, 4 g fiber), 1 g protein

Nutty Apple Streusel Dessert

PREP: 20 MINUTES • **COOK:** 6 HOURS • **YIELD:** 8 SERVINGS

Many people don't think of using a slow cooker to make dessert, but I like having this hot, scrumptious apple treat waiting to be served when we finish up our dinner. I start it in the morning and don't think about it all day.

— *Jacki Every, Rotterdam, New York*

6   cups sliced peeled tart apples
1¼   teaspoons ground cinnamon
¼   teaspoon ground allspice
¼   teaspoon ground nutmeg
¾   cup 2% milk
2   tablespoons butter, softened
¾   cup sugar
2   large eggs

1   teaspoon vanilla extract
½   cup biscuit/baking mix

TOPPING:
1   cup biscuit/baking mix
⅓   cup packed brown sugar
3   tablespoons cold butter
½   cup sliced almonds
    Ice cream or whipped cream, optional

1. In a large bowl, toss apples with cinnamon, allspice and nutmeg. Place in a greased 3-qt. slow cooker. In a small bowl, combine the milk, butter, sugar, eggs, vanilla and baking mix. Spoon over apples.

2. For topping, combine biscuit mix and brown sugar in a large bowl; cut in butter until crumbly. Add almonds; sprinkle over apples.

3. Cover and cook on low for 6–8 hours or until the apples are tender. Serve with ice cream or whipped cream if desired.

NUTRITIONAL FACTS
1 CUP: 378 calories, 16 g fat (6 g saturated fat), 75 mg cholesterol, 387 mg sodium, 57 g carbohydrate (39 g sugars, 3 g fiber), 5 g protein

Slow Cooker Spiced Poached Pears

PREP: 25 MINUTES • **COOK:** 4 HOURS • **YIELD:** 8 SERVINGS

Some of the many reasons I love this dessert recipe are: It's on the healthy side; it's easy to make; the recipe can be mostly prepared in advance of company arriving; and the presentation is lovely.

—Jill Mant, Denver, Colorado

1½ cups dry red wine or cranberry juice
⅓ cup packed brown sugar
2 tablespoons dried cherries
1 tablespoon ground cinnamon
1 whole star anise
1 dried Sichuan peppercorn, optional
4 ripe Bosc pears

GANACHE:
6 ounces bittersweet chocolate, chopped
¼ cup heavy whipping cream

TOPPINGS:
2 tablespoons pine nuts
  Fresh blackberries
  Sweetened whipped cream, optional

1. In a 3-qt. slow cooker, mix wine, brown sugar, cherries, cinnamon, star anise and, if desired, peppercorn until blended. Peel and cut pears lengthwise in half. Remove cores, leaving a small well in the center of each. Arrange pears in wine mixture.

2. Cook, covered, on low 4–5 hours or until pears are almost tender. Discard star anise and peppercorn.

3. Place chocolate in a small bowl. In a small saucepan, bring cream just to a boil. Pour over chocolate; stir with a whisk until smooth.

4. To serve, remove pears to dessert dishes; drizzle with some of the poaching liquid. Spoon ganache into wells of pears. Top with pine nuts and blackberries. If desired, serve with whipped cream.

NUTRITIONAL FACTS
1 SERVING (CALCULATED WITHOUT WHIPPED CREAM AND BLACKBERRIES): 295 calories, 12 g fat (6 g saturated fat), 8 mg cholesterol, 8 mg sodium, 30 g carbohydrate (22 g sugars, 4 g fiber), 2 g protein

Butterscotch Fruit Dip

PREP: 5 MINUTES ● **COOK:** 45 MINUTES ● **YIELD:** ABOUT 3 CUPS

If you like the sweetness of butterscotch chips, you'll enjoy this warm rum-flavored fruit dip. I serve it with apple and pear wedges. It holds up for up to two hours in the slow cooker.
— *Jeaune Hadl Van Meter, Lexington, Kentucky*

2 packages (10 to 11 ounces each) butterscotch chips

$^2/_3$ cup evaporated milk

$^2/_3$ cup chopped pecans

1 tablespoon rum extract

Apple and pear wedges

In a $1^1/_2$-qt. slow cooker, combine butterscotch chips and milk. Cover and cook on low for 45–50 minutes or until chips are softened; stir until smooth. Stir in pecans and extract. Serve warm with fruit.

NUTRITIONAL FACTS
$^1/_4$ **CUP:** 197 calories, 13 g fat (7 g saturated fat), 6 mg cholesterol, 32 mg sodium, 17 g carbohydrate (16 g sugars, 1 g fiber), 2 g protein

Pumpkin Pie Pudding

PREP: 10 MINUTES • **COOK:** 6 HOURS • **YIELD:** 6 SERVINGS

My husband loves anything pumpkin, and this creamy, comforting dessert is one of his favorites. We make this easy pudding all year long, but it's especially nice in the fall.

—*Andrea Schaak, Bloomington, Minnesota*

1 can (15 ounces) solid-pack pumpkin	2 tablespoons butter, melted
1 can (12 ounces) evaporated milk	2½ teaspoons pumpkin pie spice
¾ cup sugar	2 teaspoons vanilla extract
½ cup biscuit/baking mix	Sweetened whipped cream or
2 large eggs, beaten	vanilla ice cream, optional

1. In a bowl, combine first eight ingredients. Transfer to a greased 3-qt. slow cooker.

2. Cook, covered, on low until a thermometer reads 160°, 6–7 hours. If desired, serve with whipped cream.

NUTRITIONAL FACTS
1 EACH: 229 calories, 9 g fat (5 g saturated fat), 76 mg cholesterol, 187 mg sodium, 33 g carbohydrate (25 g sugars, 2 g fiber), 6 g protein

Caramel and Pear Pudding

PREP: 20 MINUTES • **COOK:** 3 HOURS • **YIELD:** 10 SERVINGS

This is a lovely winter dessert that uses pears that are seasonally available. It's easy to fix and a comforting treat after any meal. I enjoy snacking on it in front of the fireplace.

—Diane Halferty, Corpus Christi, Texas

1 cup all-purpose flour	4 medium pears, peeled and cubed
½ cup sugar	½ cup chopped pecans
1½ teaspoons baking powder	¾ cup packed brown sugar
½ teaspoon ground cinnamon	¼ cup butter, softened
¼ teaspoon salt	½ cup boiling water
⅛ teaspoon ground cloves	Vanilla ice cream, optional
½ cup 2% milk	

1. In a large bowl, combine flour, sugar, baking powder, cinnamon, salt and cloves. Stir in milk until smooth. Add pears and pecans. Spread evenly into a 3-qt. slow cooker coated with cooking spray.

2. In a small bowl, combine brown sugar and butter; stir in boiling water. Pour over batter (do not stir). Cover and cook on low for 3–4 hours or until pears are tender. Serve warm, with ice cream if desired.

NUTRITIONAL FACTS
½ CUP: 274 calories, 9 g fat (3 g saturated fat), 13 mg cholesterol, 164 mg sodium, 47 g carbohydrate (33 g sugars, 3 g fiber), 3 g protein

Rice Pudding

PREP: 15 MINUTES • **COOK:** 3 HOURS + CHILLING • **YIELD:** 4 SERVINGS

For an old-fashioned sweet treat just like Grandma made, try this creamy pudding. It has a rich cinnamon flavor and is made wonderfully light after whipped cream is stirred into it at the end.

—*Jennifer Bennett, Salem, Indiana*

1¼ cups 2% milk	1 teaspoon butter, melted
½ cup sugar	1 teaspoon vanilla extract
½ cup uncooked converted rice	¾ teaspoon lemon extract
½ cup raisins	1 cup heavy whipping cream, whipped
2 large eggs, lightly beaten	Additional whipped cream and ground
1 teaspoon ground cinnamon	cinnamon, optional

1. In a 1½-qt. slow cooker, combine the first nine ingredients. Cover and cook on low for 2 hours; stir. Cover and cook 1–2 hours longer or until rice is tender. Transfer to a small bowl; cool. Refrigerate until chilled.

2. Just before serving, fold in whipped cream. If desired, garnish with additional whipped cream and cinnamon.

NUTRITIONAL FACTS
¾ CUP: 437 calories, 17 g fat (10 g saturated fat), 157 mg cholesterol, 87 mg sodium, 63 g carbohydrate (39 g sugars, 1 g fiber), 8 g protein

Salted Nut Squares

PREP: 15 MINUTES + CHILLING • **YIELD:** 4½ DOZEN

A favorite of young and old, this recipe came from my sister-in-law. It's simple to prepare and delicious. There's no need to keep it warm or cold, so it's perfect for the potluck that has you traveling longer distances.

—*Kathy Tremel, Earling, Iowa*

3 cups salted peanuts without skins, divided	1 can (14 ounces) sweetened condensed milk
2½ tablespoons butter	2 cups miniature marshmallows
2 cups peanut butter chips	

1. Place half of the peanuts in an ungreased 11x7-inch dish; set aside. In a large saucepan, melt butter and peanut butter chips over low heat. Add milk and marshmallows; cook and stir until melted.

2. Pour over peanuts. Sprinkle with remaining peanuts. Cover and refrigerate until chilled. Cut into scant 1¼-inch squares.

NUTRITIONAL FACTS
1 PIECE: 115 calories, 7 g fat (2 g saturated fat), 4 mg cholesterol, 56 mg sodium, 10 g carbohydrate (8 g sugars, 1 g fiber), 4 g protein

Easy Chocolate Clusters

PREP: 10 MINUTES + STANDING ● **COOK:** 2 HOURS ● **YIELD:** 3½ DOZEN

You can use this simple recipe to make a big batch of chocolate candy without a lot of fuss. I've sent these clusters to my husband's office a number of times . . . and passed the recipe along as well.

—*Doris Reynolds, Munds Park, Arizona*

2 pounds white candy coating, broken into small pieces

2 cups (12 ounces) semisweet chocolate chips

4 ounces German sweet chocolate, chopped

1 jar (24 ounces) dry roasted peanuts

1. In a 3-qt. slow cooker, combine the candy coating, chocolate chips and German chocolate. Cover and cook on high for 1 hour. Reduce heat to low; cover and cook 1 hour longer or until melted, stirring every 15 minutes.

2. Stir in peanuts. Drop by teaspoonfuls onto waxed paper. Let stand until set. Store at room temperature.

NUTRITIONAL FACTS

2 EACH: 521 calories, 35 g fat (17 g saturated fat), 0 cholesterol, 265 mg sodium, 51 g carbohydrate (43 g sugars, 4 g fiber), 9 g protein

Slow Cooker Candied Nuts

PREP: 10 MINUTES ● **COOK:** 2 HOURS ● **YIELD:** 4 CUPS

I like giving spiced nuts as holiday gifts. This slow-cooker recipe with ginger and cinnamon is so good, you just might use it all year long.

—*Yvonne Starlin, Hermitage, Tennessee*

½ cup butter, melted	¼ teaspoon ground allspice
½ cup confectioners' sugar	1½ cups pecan halves
1½ teaspoons ground cinnamon	1½ cups walnut halves
¼ teaspoon ground ginger	1 cup unblanched almonds

1. In a greased 3-qt. slow cooker, mix butter, confectioners' sugar and spices. Add nuts; toss to coat. Cook, covered, on low 2–3 hours or until nuts are crisp, stirring once.

2. Transfer nuts to waxed paper to cool completely. Store in an airtight container.

NUTRITIONAL FACTS
⅓ CUP: 327 calories, 31 g fat (7 g saturated fat), 20 mg cholesterol, 64 mg sodium, 11 g carbohydrate (6 g sugars, 3 g fiber), 6 g protein

Quick Tip
To remove water marks from a highly glazed crockery insert, rub the surface with vegetable oil and allow to stand for 2 hours before washing with hot sudsy water.

Dark Chocolate Orange Truffles

PREP: 15 MINUTES + CHILLING ● **YIELD:** 2½ DOZEN

I love chocolate truffles, so you can imagine my delight when I came across the recipe for these dark and decadent confections. The hint of orange makes them deliciously different from other candies.

—*Theresa Young, McHenry, Illinois*

1 package (12 ounces) dark chocolate chips	1 teaspoon orange extract
¾ cup heavy whipping cream	⅓ cup sugar

In a microwave, melt chocolate; stir until smooth. Gradually stir in cream until blended. Stir in extract. Cool to room temperature, stirring occasionally. Refrigerate until firm. Shape into ¾-inch balls. Roll in sugar.

NUTRITIONAL FACTS
1 EACH: 82 calories, 5 g fat (3 g saturated fat), 7 mg cholesterol, 2 mg sodium, 8 g carbohydrate (7 g sugars, 0 fiber), 1 g protein

Peanut Butter Snowballs

PREP: 15 MINUTES + CHILLING ● **YIELD:** 2 DOZEN

These creamy treats are a nice change from the typical milk chocolate and peanut butter combination. This recipe is also an easy one for children to help with. I prepared the snowballs for a bake sale at my granddaughter's school and put them in gift boxes I share with neighbors at Christmas.

—*Wanda Regula, Birmingham, Michigan*

1 cup confectioners' sugar	3 tablespoons butter, softened
½ cup creamy peanut butter	1 pound white candy coating, coarsely chopped

1. In a bowl, combine the sugar, peanut butter and butter. Shape into 1-inch balls and place on a waxed paper–lined baking sheet. Chill for 30 minutes or until firm.

2. Meanwhile, melt the candy coating in a microwave-safe bowl. Dip balls and place on waxed paper to harden.

NUTRITIONAL FACTS
1 EACH: 164 calories, 10 g fat (6 g saturated fat), 4 mg cholesterol, 39 mg sodium, 19 g carbohydrate (18 g sugars, 0 fiber), 1 g protein

Peanut Butter Cups

PREP: 20 MINUTES + CHILLING • **YIELD:** 3 DOZEN

The classic combination of peanut and chocolate is one my children, grandchildren and great-grandchildren can't resist. They gobble up this candy all year long!

—*Doris Price, St. John, New Brunswick*

1½ cups confectioners' sugar
1 cup creamy peanut butter
½ cup packed brown sugar
2 tablespoons butter, softened

1 teaspoon vanilla extract
2 cups (12 ounces) semisweet chocolate chips
¼ cup shortening

1. In a small bowl, combine the confectioners' sugar, peanut butter, brown sugar, butter and vanilla; cover and set aside.

2. In a microwave, melt chocolate chips and shortening; stir until smooth. Pour teaspoonfuls into paper-lined miniature muffin cups.

3. Drop a rounded teaspoonful of peanut butter mixture into each cup; top with another teaspoonful of chocolate mixture. Refrigerate until set. Store in an airtight container.

NUTRITIONAL FACTS
1 CANDY: 182 calories, 11 g fat (5 g saturated fat), 2 mg cholesterol, 41 mg sodium, 21 g carbohydrate (19 g sugars, 2 g fiber), 3 g protein

Candy Bar Fudge

PREP: 20 MINUTES + CHILLING • **YIELD:** 2¾ POUNDS (64 PIECES)

My manager at work, who knows I like to try new treat recipes, shared this one with me. I've made this chewy and chocolaty fudge many times since. Packed with nuts and caramel, it's like a candy bar. Everyone who's tried it loves it.

—Lois Freeman, Oxford, Michigan

½ cup butter	30 caramels, unwrapped
⅓ cup baking cocoa	1 tablespoon water
¼ cup packed brown sugar	2 cups salted peanuts
¼ cup milk	½ cup semisweet chocolate chips
3½ cups confectioners' sugar	½ cup milk chocolate chips
1 teaspoon vanilla extract	

1. In a microwave-safe bowl, combine the butter, cocoa, brown sugar and milk. Microwave on high until mixture boils, about 2 minutes. Stir in confectioners' sugar and vanilla. Pour into a greased 8-inch square dish.

2. In another microwave-safe bowl, heat caramels and water on high for 1¼ minutes or until melted. Stir in peanuts; spread over chocolate layer. Microwave chocolate chips on high for 30 seconds or until melted; spread over caramel layer. Chill until firm.

NOTE: This recipe was tested in a 1,100-watt microwave.

NUTRITIONAL FACTS
1 PIECE: 101 calories, 5 g fat (2 g saturated fat), 5 mg cholesterol, 48 mg sodium, 14 g carbohydrate (12 g sugars, 1 g fiber), 2 g protein

Easy Double-Decker Fudge

PREP: 15 MINUTES + CHILLING ● **YIELD:** ABOUT 1½ POUNDS

Microwave-quick and peanut buttery, this easy fudge is just the thing to have on hand for after-school treats or dessert. And don't forget about it for your cookie plates at the holidays.

—*Sherri Melotik, Oak Creek, Wisconsin*

1 teaspoon butter	1 teaspoon vanilla extract, divided
1 cup peanut butter chips	1 cup (6 ounces) semisweet chocolate chips
1 can (14 ounces) sweetened condensed milk, divided	

1. Line an 8-inch square pan with foil; butter foil and set aside.

2. In a microwave-safe bowl, combine peanut butter chips and ⅔ cup milk. Microwave on high for 1 minute; stir. Microwave at additional 15-second intervals, stirring until smooth. Stir in ½ teaspoon vanilla. Pour into prepared pan. Refrigerate for 10 minutes.

3. Meanwhile, in a microwave-safe bowl, combine chocolate chips and remaining milk. Microwave on high for 1 minute; stir. Microwave at additional 15-seconds intervals, stirring until smooth. Stir in remaining vanilla. Spread over peanut butter layer.

4. Refrigerate for 1 hour or until firm. Using foil, remove fudge from pan. Cut into 1-inch squares.

NUTRITIONAL FACTS
1 PIECE: 47 calories, 2 g fat (1 g saturated fat), 2 mg cholesterol, 15 mg sodium, 6 g carbohydrate (6 g sugars, 0 fiber), 1 g protein

Mocha Nut Balls

PREP: 20 MINUTES ● **BAKE:** 15 MINUTES/BATCH ● **YIELD:** 4½ DOZEN

These tender, flavorful cookies are so addictive, I always know I have to make a double batch. The family demands it!

—*Janet Sullivan, Buffalo, New York*

1 cup butter, softened	⅓ cup baking cocoa
½ cup sugar	1 tablespoon instant coffee granules
2 teaspoons vanilla extract	1 cup finely chopped pecans or walnuts
1¾ cups all-purpose flour	Confectioners' sugar

1. Preheat oven to 325°. In a large bowl, cream butter and sugar until light and fluffy. Beat in vanilla. In another bowl, whisk flour, cocoa and coffee granules; gradually beat into creamed mixture. Stir in pecans. Shape dough into 1-inch balls; place 2 inch apart on ungreased baking sheets.

2. Bake 14–16 minutes or until set. Cool on pans 1–2 minutes. Roll warm cookies in confectioners' sugar. Cool on wire racks.

NUTRITIONAL FACTS
1 COOKIE: 69 calories, 5 g fat (2 g saturated fat), 9 mg cholesterol, 24 mg sodium, 6 g carbohydrate (2 g sugars, 0 fiber), 1 g protein

Crisp Sugar Cookies

PREP: 15 MINUTES + CHILLING ● **BAKE:** 10 MINUTES ● **YIELD:** 8 DOZEN

My grandmother always had sugar cookies in her pantry, and we grandchildren would empty that big jar quickly because they were the best! I now regularly bake these wonderful cookies to share with friends.

—*Evelyn Poteet, Hancock, Maryland*

1 cup butter, softened	1½ teaspoons baking powder
2 cups sugar	1 teaspoon baking soda
2 large eggs	½ teaspoon salt
1 teaspoon vanilla extract	¼ cup 2% milk
5 cups all-purpose flour	

1. In a large bowl, cream butter and sugar until light and fluffy. Add eggs and vanilla; mix until combined. In another bowl, combine flour, baking powder, baking soda and salt; add to creamed mixture alternately with milk. Cover and refrigerate 15–30 minutes or until easy to handle.

2. Preheat oven to 350°. On a floured surface, roll out dough to ⅛-inch thickness. Cut out cookies into desired shapes. Place 2 inches apart on greased baking sheets.

3. Bake 10 minutes or until edges are lightly browned. Remove from pans to wire racks to cool completely.

NUTRITIONAL FACTS
2 EACH: 117 calories, 4 g fat (2 g saturated fat), 19 mg cholesterol, 105 mg sodium, 18 g carbohydrate (8 g sugars, 0 fiber), 2 g protein

Quick Cranberry Chip Cookies

PREP: 25 MINUTES • **BAKE:** 10 MINUTES/BATCH • **YIELD:** 6 DOZEN

I received these delightful cookies for Christmas a few years ago. I was watching my diet, but I couldn't stay away from them! The tart cranberries blend beautifully with the sweet chocolate and vanilla chips.

—*Jo Ann McCarthy, Canton, Massachusetts*

- 1/2 cup butter, softened
- 1/2 cup shortening
- 3/4 cup sugar
- 3/4 cup packed brown sugar
- 2 large eggs
- 1 teaspoon vanilla extract
- 2 1/4 cups all-purpose flour
- 1 teaspoon baking soda
- 1/2 teaspoon salt
- 1 cup semisweet chocolate chips
- 1 cup white baking chips
- 1 cup dried cranberries
- 1 cup chopped pecans

1. Preheat oven to 375°. In a large bowl, cream butter, shortening and sugars until light and fluffy. Add eggs, one at a time, beating well after each addition. Beat in vanilla. In another bowl, combine the flour, baking soda and salt; gradually add to the creamed mixture and mix well. Stir in the chips, cranberries and pecans.

2. Drop by tablespoonfuls 2 inch apart onto ungreased baking sheets. Bake 9–11 minutes or until golden brown. Cool on pans 2 minutes before removing to wire racks.

NUTRITIONAL FACTS
1 EACH: 97 calories, 5 g fat (2 g saturated fat), 10 mg cholesterol, 48 mg sodium, 12 g carbohydrate (8 g sugars, 0 fiber), 1 g protein

Freeze It
Freeze cookies, layered between waxed paper, in freezer containers. To use, thaw before serving or, if desired, reheat on a baking sheet in a preheated 350° oven 3–4 minutes.

White Chocolate Macadamia Cookies

PREP: 15 MINUTES ● **BAKE:** 10 MINUTES/BATCH ● **YIELD:** 4¹⁄₂ DOZEN

White baking chips and macadamia nuts are a fantastic duo in these buttery cookies. They are a nice change from the classic chocolate chip ones.

—*Cathy Lennon, Newport, Tennessee*

¹⁄₂ cup butter, softened	1 cup plus 2 tablespoons all-purpose flour
²⁄₃ cup sugar	¹⁄₂ teaspoon baking soda
1 large egg	1 cup macadamia nuts, chopped
1 teaspoon vanilla extract	1 cup white baking chips

1. Preheat oven to 350°. In a large bowl, cream butter and sugar until light and fluffy. Beat in egg and vanilla. In another bowl, whisk flour and baking soda; gradually beat into creamed mixture. Stir in nuts and baking chips.

2. Drop by heaping teaspoonfuls 2 inch apart onto ungreased baking sheets. Bake 10–12 minutes or until golden brown. Cool on pans 1 minute. Remove to wire racks to cool completely.

NUTRITIONAL FACTS
1 COOKIE: 70 calories, 5 g fat (2 g saturated fat), 9 mg cholesterol, 38 mg sodium, 7 g carbohydrate (4 g sugars, 0 fiber), 1 g protein

Oat-Rageous Chocolate Chip Cookies

PREP: 25 MINUTES ● **BAKE:** 10 MINUTES/BATCH ● **YIELD:** ABOUT 3 DOZEN

My aunt gave me this recipe, and my family thinks these cookies are delicious. We enjoy all different kinds of cookies, and with this recipe, we can combine three of our favorite kinds—oatmeal, peanut butter and chocolate chip—in one!

—*Jaymie Noble, Kalamazoo, Michigan*

¹⁄₂ cup butter, softened	1 cup all-purpose flour
¹⁄₂ cup creamy peanut butter	¹⁄₂ cup quick-cooking oats
¹⁄₂ cup sugar	1 teaspoon baking soda
¹⁄₃ cup packed brown sugar	¹⁄₄ teaspoon salt
1 large egg	1 cup (6 ounces) semisweet chocolate chips
¹⁄₂ teaspoon vanilla extract	

Preheat oven to 350°. In a bowl, cream butter, peanut butter and sugars; beat in egg and vanilla. In another bowl, combine flour, oats, baking soda and salt. Add to the creamed mixture and mix well. Stir in chocolate chips. Drop by rounded tablespoonfuls onto ungreased baking sheets. Bake for 10–12 minutes or until lightly browned.

NUTRITIONAL FACTS
2 EACH: 207 calories, 12 g fat (6 g saturated fat), 25 mg cholesterol, 194 mg sodium, 24 g carbohydrate (15 g sugars, 1 g fiber), 4 g protein

Wyoming Whopper Cookies

PREP/TOTAL TIME: 30 MINUTES • **YIELD:** 2 DOZEN

These big country cookies are made to travel—in fact, I came up with this recipe while trying to match a commercial cookie that was good, but too crumbly to carry.

—Jamie Hirsch, Powell, Wyoming

$\frac{2}{3}$ cup butter, cubed

$1\frac{1}{4}$ cups packed brown sugar

$\frac{3}{4}$ cup sugar

3 large eggs, beaten

$1\frac{1}{2}$ cups chunky peanut butter

6 cups old-fashioned oats

2 teaspoons baking soda

$1\frac{1}{2}$ cups raisins

2 cups (12 ounces) semisweet chocolate chips

1. Preheat oven to 350°. In a large saucepan, melt butter over low heat. Stir in the sugars, eggs and peanut butter until smooth. Add oats, baking soda, raisins and chocolate chips (dough will be sticky).

2. Drop on a greased baking sheet with an ice cream scoop or large spoon. Flatten slightly. Bake for 15 minutes. Remove cookies to a wire rack to cool.

NOTE: Reduced-fat peanut butter is not recommended for this recipe.

NUTRITIONAL FACTS
2 EACH: 768 calories, 39 g fat (15 g saturated fat), 80 mg cholesterol, 499 mg sodium, 101 g carbohydrate (65 g sugars, 8 g fiber), 17 g protein

Quick Tip   **For uniform-size cookies, use an ice cream scoop. A 1-tablespoon size scoop is perfect to make 2-inch cookies. Scrape the excess dough from the top of the scoop, or the cookies will not be identical.**

Mocha Cookies

PREP: 15 MINUTES • **BAKE:** 10 MINUTES + COOLING • **YIELD:** 15 COOKIES

Crisp on the outside, gooey on the inside, these mocha-flavored cookies are the perfect treat for chasing away winter doldrums. Why not invite a friend over some snowy afternoon to share a plateful and a cup of coffee?

—*Pamela Jessen, Calgary, Alberta*

$\frac{1}{4}$ cup butter, cubed
$\frac{1}{4}$ cup semisweet chocolate chips
$1\frac{1}{2}$ teaspoons instant coffee granules
$\frac{1}{3}$ cup sugar
$\frac{1}{3}$ cup packed brown sugar
1 large egg, lightly beaten
1 teaspoon vanilla extract
1 cup all-purpose flour

2 tablespoons plus 2 teaspoons baking cocoa
$\frac{1}{4}$ teaspoon baking powder
$\frac{1}{8}$ teaspoon salt
$\frac{1}{3}$ cup English toffee bits or almond brickle chips
1 ounce milk chocolate, melted

1. Preheat oven to 350°. In a microwave-safe bowl, melt butter and chocolate; stir until smooth. Stir in coffee granules until dissolved; cool for 5 minutes. Transfer to a small bowl. Add the sugars, egg and vanilla.

2. In another bowl, combine the flour, cocoa, baking powder and salt; add to chocolate mixture and mix well. Stir in toffee bits. Drop by rounded tablespoonfuls 2 inch apart onto a baking sheet lightly coated with cooking spray.

3. Bake for 8–10 minutes or until set. Cool for 1 minute before removing to a wire rack to cool completely. Drizzle with melted milk chocolate.

NUTRITIONAL FACTS
1 EACH: 152 calories, 7 g fat (4 g saturated fat), 25 mg cholesterol, 94 mg sodium, 22 g carbohydrate (15 g sugars, 1 g fiber), 2 g protein

Chocolate Maple Bars

PREP: 20 MINUTES ● **BAKE:** 25 MINUTES + COOLING ● **YIELD:** 3 DOZEN

My family runs a maple syrup operation, and I'm always looking for new ways to incorporate maple syrup into my cooking and baking. These bars are delicious!

—*Cathy Schumacher, Alto, Michigan*

½ cup shortening
¾ cup maple syrup
½ cup sugar
3 large eggs
3 tablespoons milk
1 teaspoon vanilla extract
1¼ cups all-purpose flour
¼ teaspoon baking powder
¼ teaspoon salt

1½ ounces unsweetened chocolate, melted
½ cup chopped pecans
½ cup flaked coconut

FROSTING:
¼ cup butter, softened
1 cup confectioners' sugar
½ cup baking cocoa
½ cup maple syrup
1 cup miniature marshmallows

1. Preheat oven to 350°. In a large bowl, cream the shortening, syrup and sugar until light and fluffy. Beat in the eggs, milk and vanilla. In another bowl, combine the flour, baking powder and salt; add to creamed mixture and mix well. Remove half of the batter to another bowl.

2. Combine melted chocolate and pecans; stir into one bowl. Spread into a greased 13x9-inch baking pan. Add coconut to remaining batter. Spread carefully over chocolate batter.

3. Bake for 25 minutes or until a toothpick inserted near the center comes out clean. Cool completely on a wire rack.

4. For frosting, in a small bowl, beat butter until smooth. Gradually add the confectioners' sugar and cocoa. Gradually add syrup, beating until smooth. Fold in marshmallows. Frost bars.

NUTRITIONAL FACTS
1 EACH: 143 calories, 7 g fat (3 g saturated fat), 21 mg cholesterol, 43 mg sodium, 20 g carbohydrate (14 g sugars, 1 g fiber), 2 g protein

Triple-Layer Cookie Bars

PREP: 15 MINUTES • **BAKE:** 30 MINUTES • **YIELD:** 3 DOZEN

My family just loves these chewy chocolate and peanutty bars. They're perfect for dessert and snacks. I make them whenever I get a craving for something sweet and special.

—*Diane Bradley, Sparta, Michigan*

1¼ cups all-purpose flour
⅔ cup sugar
⅓ cup baking cocoa
¼ cup packed brown sugar
1 teaspoon baking powder
¼ teaspoon salt
½ cup cold butter
2 large eggs

TOPPING:

1 package (7 ounces) flaked coconut
1 can (14 ounces) sweetened condensed milk
2 cups (12 ounces) semisweet chocolate chips
½ cup creamy peanut butter

1. Preheat oven to 350°. In a large bowl, combine the first six ingredients. Cut in butter until crumbly. Beat in eggs. Spread in a greased 13x9-inch baking pan.

2. Bake for 8 minutes. Sprinkle coconut over crust; drizzle with milk. Bake 20–25 minutes longer or until lightly browned.

3. Meanwhile, in a microwave, melt chocolate chips and peanut butter; stir until smooth. Spread over brownies. Cool on wire rack. Cut into bars.

NUTRITIONAL FACTS
2 EACH: 290 calories, 16 g fat (9 g saturated fat), 34 mg cholesterol, 155 mg sodium, 36 g carbohydrate (28 g sugars, 2 g fiber), 5 g protein

Quick Tip

Measuring with a ruler before cutting a pan of bars helps create even servings. Use a sharp knife when cutting bars, and be sure to slice all the way through to the bottom of the pan. Consider cutting your bars into diamond shapes to help them stand out on a dessert buffet.

Glazed Peanut Butter Bars

PREP: 15 MINUTES ● **BAKE:** 20 MINUTES + COOLING ● **YIELD:** 4 DOZEN

Memories of lunchtime at school and my Aunt Shelly's kitchen come to mind when I bite into these sweet, chewy bars. My husband is the biggest fan of these peanut butter and chocolate treats.

—*Janis Luedtke, Westminster, Colorado*

$\frac{3}{4}$ cup butter, softened
$\frac{3}{4}$ cup creamy peanut butter
$\frac{3}{4}$ cup sugar
$\frac{3}{4}$ cup packed brown sugar
2 large eggs
2 teaspoons water
$1\frac{1}{2}$ teaspoons vanilla extract
$1\frac{1}{2}$ cups all-purpose flour

$1\frac{1}{2}$ cups quick-cooking oats
$\frac{3}{4}$ teaspoon baking soda
$\frac{1}{2}$ teaspoon salt

GLAZE:
$1\frac{1}{4}$ cups milk chocolate chips
$\frac{1}{2}$ cup butterscotch chips
$\frac{1}{2}$ cup creamy peanut butter

1. Preheat oven to 325°. In a large bowl, cream the butter, peanut butter and sugars until light and fluffy, about 4 minutes. Beat in the eggs, water and vanilla. In another bowl, combine the flour, oats, baking soda and salt; gradually add to creamed mixture and mix well.

2. Spread into a greased 15x10x1-inch baking pan. Bake for 18–22 minutes or until lightly browned.

3. For glaze, in a microwave, melt chips and peanut butter; stir until smooth. Pour over warm bars; spread evenly. Cool completely on a wire rack before cutting.

NUTRITIONAL FACTS
1 EACH: 153 calories, 9 g fat (4 g saturated fat), 18 mg cholesterol, 114 mg sodium, 17 g carbohydrate (11 g sugars, 1 g fiber), 3 g protein

Caramel Pecan Bars

PREP: 15 MINUTES ● **BAKE:** 20 MINUTES + COOLING ● **YIELD:** 4 DOZEN

This pecan bar recipe won first place at a cookie contest held where I work. These rich bars really capture the flavor of pecan pie.

—*Emma Manning, Crossett, Arkansas*

1 cup butter, cubed	1½ cups all-purpose flour
2¼ cups packed brown sugar	2 teaspoons baking powder
2 large eggs	2 cups chopped pecans
2 teaspoons vanilla extract	Confectioners' sugar, optional

1. Preheat oven to 350°. In a large saucepan, combine butter and brown sugar over medium heat until sugar is dissolved. In a large bowl, beat eggs and vanilla. Gradually add hot sugar mixture, stirring constantly. Combine flour and baking powder; gradually add to the butter mixture and mix well. Stir in pecans.

2. Spread into a greased 13x9-inch baking pan. Bake for 20–25 minutes or until a toothpick inserted near the center comes out with moist crumbs and edges are crisp. Cool on a wire rack. Dust with confectioners' sugar if desired. Cut into bars.

NUTRITIONAL FACTS
1 EACH: 124 calories, 8 g fat (3 g saturated fat), 19 mg cholesterol, 62 mg sodium, 14 g carbohydrate (10 g sugars, 1 g fiber), 1 g protein

Frosted Banana Bars

PREP: 15 MINUTES ● **BAKE:** 20 MINUTES + COOLING ● **YIELD:** 3 DOZEN

These bars are always a hit at potlucks here in the small rural farming community where my husband and I live. I also like to provide them for coffee hour after church. They're so moist and delicious that wherever I take them, they don't last long.

—Karen Dryak, Niobrara, Nebraska

½ cup butter, softened
2 cups sugar
3 large eggs
1½ cups mashed ripe bananas (about 3 medium)
1 teaspoon vanilla extract
2 cups all-purpose flour
1 teaspoon baking soda
Dash salt

FROSTING:

1 package (8 ounces) cream cheese, softened
½ cup butter, softened
4 cups confectioners' sugar
2 teaspoons vanilla extract

1. Preheat oven to 350°. In a large bowl, cream butter and sugar until light and fluffy. Beat in the eggs, bananas and vanilla. In another bowl, combine the flour, baking soda and salt; stir into creamed mixture just until blended.

2. Transfer to a greased 15x10x1-inch baking pan. Bake for 20–25 minutes or until a toothpick inserted near the center comes out clean. Cool in pan on a wire rack.

3. For frosting, in a small bowl, beat cream cheese and butter until fluffy. Add confectioners' sugar and vanilla; beat until smooth. Frost bars.

NUTRITIONAL FACTS
1 EACH: 202 calories, 8 g fat (5 g saturated fat), 38 mg cholesterol, 100 mg sodium, 32 g carbohydrate (25 g sugars, 0 fiber), 2 g protein

Peanut Butter Cake Bars

PREP: 15 MINUTES ● **BAKE:** 45 MINUTES + COOLING ● **YIELD:** 2 DOZEN

These cake-like bars are packed with peanut butter and chocolate chips, and they are perfect for any occasion. Kids and adults alike are in for a treat with these gems.

—*Charlotte Ennis, Lake Arthur, New Mexico*

$^2/_3$ cup butter, softened	2 teaspoons vanilla extract
$^2/_3$ cup peanut butter	2 cups all-purpose flour
1 cup sugar	2 teaspoons baking powder
1 cup packed brown sugar	$^1/_2$ teaspoon salt
4 large eggs	1 package (11$^1/_2$ ounces) milk chocolate chips

1. Preheat oven to 350°. In a large bowl, cream butter, peanut butter, sugar and brown sugar. Add eggs, one at a time, beating well after each addition. Beat in vanilla. In another bowl, combine the flour, baking powder and salt; gradually add to creamed mixture. Stir in chocolate chips.

2. Spread into a greased 13x9-inch baking pan. Bake 45–50 minutes or until a toothpick inserted near the center comes out clean. Cool on a wire rack. Cut into bars.

NUTRITIONAL FACTS
1 EACH: 277 calories, 14 g fat (6 g saturated fat), 52 mg cholesterol, 178 mg sodium, 35 g carbohydrate (25 g sugars, 1 g fiber), 5 g protein

Fudge Nut Brownies

PREP: 15 MINUTES ● **BAKE:** 25 MINUTES ● **YIELD:** ABOUT 24 BROWNIES

There's no brownie recipe or mix I've ever tried that's better than this! And it's so easy—you can mix it in one bowl in just a few minutes. My husband's grandmother passed the recipe on; now our son makes these brownies for after-school snacks.

—*Becky Albright, Norwalk, Ohio*

1⅓	cups all-purpose flour	½	cup chopped nuts
2	cups sugar	⅔	cup vegetable oil
¾	cup baking cocoa	4	large eggs, lightly beaten
1	teaspoon baking powder	2	teaspoons vanilla extract
½	teaspoon salt	1	cup chopped nuts, optional

1. Preheat oven to 350°. In a bowl, combine the first six ingredients. In another bowl, combine oil, eggs and vanilla; add to dry ingredients. Do not overmix.

2. Spread in a 13x9-inch baking pan. Sprinkle with nuts if desired. Bake 20–25 minutes or until a toothpick inserted in center comes out clean. Cool in pan on a wire rack.

NUTRITIONAL FACTS
1 EACH: 180 calories, 9 g fat (1 g saturated fat), 35 mg cholesterol, 77 mg sodium, 24 g carbohydrate (16 g sugars, 1 g fiber), 3 g protein

Index

Boldface page numbers indicate photographs. <u>Underscored</u> references indicate boxed text, charts, and graphs.